Changing Minds in Therapy

The Norton Series on Interpersonal Neurobiology
Allan N. Schore, PhD, Series Editor
Daniel J. Siegel, MD, Founding Editor

The field of mental health is in a tremendously exciting period of growth and conceptual reorganization. Independent findings from a variety of scientific endeavors are converging in an interdisciplinary view of the mind and mental well-being. An interpersonal neurobiology of human development enables us to understand that the structure and function of the mind and brain are shaped by experiences, especially those involving emotional relationships.

The Norton Series on Interpersonal Neurobiology will provide cutting-edge, multidisciplinary views that further our understanding of the complex neurobiology of the human mind. By drawing on a wide range of traditionally independent fields of research—such as neurobiology, genetics, memory, attachment, complex systems, anthropology, and evolutionary psychology—these texts will offer mental health professionals a review and synthesis of scientific findings often inaccessible to clinicians. These books aim to advance our understanding of human experience by finding the unity of knowledge, or consilience, that emerges with the translation of findings from numerous domains of study into a common language and conceptual framework. The series will integrate the best of modern science with the healing art of psychotherapy.

A Norton Professional Book

Changing Minds in Therapy

*Emotion, Attachment, Trauma,
and Neurobiology*

Margaret Wilkinson

W. W. Norton & Company
New York • London

Contents

Acknowledgments

MY EXPLORATION OF THE NEUROBIOLOGY OF EMOTION and its relevance to the process of changing minds in therapy has been immeasurably enriched by my teachers, colleagues, and friends. I have been stimulated by the thinking of colleagues from the Neuroscience Research and Reading Groups that I lead at the Northern School of Child and Adolescent Psychotherapy in Leeds and at the Society of Analytical Psychology in London. I am particularly indebted to Chris Driver, Alan and Sally Galbraith, Carolyn Hart, Ruth Lanius, Linda Neal, Anna Nowasielska-Carey, Ursa and Janko Mrevlje-Lozar, Susie Orbach, Joy Schaverien, Valerie Sinason, and Sandra Walline. I am especially grateful to Pramila Bennett and Christine Firth for their willingness to help with the preparation and checking of the text before submission for publication. I have very much valued the interest, advice, and warm encouragement provided by Deborah Malmud and her colleagues at W. W. Norton. Finally, this book would never have been written without the continued encouragement and stimulus toward creative thought provided by Allan Schore, to whom I am immensely grateful.

I have a passion for this subject that sustained me throughout the writing process and a wish to make complex concepts accessible to a wide range of colleagues working in the mental health field, so that they may more easily absorb them and apply them to therapy in their own setting. For simplicity I have tended to use the terms *therapist* and *patient* to explore the therapeutic relationship. I trust that readers will translate these terms into the words that most adequately describe their own working relationships. This book is, in a sense, a record of my own exploration of some specific aspects of the process of changing minds through therapy and my growing understanding of the relevance of an interdisciplinary approach to the process.

Over the years I have come to specialize in clinical work with patients who have experienced early relational trauma. Many of these patients explore the changes in their inner world in extremely creative ways. Clinical case studies run throughout the book, and some patients whom the reader encounters in the early chapters are met again in later ones. All the case studies included in this book are composites of material from more than one patient. I am fortunate to have patients who have produced pictures that illustrate the changes that have occurred in their psyches at a very deep level. Some of these pictures are included in the book to illustrate the process of change in attachment and in the sense of self. All biographical material is disguised in order to preserve confidentiality. I would like to thank all those who have allowed their material and artwork to be used. Their generosity has enabled me to create the composite characters that help us to consider the process of changing minds in therapy throughout the book.

Changing Minds in Therapy

PART I
Containment:
The Neurobiology of Attachment, Affect Regulation, and Patterning in the Therapeutic Process

1

Creating Connections

RECENT DEVELOPMENTS IN THE NEUROBIOLOGY of emotion have provided us with new insights concerning the process of changing minds that occurs in therapy. It has become clear that mind, brain, and body are inextricably linked; that the developing self and mind reflect the developing brain and body; and that both affect their development, just as their development affects the mind. In Cozolino's words, we should understand the brain "not as a fully formed structure but as a dynamic process undergoing constant development and reconstruction across the lifespan" (Cozolino, 2006, p. 50). What insight, then, does neuroscience offer to our clinical understanding of these inner world experiences? While for the purposes of neuroscience mind may be perceived as an "epiphenomenon" of the brain, in clinical work mind "is the central phenomenon: that which experiences and is experienced, embedded in and shaped by its interactions in its physical, relational and intrapsychic networks" (Zabriskie, 2004, p. 235). How can we better understand the relationship of brain to mind? Does the plasticity of the brain contribute to therapeutic change, and if so, how? These are some of the questions I seek to explore.

Ian McEwan, in his acclaimed exploration of the inner being of a talented neurosurgeon in the novel *Saturday*, muses about how the central character, Henry Perowne, remains in awe of the relationship between brain and the inner exploration and encoding of experience:

> For all the recent advances it's still not known how this well-protected one kilogram or so of cells actually encodes information, how it holds experiences, memories, dreams and intentions.

He doesn't doubt that in years to come, the coding mechanism
will be known, though it might not be in his lifetime. . . . But even
when it has, the wonder will remain, that mere wet stuff can make
this bright inward cinema of thought, of sight and sound and
touch bound into a vivid illusion of an instantaneous present, with
a self, another brightly wrought illusion, hovering like a ghost at
its centre. . . . There's a grandeur in this view of life. (from
Saturday by Ian McEwan, published by Jonathan Cape. Reprinted
by permission of The Random House Group Ltd., pp. 254–255)

How does this amazing, dynamic process occur? Bar-Yam (1993)
explains that we can think of the brain as made up of neurons that are in
either an excited or passive state. Neurons affect the activity of other
neurons as electrochemical conversations take place between them
whereby new synaptic connections are made. One's current state of mind
is the result of a particular pattern of neuronal activity developed from
earlier patterns of activity. Patterns in the mind–brain become the essential key to our understanding of the processes underlying the change that
occurs in therapy. These patterns are the product of the activity of each
neuron, which is determined by the activity of all neurons at an earlier
time and the excitatory or inhibitory synapses between them. Many
synaptic connections are "hard-wired," performing functions that are
prespecified. However, their change and development are triggered by
experience such that new connections arise directly out of new experience. Thus the experience-dependent plasticity of the mind–brain–body
becomes key to understanding the possibility of changing minds and the
learning that can take place in psychotherapy (Mundo, 2006; Wilkinson,
2004, 2006a; Pally, 2007).

Mind, brain, and body are inextricably linked; no one who seeks to
work with any one of these can afford to ignore the other two. I explore
the contribution that not only neuroscience but also attachment and
trauma theories are fast making to our understanding of the grandeur of
these complex relationships and their significance for clinical work.

Emotion

Antonio Damasio (1994) conceptualizes emotion as the sum total of
somatic and autonomic changes that take place in the body as a result of
some particular stimulus, whether from the external world of sensory

experience or the internal world of imagination. Emotions involve the whole body in an adaptation to its environment and whatever new challenge occurs at any given moment. Feelings are the mental representations of our emotional responses. Damasio observes that "emotions play out in the theater of the body. Feelings play out in the theater of the mind" (Damasio, 2003, p. 28). He defines the essential content of a feeling as the mapping of a particular body state and explains that the substrate of a feeling is the set of neural patterns that map that particular body state from which a mental image can emerge (Damasio, 2003, p. 88).

Attachment

What is becoming more and more evident from research in both contemporary neuroscience and attachment is that the individual mind can no longer be explored in isolation; a young person's brain and mind owe a huge amount to the infant's and growing child's experiences of nurture, with mother, with father and with significant others, and later with the world of school and the wider world beyond. It is much more than merely the young person's brain that is the outcome of successful affect regulation and the development of emotional competence in the earliest years. Rather it is the development of an ever-increasing neuronal connectivity resulting in the complexity that is mind, which in turn gives rise to varied but interlinked self states. Ultimately it is on issues around attachment and affect regulation that a person's capacity to experience a sense of self that is "simultaneously fluid and robust" depends (Bromberg, 2006, p. 32).

A further related issue centers on the notions of vulnerability and resilience. Lanius (2008) defines resilience as "the capacity of a system exposed to hazards to adapt, by resisting or changing, in order to reach and maintain an acceptable level of functioning and structure." One may ask, "Why are some patients more resilient than others in the aftermath of trauma?" I locate the origins of this vital life skill in the earliest experience of empathic relating by another, but I also note that, where that has failed, patients may still exhibit a capacity for resilience that has developed out of a more fleeting relationship with a caring adult. Fosha (2003) suggests that "through just one relationship with an understanding other, trauma can be transformed and its effects neutralized or counteracted" (p. 223) and stresses that "the roots of resilience are to be found in the sense of being understood by and having the sense of existing in the mind and heart of a loving, attuned, and self-possessed other" (p. 228). This "other" may have been a family member or friend, a teacher or a neighbor. The resilience shown by some patients with less than straightforward early beginnings offers evidence that even a transient experience of being cared for may enable a child to go more confidently into the world. Such an experience of being cared for not only gives rise to resilience but also keeps alive within an individual the hope that there may be a possibility of learning to relate in a meaningful, satisfying way.

Affect regulation and attunement, twin regulatory processes identified by attachment theory, are key foci for me as I explore interactions in the consulting room. For many patients arrival at a more secure attachment is the unconscious goal of therapy—one that yields a safe sense of separateness and an ability to live life with curiosity and confidence. To develop what I think of as a "learned" secure attachment, past baggage may need to be discarded, and an integral part of this process is the mourning of, and ultimately a detaching from, what was not possible to achieve in early relationships. I describe a newly developed secure attachment that is the result of successful therapy as being "learned," rather than using the more familiar term "earned" (Pearson, 1994; Neborsky, 2003). I do so because I wish to emphasize that affective engagement in therapy enables new emotional learning to occur, and that such learning may bring about a profound change in the way the patient relates to others.

Trauma

Much of this book is concerned with early relational trauma, that which I often describe to patients as "the old present"—those difficult early experiences that remain buried within, unknown and unknowable, but carrying an instantly recognizable feeling tone that is often a meld of helplessness, rage, terror and dread. This feeling tone can be recreated in an instant by a triggering event or sensation. Such a feeling tone comes with a sense of *now*, not *then*. Why and how does difficult early experience affect the emotional, intellectual, and imaginative life of the individual in this way? What sort of experience gives rise to early relational trauma? Some difficulties occur unintentionally simply from the problems and sometimes failures of everyday parenting, or from well-meaning, necessary, but intrusive medical procedures and hospitalization early in life. At

such times an infant's simultaneous experience of intrusion and abandonment may be overwhelming. There are also the well-documented difficulties that arise from early experiences that are abusive. Whether the abuse
is psychological, physical, or sexual in nature, if it occurs early in life the
brain becomes hard-wired to cope in a hostile world. If traumatic experience is prolonged, multilayered, and experienced at the hands of a caregiver, negative persecutory patterns accumulate in the mind that predict
the likelihood of dire future experiences of relating. Bromberg (2008)
explains that a person's core self is defined by whom the parents (or caregivers) perceive the child to be and, just as importantly, who they deny the
child to be. When parents deny certain aspects of their child's self, they
disconfirm those aspects, which then become dissociated and unavailable
to the child. Bromberg concludes that "disconfirmation, because it is relationally non-negotiable, is traumatic by definition, and I believe accounts
for much of what we call developmental trauma" (2008, p. 424).

The effects of some early relational traumas do not manifest until a
difficult experience later in life acts as a reminder of the as-yet
unprocessed difficulties. An accumulation of difficulties in adulthood or
an overwhelmingly frightening experience may also give rise to trauma-
based responses and may require help through the medium of therapy,
even though the patient had a good start in life and is able to relate to
others in a securely attached manner. Such trauma will be processed
more easily if the person concerned had a secure start in life.

When early relational trauma remains unresolved, that damaged
child aspect of the self may remain metaphorically shut away, locked up,
locked away, indeed imprisoned. The patient may be seemingly very
successful both professionally and in relationships, but his or her core self
may still be in hiding. Kalsched (1996) notes that a powerful
protector/persecutor figure is often part of the imagery that emerges
from the internal world of such patients. Such patients may find themselves hypervigilant, perceiving threat where no threat now exists and
responding in an unnecessarily assertive or aggressive way. Such patients
easily become overaroused or may shift into "switched off" states that
may result in depersonalization and derealization. Such reaction patterns
inevitably get played out in the therapy. I understand the childlike or
fierce judgmental aspects of the personality as attempts of the mind to
represent aspects of traumatic experiences that have remained encapsulated in implicit memory.

In normal circumstances the explicit or declarative memory store of
the hippocampus in the later developing left hemisphere is easily accessible; indeed, it tags time and place to memories to facilitate their
retrieval. But if information has not been adequately processed by the
hippocampus (which becomes inactive in circumstances of severe
trauma), the person cannot easily remember what happened. Events
which are distressing emotionally, which inactivate the memory store of
the left hemisphere in this way, leave the strong emotion to be stored
principally in the emotional storehouse of the amygdala, which is located
in the earlier developing right hemisphere. It remains unavailable to
recall but may come to govern ways of being and behaving in relation to
others. Subsequently, if an environmental stimulus triggers reactivation
of an emotional memory, aspects of it may then become available to the
conscious mind; the patient becomes able to think and begins to process
their hitherto dissociated experience. In Damasio's (2003) terms the
emotion has never become a feeling, a mental representation which can
then be processed. Such processing occurs only with difficulty.
Rosenbaum uses a vivid image to describe the dissociative defense of the
sufferer of trauma:

> Shutting the door of your own home won't make it safe. But
> maybe you can shut the door on yourself. Hide in one of those
> rooms, maybe even in the attic. Crawl inside and take cover from
> the hurt. After a while, with any luck, no one will even notice that
> you have been gone. . . . All that's left to decide is when, if ever, to
> re-emerge. (cited in Bromberg, 2003, p. 707)

Throughout the book I emphasize the primitive levels at which relational development needs to occur in therapy for patients with early relational trauma to experience a change in the underlying fundamental
patterns of feeling, being, and behaving that persist and cause distress.
Schore (2007b) stresses that attachment communications of trauma
patients are implicit, affective, and nonverbal, and that unconscious
affect regulation "expressed in rapid nonverbal emotional communications at levels beneath conscious awareness within the dynamic intersubjective field" play a critical psychobiological role within patient–therapist
dyads (p. 762). It is these unconscious processes in therapy that lead to
changes in the way a patient becomes able to relate not only to others but
also to his or her own inner world. As Schore (2007a) points out, even

cognitive neuroscientists now require a theory of unconscious subjectivity to deal with the question of unconscious emotion.

Anxiety, depression, or difficult life circumstances may bring patients into therapy, and hope may enable them to engage affectively in this experience—which may then provide a series of new attachment experiences. When Holly, a new patient, brings a dream to her first session, she makes it clear that she hopes to find a therapist who can engage with her.

Case Example: Holly

Holly, a patient in her 30s who had come for an assessment interview prior to beginning therapy, recounted a dream that illustrated to me, through an extended metaphor, that the work ahead would center around issues of early attachment.

> I am trying to separate from my family after long years of being together. I know I must go in a different direction from my mother. I must leave her and go to find my new destination. I am carrying too much luggage to manage on my own; I have one very heavy suitcase that I can barely lift. I have three other pieces. I see a taxi with an empty sign coming. I say to my mother that I will get a taxi to my different destination. My mother is surprised that I could actually leave separately from her. She went off. I turned to begin to lift the heavy luggage into the taxi. I feared that when the taxi driver saw how much luggage I had, he would drive off. I felt I wouldn't have taken the radical step of leaving my mother if I hadn't seen the taxi actually stop for me. I feared I would not be able to struggle across the road to where other taxis might stop; I feared none of them would be willing to take me. I wondered whether the taxi would take me after all.

Holly added that she had thought afterward that the big, heavy suitcase reminded her of the large family suitcase of early childhood. In the dream she could only drag it a few feet at a time on her own. This patient would indeed need to separate from her mother and "the family baggage" that she was carrying. She had experienced early relational trauma that she thought had centered on her relationship with her mother but had actually extended into the immediate family (the large suitcase). Now the patient had come to explore the possibility of beginning therapy with me and wondered whether I would take her on with all her baggage. I learned that a previous therapist had seen her for one session and had not taken her as a patient. Gradually, as we worked together, we found that the heart of her therapy would be to grieve and mourn the mother that her mother had not been able to be for her, and to develop the necessary self-regulatory control of affect that would enable her to mother herself more adequately.

Neurobiology

As this book unfolds the reader will notice that I emphasize the influence of the brain's right-hemispheric processes through an exploration of the way in which the neural systems that encode attachment are shaped by our earliest relationships (Chapters 2 and 3). The patterns of relating established in early development and the role of the right hemisphere in the persistence of these patterns as ways of being, feeling, and relating that are held in the body and in implicit memory are explored in Chapters 3 and 4. The pivotal role of the right hemisphere in relational areas is then explored further as we examine the neurobiology of emotion (Chapter 5), the ways in which change may occur in the consulting room and be revealed through metaphor (Chapter 6), through the coconstruction of narrative (Chapter 7), and through working with dissociative experience (Chapter 8). Finally, I apply a neuroscience perspective to the process of supervision and the particular issues raised by supervising work with patients who have early relational trauma (Chapter 9). The right brain is understood as the facilitator not only of the therapeutic process that is under scrutiny but also the phenomena of mirroring, resonance, and empathy, which underpin the "parallel processing" that enables the supervisory process.

Schore has argued consistently and cogently for recognition of the central role of the right hemisphere in early development, particularly in the mother–infant interaction that stimulates the growth and development of the infant's brain. Howard and Reggia (2007) assert that the earlier maturation of the right hemisphere is supported by evidence from both anatomical and imaging research. Recent exciting advances in the use of near-infrared spectroscopy (NIRS) has made possible measurement of the hemodynamic response in both infants and mothers enabling elegant studies such as that of Minagawa-Kawai et al. (2008), which examines the role of the orbitofrontal cortex in mother–infant affective exchanges. They note that, although their study revealed bilateral activation of the orbitofrontal cortex, the *statistically significant responses* with strict thresholds *were limited to the channels on the right*" (p. 6, emphasis added). The authors note the relative consistency of these results with Schore's work (1994, 2003a, 2003b), particularly with his central thesis that "the mother–infant affective system is psychobiologically regulated by the orbitofrontal system and its cortical and sub-cortical connections" (Minagawa-Kawai et al., 2008, p. 1). Cozolino reminds us that the orbital medial prefrontal cortex is the earliest developing region of the frontal lobe and is larger in the right hemisphere than the left (2006, p. 71).

It is through my clinical encounters in the consulting room that I have come to understand the later developing left hemisphere to be the facilitator, not the master, of the right hemisphere. Schore (2008b) observes that "the ongoing paradigm shift across all the sciences is from conscious, explicit, analytical, verbal, and rational left brain to unconscious, integrative, nonverbal, bodily-based emotional processes of the right brain." The right hemisphere, the seat of the bodily based self system with its store of early relational patterning, is the source of originality, creativity, and emotional growth and development; it is also the source of all transference and countertransference experience. Unconscious emotional processing of current experience is undertaken by the right hemisphere and measured against earlier experience in order to determine the degree of threat. This processing inevitably leads to an unconscious emotional response that is based on earlier patterning.

Integration and communication are vital between and within the complex structures that are the right and left hemispheres of the brain both at a conscious and unconscious level as well as intrapsychically and interpsychically. An adequately developed corpus callosum is the structure that enables this integration and communication between the two sides of our brain. The salience of the corpus callosum in our daily lives can be illustrated with an example of an encounter with a frightening face. Because of the negative fearful emotion associated with it, a frightening face will be processed initially in the right hemisphere, but for a name to be put to that face, then the left hemisphere must also become involved (Cozolino, 2006, p. 58)—and that requires a functioning corpus callosum. Ultimately, the combined processing activity of the right and left hemispheres gives rise to a more coherent sense of self in the world

(Cozolino, 2002, 2006). Teicher's work has illustrated the damaging effects that childhood sexual trauma may have on the development of the corpus callosum and its function as the main information highway between right and left hemispheres (Teicher, 2000; Teicher et al., 2002). Equally vital is the linking that needs to occur throughout the right hemisphere, especially of the attachment and affect-regulating networks of the orbital medial prefrontal cortex, the amygdala, and associated structures (more on these later).

Therapy

Why and how might clinicians want to use a new multidisciplinary approach that integrates psychoanalytic theory with research insights from neuroscience, attachment theory, and trauma theory? Ginot (2007) stresses that therapists have become increasingly aware that "explicit content, verbal interpretations, and the mere act of recovering memories are insufficient venues for curative shifts" and that what is needed to change minds is the "transformational power embedded in unconscious affective interactions" (p. 317). Mundo (2006) cites Kandel's work to argue that effects of psychotherapy on the brain will be found in areas concerned with implicit processes, "that is, the neocortex, the amygdala and the cerebellum" (p. 684) and concludes that "the processes of dynamic psychotherapy may influence gene expression, synaptic plasticity, and brain metabolism in specific areas" (Mundo, 2006, p. 687).

For those whose earliest patterns are derived from relational trauma, an experience in therapy must seek to modify such responses by providing a different affective experience through relating with another at the deepest levels both consciously and unconsciously. Crucial are the unconscious affective exchanges between therapist and patient, patient and therapist, in the service of remaking the patient's experience of relationship. Although cognitive approaches, including interpretation and verbal response to interpretation in therapy, are the left hemisphere's necessary contribution, they are never in themselves enough (Schore, 2007b). Nevertheless, the left hemisphere does enable us to understand the symbolic material and the complexity of self and self states.

How does the therapist actually approach the therapeutic task? Chused (2007) suggests that "presenting oneself as curious, interested in connecting, without an agenda, without intrusion, is how we try to approach every patient" (p. 875). Brown (2001) draws attention to the observational skill necessary to read the emotional body language of the patient, which often speaks louder than any words are able to in the early stages of therapy. She suggests that "it requires a finely attuned consciousness to discern and comprehend . . . changes within the body which are also the signal to changes in the psyche" (p. 137). De Gelder (2006) puts forward a sophisticated two-systems model as a way of understanding our processing of the emotional body language of the other: she posits an automated reflex such as a sub-cortical circuit and a cortically controlled circuit which enables recognition and reflection (pp. 246–47). Such comments may seem rather mystifying to the reader who wishes to learn exactly how to engage patients in the empathic way that is advocated by those who stress the value of the relational aspects of the therapeutic encounter. What is required to achieve a relationally thera-peutic encounter will vary from patient to patient and from session to session as well as within a session. However, neurobiology and attach-ment and trauma theories provide useful pointers for the therapist to bear in mind.

Trauma may affect hippocampal functioning and explicit memory and leave the patient with a highly sensitized amygdala store of painful emotional memories that might even be held only in the body. Such memories make it difficult to regulate affect and to function well in life and in relationships, and they often bring patients to therapy. The ther-apist with a good understanding of these memory systems and the issues concerning affect regulation and attachment will search to find the most effective way to help patients process such painful affects and to gradu-ally build a personal narrative that is not so unbearable that it has to be split off again. Instead, this new narrative becomes storable in the hippocampus and retrievable in a bearable form because it is based on current experience in the consulting room. Material from implicit memory may be difficult to retrieve, but the therapist whose work is grounded in insights concerning the neurobiology of emotion, and particularly the role of the right hemisphere in processing it, will pay attention to dissociative states of mind, and to the patient's use of metaphor, which through vivid, visual images will carry emotional truth from the world of the implicit. Knox (2003) points out that meanings held in the inner world of imagination and metaphor arise from mental representations or image schemas which develop out of bodily experience. Such image schemas provide "the invisible scaffolding for a whole range of metaphorical extensions that can be expressed in conscious imagery" (p. 62). Visual experience and expression as well as emotional experience all arise in the right hemisphere, and it is the right hemisphere that is also densely connected into the body and involved in the processing of bodily experience. With less "background noise" from past trauma and an experience of a good attachment in the present, the patient gradually becomes more able to self-regulate affect and to move more confidently into relationships.

One patient has described in detail how helpful she found her therapist's ability to explore what would work for her and to draw from a wide range of therapeutic techniques to meet her particular need of the moment. The patient recounts:

> She tried several approaches with me before she found the one that worked best for me. The approach was eclectic and focused on trauma but in a way that was humane and minimized triggering further trauma. My psychotherapist used different techniques as the need arose and was able to hear what I needed without imposing theoretical models that would have been unworkable for me. It was a partnership, and was important because it meant an early foundation of trust was laid. (McQueen et al., 2008, p. 59, adapted from Royal College of Psychiatrists and the British Psychological Society, 2005)

Such trust is difficult to achieve yet crucial to successful work with those whose early attachments are filled with pain. There is a proliferation of new techniques in psychotherapy and recommendations concerning ways of working that seek to utilize the insights that are emerging from the new disciplines. Together they provide a rich storehouse for each therapist to explore in order to achieve the therapeutic efficacy described by this patient.

This multiplicity of new techniques confronts creative therapists with new challenges as they consider how to apply such techniques in their clinical practice. Here again insights from neurobiology may help to ground their choices. My aim here is not to offer another set of guidelines for practices that should be adopted but rather to enable therapists to develop *ways of thinking about the insights that are emerging from the fields of neurobiology, attachment, and trauma* in relation to the new emphases that are emerging in clinical practice. Therapists can enrich their therapeutic practice as they begin to utilize insights from a wide range of sources. Each therapist brings his or her uniqueness to the therapeutic task, and the way in which each works with each patient will be different as a particular relationship emerges, and will change and change again, as the therapy develops. Integral to this book is the clinical case material that demonstrates the way that affective engagement enables benign therapeutic change and the development of mind. Certain basic considerations will always need to be held in mind as the therapist approaches work with a new patient. They are the particular ways in which intersubjective experience has given rise to the patient's unique inner world. Many patients will come to therapy because the anxiety or depression they are experiencing is unbearable. Some will struggle with despair and yet long for change both in their inner and outer worlds. Others will be struggling with somatic difficulties that they perceive may actually be intimately linked to mind. Any contemporary approach to changing minds involves judicious consideration of the relative weight to be given to the affective and cognitive alongside the intra—and intersubjective domains at any given moment.

Intra- versus Intersubjective Emphases

Some seek to emphasize the importance of the intrasubjective experience in relation to early memories. Mayman (1968) regarded early memories as a source of information about a person's inner world rather than primarily as an accurate account of past experience.

Fowler et al. (2000) describe his way of working as a "projective technique" with roots in learning theory, ego psychology, and object relations theory. In an earlier paper they explained that in their view "inner object constellations intrude into the content and structure of early memories, just as they occur repetitively in important interpersonal relationships" (Fowler et al.,1996, p. 401). Clearly such material is an invaluable tool for understanding mechanisms of projection and of transference.

What I am aware of here is the emphasis that is given to the intrasubjective domain as determining recall of past intersubjective experience and as affecting present experience as well as being a predictor of relational patterns that will stretch into the future. Others, including attachment theorists, will place greater stress on early intersubjective experience as determining intrasubjective states of mind, thus affecting present experience and predicting future responses, returning us again to the importance of nonconscious predictive patterns in the mind, by which past events tend to determine future experience, or at least determine the way in which future experience is understood. Pally (2007) comments: "We learn from the past what to predict for the future and then live the future we expect. . . . What a young child learns about how relationships tend to go with early caretakers can leave an enduring impact on the child's nonconscious expectation of how relationships will tend to go with people in general" (pp. 863–863).

Hope

Cheavens and Dreer (2008) report research that suggests that hope is a key factor in bringing about purposeful change in therapy and protecting against depression. As I noted earlier, hope and resilience are intimately linked; the experience of one makes the other possible even in difficult circumstances. Therapy that seeks to maximize the transformative nature of hope is understood by these researchers as having two components: the development of the ability to recognize and map what one wants, and the strengthening of the desire and ability to achieve it. An approach in which the therapist seeks to build on patients' recognized strengths and to teach them how to develop unrecognized ones is essential.

Soma

The somatic domain is understood as the source of the earliest relational experienced with the primary caregiver. Our approach to the patient then must surely include a mind–brain–*body* focus. The therapist may specialize in mind, but mind can be treated properly only if it is treated as one aspect of the varied and complex system that is the whole living organism. As van der Kolk (1996) has suggested, "the body keeps the score" (p. 214). Coming from the opposite direction, body therapists, dance therapists, and movement therapists are increasingly utilizing techniques that consider not just the body but rather the whole body–mind–brain being. Therapists in both "hemispheres" have much to learn from each other. De Gelder (2006) argues that, in particular, the research into emotional body language that is a rapidly developing new field in neuroscience will have much to contribute to our understanding of the importance of mind–brain–body—and body–mind–brain—interaction (de Gelder, 2006).

Sensorimotor psychotherapy (Ogden, Minton, & Pain, 2006) is a thoughtful approach developed to address the somatoform symptoms that indicate unresolved trauma. Bodily experience is the focus of the therapist's work and is understood as a way to help resolve lingering trauma symptoms. Emotional expression and meaning-making arise out of attending to the patient's bodily sensations. It becomes possible to address the more primitive, automatic reactions that underlie traumatic and posttraumatic responses by means of this promising therapeutic approach. Consideration is also being given to somatoform dissociation (Van der Hart et al., 2006), its links to early relational trauma, and the way in which this response may damage every aspect of mind–brain and body, including the development of a stable core self.

I work with the mind primarily, yet I increasingly realize just how much attention I need to pay to the body, indeed just how much attention I *do* pay to the body as I work. I understand the mind–brain–body system as building and rebuilding its structures through relating to others at every level of experience. One significant memory I have of this relational impact concerns an experience with a colleague as part of our professional development. We were working in pairs; he was looking inward, reaching into bodily experience to focus on an earlier frightening experience. I sought to gain some sense of it using my own mind–brain–body system. As I sought to attune to him, I suddenly found myself physically and emotionally aware of a seemingly long forgotten incident from my own early childhood. I was in a cot in my parents' room. My mother and I were visiting my father, who was working away from home at that time. My father gave me a large, flat green boiled sweet that was shaped like a penny. I had not been used to such a sweet and almost immediately tried to swallow it, whereupon it got stuck in my throat. I remembered vividly the physical pain of it. I didn't remember much else except how cross my mother was with my father for giving me such a thing. I was startled by the vivid recall; I said nothing, endeavoring to stay on task, to focus on the other and to intuit what he might be experiencing. To my surprise afterward he told that he had found himself focusing on a forgotten but very scary incident when, as a child, he had choked on a boiled sweet. He had become very frightened until finally it was dislodged. Both of us had accessed memories held only in the body that we still needed to allow into the mind in order to process in a healing way. For me the route to my own self-knowledge had come through this experience of attunement to another.

Assessment Issues

Assessment and treatment of people who have been abused as children are complex undertakings and may prove to be emotionally disturbing to the therapist. As a consequence he or she may wish to use supervision to give due consideration to the type, timing, duration, and intensity of the therapy, which may vary from patient to patient in this client group; for example, separate courses of treatment may be required at times of change or major life events throughout the lifespan (McQueen et al., 2008).

At assessment, which may require several sessions depending on the complexity of the patient's needs, the therapist and patient are probably both trying to absorb quite a lot of information about each other. For the patient not least will be the task of gradually making a decision as to whether this particular therapist is someone with whom the patient would feel comfortable working. The patient may have very relevant questions to ask about the qualifications of the therapist and the nature of the therapy being offered. As the therapist, I have a series of questions that will help me explore whether the person will be able to use this therapy. I try to allow the patient to tell his or her story. I may ask brief open-ended questions to help the person to say what he or she needs to say. I may perhaps encourage the patient to attend to the affect if he or she is very switched off by asking "How did you feel?" I may intervene to help the person to control and contain affect that threatens to overwhelm him or her, perhaps by saying "That must have been very difficult for you." Such a simple remark acknowledges the pain and may help the person feel more contained without interrupting the flow of his or her material. Meanwhile I am evaluating issues, such as:

- What has brought this patient to therapy?
- Is the kind of therapy I offer appropriate for this patient at this time?
- Would another form of treatment be more appropriate?
- Is the patient able to demonstrate any capacity for insight into his or her current distress?
- Are early factors contributing to the patient's current state of mind?
- What was the patient's original family like? What was his or her place in it in relation to mother, father, siblings, significant others?
- How has the patient met the ordinary developmental hurdles that life presents?

- What about his or her current circumstances?
- Is the patient in a relationship currently? Has he or she ever been?
- Does the patient have children?
- How do relationships work in the patient's current family or with his or her friends?
- Is the patient working? If not, how is he or she managing the unstructured time that arises from this?
- What are his or her unconsciously determined ways of dealing with difficulties?
- Does he or she dissociate, and if so, in what way?
- What capacity does the patient have to self-regulate his or her affect?
- Will the patient be able to work in therapy?
- What level of inner strength does the patient have?
- What capacity is the patient demonstrating for tolerating or embracing change?
- How is this patient affecting me: by what he or she says, by what he or she makes me feel emotionally, and by what bodily sensations he or she is able to evoke in me?

I do not address these questions, which concern attachment style, traumatic experience, the nature of the patient's defense system, and his or her ego strength, to the patient as such. For me the most important aspect of the session is not information gathering but rather an exploration of the patient's capacity to begin to engage in a therapeutic relationship. I want the patient to feel heard so I start by asking what brings the patient to see me. Nevertheless I will be looking for the answers to each of those other questions and after the session will note carefully not only the relevant information that emerged but any areas that we failed to cover so that I may bear them in mind in future sessions. If the patient seems to have developed dissociative ways of managing trauma, I may need to ask some specific questions (McQueen et al., 2008), such as, "Have you ever felt as if you were outside your own body or a bit unreal, maybe as if you were observing yourself from outside?" An affirmative answer inevitably leads to further discussion of how often and in what circumstances. I might question "Do you ever feel you have lost track of what happened for a few minutes or perhaps for longer chunks of time?" If the patient tells of a traumatic incident or difficult experiences spread over time, I might ask "Do you get overtaken by flashbacks to that?"

Questions related to risk assessment and self-harm will also be in the back of my mind and will be asked if necessary.

Structure and Setting

Although such a session might seem unstructured, it is actually structured fairly tightly. I practice what I think of as the "law of thirds" in relation to any session:

1. The first part allows the patient to settle into the room and into the work.
2. The middle of the session is the part where grappling with difficult material, sometimes arising out of transference projections, may be done most effectively.
3. The last third is the time needed to allow the patient to leave in a manageable state of mind; this period is ignored at the patient's peril, particularly with those who have experienced early relational trauma and where affective engagement with the therapist may occur rapidly and involve very primitive levels of mind.

For these patients the "holding" environment that the therapist creates initially will be crucial. Sessions that happen reliably and that begin and end on time give a sense of security. The setting also needs to remain as constant as possible; sometimes the therapist's room is the first place that has ever felt like a really safe place to be for patients whose underlying fear and anxiety may have penetrated almost every aspect of their lives. Even the arrangement of the room has a part to play in enabling the patient to feel safely held in a nonthreatening way. If a patient is easily overwhelmed by fear or angry feelings, he or she will feel less prey to these emotions if the therapist is not seated in a way that blocks their way out of the room. The seating arrangement needs to permit emotional space but should also allow the patient and therapist to engage each other's gaze in a natural way. This experience of looking, of gazing, may well become an important part of the ensuing therapy. Gaze plays a crucial part in the development of a sense of self and a sense of the other and underpins all social relating that develops out of the earliest relationship (Schore, 1994, 2003a, 2003b). Now I turn to an initial session with a patient whom I call Clare.

Case Example: Clare

Clare entered the room somewhat shyly, it seemed. I had the fleeting impression of a teenager with long loose hair, but then was somewhat more able to perceive the reality of the slender woman in her 30s who stood uncertainly just inside the door. After a moment or two of introduction she sat down and began to look a little more relaxed as she settled into the room. In response to my initial open-ended question "What brings you to see me?" Clare told of her growing unhappiness through her late 20s as no relationship seemed to last. She was finding it increasingly difficult to believe that a man might find her attractive enough to pursue seriously. When asked "Can you say more about how you feel?," it became clear that she was struggling with feelings of depression and sometimes had suicidal feelings, but that she had made no plans around them, nor had she ever taken any directly suicidal action. However, she did tell of walking through a red light and finding herself nearly under the wheels of a car.

It became clear that her father's attitude was one of unrelenting hostility, the only way she had ever known him to be with her. She loved her mother and liked to spend time with her, but her mother was unhappy in her marriage; nevertheless, she stayed with her husband. Her mother's distress manifested itself in sudden and unpredictable mood swings and outbursts of temper, which always took her daughter by surprise and terrified her.

Her father had left 3 months before her birth for a long spell working onboard a ship, and he was away for most of the first 3 years of her life. Much of her earliest experience with her mother was happy; her mother's family were nearby and provided support to the young mother and baby in the absence of her husband. Later her mother told her that when she was in her stroller and they passed a sailor in uniform, which happened often as they lived in a port, she would wave and say "That's my daddy," much to her young mother's embarrassment. What the tale seems to show is a child in whom the hope of a daddy to love had been kept alive.

Reality had provided a very different experience, and my patient's initial hesitant telling of it provided a cameo of a young child's painful swing toward disillusionment. When he returned from his spell in the merchant navy, Clare's young father was hostile and rejecting of the child whom he clearly resented as having displaced him in his wife's affections. When asked about her early memories of her father, Clare reported that her first clear memory was of coming home for lunch, having just started at nursery school. She remembered being in the dining room, a sense of her father's looming face, his hostile eyes, his shouting and shouting at her, and that then the room seemed to go dark. The next thing she knew she was standing at the bottom of the sunlit garden, under the lilac tree which was in full flower. She looked back momentarily at the open doors that led to the dark space that was the dining room from which she had fled, or been banished. She recalled standing under the tree for a long time, slowly tracing the design of the badge on her new school blazer pocket with her finger over and over again. She had been so proud of her uniform and of starting school. It was as if she had tried to hang on to something good as she stood under the sweet-smelling tree and traced the design with her finger. The design on her school blazer badge was also of a tree, an oak tree. Recalling the experience in therapy, she commented that the oak tree was masculine in its strength but provided protection, not threat. She couldn't remember anything else.

Some time into the therapy, during her mother's last illness, Clare recounted that as her mother lay dying she had said to her, "I am so sorry for what happened to you . . . I should have left him . . . You didn't understand what was happening . . . You were so frightened when he shouted at you . . . I remember the day when you came home from school. . . ." Clare was amazed to find that her mother still remembered and recounted the incident almost as she herself remembered it. But Clare had forgotten her mother's presence in the room on that fateful day. A mother so unable to protect her had been clearly too unbearable for the young Clare to keep in mind. Yet down the years this patient had sought a mother figure who would be there for her. It was only with much difficulty and continued support in therapy that she could become separate enough from her parents in her internal world to be able to begin to live her life.

Conclusion

There is an increasing application of insights from the research on the neurobiology of emotion to the basic principles of psychotherapeutic technique among practitioners in the psychological therapies as well as in the wider field of mental health practitioners in general. The study of the neurobiology of emotion may inform matters of practice as basic as the effects of the arrangement of the consulting room and those as complex as experiencing affective engagement with the therapist and the transference and countertransference. Nevertheless, "the subtlety of communication that can be transformative as a result of analysis lies in the uniquely human realm of the symbolic" (Lichtenberg, 2003, p. 141). It is to address the needs of patients such as Holly and Clare in the most appropriate way possible that I seek to clarify, in this book, the complex relationship between several strands of psychological understanding and the neural complexities of the process by which minds may change in therapy.

2

Attachment and Affect Regulation

Early Attachment

THE INITIAL ENGAGEMENT IN THERAPY with trauma patients requires an understanding of the earliest ways of relating that give rise to patterns of feeling, being, and behaving that persist throughout life unless another meaningful relationship can harness the plasticity of the brain to bring about lasting change. It is in the context of relationship that healing change can occur.

From birth, and even before birth, the provision of a nurturing environment is the key to emotional well-being and the realization of the full developmental potential of an individual because genetic potentialities can only become activated by actual early experience of secure and loving caregiving. Hart (2008) notes that first relationships influence the internal hormonal environment of the infant and that these hormones in turn influence the way in which the baby's genetic material manifests itself. Thus the early development of mind is dependent on each individual's experiences of relating to others. I summarize below Gergely and Unoka's (2008) list of the species-specific characteristics of human mother–baby interactions:

- A "proto-conversational" turn-taking contingency structure
- Baby's preference for eye contact, contingent reactivity, and "motherese"
- Baby's attention to and gaze-following activities
- Frequent exchanges of rich and varied facial–vocal displays of emotion
- Empathic affect-mirroring displays of emotion
- Baby's capacity to reenact parents facial–vocal displays of emotion

Schore (2003b) explains that in such face-to-face interactions the child uses the output of the mother's emotion-regulating right cortex as a template for the imprinting of his or her own right cortex that will mediate his or her own expanding abilities. Bucci (1997) notes that as "repeated observations of an object form functionally equivalent classes and prototypic images, so repeated episodes with a common affective core, involving other persons in relation to the self, also form functionally-equivalent classes" (p. 195). The baby internalizes models of emotion schemas for self in relation to others based on his or her particular experiences of interactions with the caregiver. The care offered will reflect, to a great extent, the parent's own early experience of being cared for and his or her own attachment style. Cozolino (2006) notes that poor early experience may have an adverse effect on the development and organization of the spindle cells in the anterior cingulate, with lifelong consequences for cognitive and emotional functioning. These consequences will include the child's own future parenting style—which means that poor early experience may be passed on from generation to generation.

In good-enough circumstances caregivers establish a warm, empathic way of being with a child that forges a secure attachment, from which the growing child steps confidently into the wider world. The very rapid form of learning that occurs through the holding and smiling and vocal exchanges of the first months of life "irreversibly stamps early experience upon the developing nervous system and mediates attachment bond formation" (Schore, 2003a, p. 277). In good-enough circumstances this earliest emotional learning happens naturally as mother and baby begin to get to know each other. Such an experience inevitably includes the sensitive regulation of affect that an attentive and secure mother is able to offer to her baby and which leads, in due time, to the development of the ability to self-regulate affect.

Neural Substrates of Early Attachment

Relating to another in this healthy way is an early right-hemisphere activity that stimulates the growth of the centers for speech and language in the later developing left hemisphere of the brain, leading ultimately to the development of the child's own mind (Tzourio-Mazoyer et al., 2002). In this respect the affectionate interaction with caregivers literally "grows" the baby's brain (Gerhardt, 2004). Research with infants shows that the brain tissue where language is localized begins to develop as early as 3 months of age, that the functional cortical specialization involved in face recognition and processing is "online" at 6 months of age (de Haan & Nelson, 1999), and that by 1 year it is possible to identify the significant role played by the orbitofrontal cortex in positive exchanges between a mother and her infant (Minagawa-Kawai et al., 2008).

As the right brain is online from birth, it is a key player in these early emotional learning processes. Right-brain learning is primarily relational in nature; therefore, successful learning will inevitably be personalized. Patterns of expectation of how relationships will go begin to accumulate in the young child's brain; they are stored in implicit or emotional memory and have a lasting effect on the way a young person begins to expect interactions to be with another, indeed all others. The sparse connections in the infant brain–mind mean that the child is much like a play about to be written: to a certain extent the content is already determined (genetically), but the drama that will emerge is as yet unknown and will be shaped by environmental influences. The baby's brain responds to healthy interaction with another brain–mind by growing more neuronal connections than will ultimately be needed, so a neural pruning takes place in which cells without inputs die. The "use it or lose it" principle of learning is at work from the very beginning: appropriate levels of stimulation and interaction with another are key in this crucial developmental process (Wilkinson, 2006a).

The new "non-invasive neuroimaging techniques that allow three-dimensional spatial mapping of metabolic activity (which reflects level of neuronal activity) in real time" (Sherwood, 2006, p. 63) allow us "to measure *in vivo* subtle inter-individual differences in brain structure and to assess activity in distinct neural circuits from birth to adulthood" (Paus, 2005, p. 60). Knickmeyer et al. (2008) carried out a large-scale study using functional magnetic resonance imaging (fMRI) on brain development in the first 2 years after birth. They reported earlier work that identified a dramatic increase in overall brain size with, by age 2, the brain reaching 80–90% of adult volume, rapid elaboration of new synapses, an increase in overall gray matter volume, and myelination of white matter. Their own study revealed the following:

> Total brain volume increased 101% in the first year, with a 15% increase in the second. The majority of hemispheric growth was accounted for by gray matter, which increased 149% in the first year; hemispheric white matter volume increased by only 11%.

Cerebellum volume increased 240% in the first year. Lateral ventricle volume increased 280% in the first year, with a small decrease in the second. The caudate increased 19% and the hippocampus 13% from age 1 to age 2. (p. 12,176)

Early Attachment and A Robust Sense of Self

Further research has indicated that securely attached mothers are more able to match their babies' moods than those with less secure or disorganized attachments (Haft & Slade, 1989). Researchers also observe the importance of therapeutic intervention in the first year of life for those most at risk, citing data from the Bucharest Early Intervention Project, which is studying a group of Romanian children in foster care who had earlier experienced extreme deprivation in orphanages. They note that children placed in foster care before 2 years of age appear to be making far better improvements in cognitive development than those placed in foster care after the age of 2. Chugani's earlier study of Romanian orphans had shown that these children, "cut off from close bonds with an adult by being left in their cots all day, unable to make relationships, had a virtual black hole where their orbitofrontal cortex should be" (as cited in Gerhardt, 2004, p. 38).

What is becoming more and more evident from research in both contemporary neuroscience and attachment is that a young person's brain and mind will owe a huge amount to the infant's and growing child's experiences of nurture with the mother, with the father, and with significant others, and later with the world of school and the wider world beyond it. It is much more than merely the young person's brain that is the outcome of successful affect regulation and the development of emotional competence in the earliest years. Rather it is the interactive development of an ever-increasing connectivity resulting in the complexity that is mind, which in turn gives rise to varied but interlinked self states. Ultimately it is on issues around attachment and affect regulation that a person's capacity to experience a sense of self that is, as noted previously, "simultaneously fluid and robust" depends (Bromberg, 2006, p. 32).

Research indicates not only that the right hemisphere is dominant for face recognition and sense of self throughout life but also that even 2-month-old infants looking at their mother's face utilize what, in the left hemisphere, will later become their language network. Tzourio-Mazoyer et al. (2002) note that "co-activation of the face and the future language network sustains the facilitative efforts of social interactions, such as looking at the mother's face, on language development" and establishes a sense of self and others (p. 460). The capacity of the young child to develop a secure and robust sense of self and of personal identity as well as of the identity of another was brought home to me recently in a rather charming way by Naja, the young daughter of close friends. This young family spoke a language that I had struggled (rather unsuccessfully) to acquire. Naja had seen me every month or so since she was born and almost always greeted me with delight, gurgling away as I lalled to her in English. She was about 1 year old when I began using some words of her own language to speak to her, and the look of recognition was clear to behold in contrast with our encounters in English, which relied heavily on affect for our sense of being in touch with one another. At 15 months her father spoke to her in English on one occasion when I had not been there for several weeks. To his surprise Naja immediately smiled broadly and exclaimed "Maggie!," demonstrating that both receptive and expressive language have their roots firmly in relationship (Figure 2.1).

Early Patterns of Attachment and Their Effect on Affect Regulation

Given that the mind is fundamentally associative and its development based on psychological identification, these early patterns of relating are inevitably transferred to significant others in the outside world. The teacher who looks after children in their first year in school may hardly recognize herself in the eyes of a frightened or angry child who is reacting to her so badly on the basis of earlier traumatic experience. In contrast, the boy or girl whose early experience has led to secure attachments will go forth confidently into the world, aware of how to engage with others in a comfortable way. In other words, in the important new relationships that they make, children mirror ways of being with others and expecting others to be that are already firmly established inside. These processes are early, implicit, and emotional in nature. Emotional competence is achieved through healthy interaction with another mind, which provides a secure base from which further emotional learning may take place. When a mother is depressed or withdrawn, she may not be able to respond adequately to her baby's needs, and her baby's state of distress will escalate. When the mother repeatedly responds in a fearful, angry, terrifying, or inconsistent, unpredictable way, then the child that baby becomes will be affected throughout his or her whole mind–brain–body.

When a mother is unable to protect a child from abuse, the world becomes a terrifying place, and secure attachment moves out of reach without skilled intervention. If sustained trauma is experienced at the hands of those closest to the child, then there are far-reaching effects on the development of mind. Fonagy (1991) suggests that "the parent's abuse undermines the child's theory of mind, so that it is no longer safe for the child . . . to think about wishing, if this implies the contemplation of the all too real wishes of the parent to harm the child" (p. 649).

Case Example: Harriet

A little girl of about 4 years old, whom I will call Harriet, was part of a happy group of children in short-term fostering going to a *son et lumière* show in the local park. Harriet was in care while her mother was in the hospital and her father was working abroad. She chattered happily to her foster carer who was pushing her in her buggy, enjoying the colored lights, strung through the trees, which came on as they passed them. Harriet enjoyed music and sang along happily to some tunes that were familiar to her. Suddenly the park darkened and the first few notes of some rather scary music came out of the darkness; a sense of urgency and foreboding in the music grew rapidly. Suddenly bright lights flashed out of the darkness at about the height of the child's face. Harriet became absolutely rigid; the change was noted instantly by the foster carer, who knew that the child had a history of early relational trauma. The group walked away as quickly as possible, rapidly making their way to the well-lit area around the café in the park. As they walked, the foster carer leaned forward, touched Harriet's head gently, and soothed her saying, "It's all right, you're with me now and John and Alice are here, and we're all going to get a drink of hot chocolate." Slowly the rigidity left the child's body and gradually she began to relax once again. The foster carer had regulated the level of arousal and averted what appeared to be the beginning of a catastrophic reexperiencing of trauma, triggered by the sudden flashing of bright lights in the darkness and the music that was frightening to the child.

The next day when they were in the car on the way to nursery, Harriet said to the foster carer, "What happened to me when we went to the park?" The foster carer thought for a moment and replied calmly, "I think you were reminded of scary times." "Yes, what did you say?" asked Harriet. "I said that you were safe, and you were with John and Alice and me," replied the carer. "Mmm . . . and?" "And we went to get the hot chocolate." Enough had been said for the moment and the child moved on to talk about school. The careful way the carer responded to the child's rather frightened questioning regulated the affect that the child experienced at the transition moment of leaving the carer and going into nursery. This intervention would help her create a coherent narrative of her immediate experience without foreclosing on the exploration of more painful aspects when the child became ready to do so. Later the social worker told the foster carer that new evidence had emerged that the child had been abused in the illicit video industry. Sadly the reasons for Harriet's intense reaction to the sudden bright light and music were now all too apparent.

The vivid visual and emotional "pictures," such as may have come to Harriet's mind in the park revealing aspects of early traumatic affective experience, are products of right-brain activity, recorded in implicit memory. The early traumatic experience is not encoded as part of an autobiographical narrative that is easily accessible because the hippocampus that tags time and place to memory would not have been online yet. Rather the experience would have remained as part of Harriet's implicit memory, only to emerge when a stimulus such as similar feeling tone, sight, or smell awakens it, much in the way her traumatic experience was reevoked by the light and music in the park.

The method that the foster carer demonstrated will resonate with those who look to regulate levels of arousal within therapy.

- She was alert to the child's level of arousal.
- She sought to regulate that level.
- She used the rhythm, lilt, and melody of her voice to calm the child.
- She moved the child's attention away from the environmental triggers rather than allowing the triggering to continue, leading to further arousal.
- She steadied the child by returning her to positive present sensory experience and to current nurturing relationships.
- Later she steadied the child again by answering her questions in a way that enabled the child to remain regulated at a moment of transition when reengaging with the outside world of school.
- She sought to help the child to think about her experience in a manageable way so that the processes of mentalization were assisted rather than discouraged.

Overview of Memory Systems

Encoding

Memory processing consists of encoding and retrieval, and plays a vital part in allowing us to develop a sense of self as well as a sense of self in relation to others over time. Memory makes possible the pattern-matching and meaning-making processes that allow us to build on earlier experience in a creative way, that enable us to make sense of current experience, and to regulate our affect in the light of past experience. LeDoux (2002) describes memory as the maintenance and stabilization of changes in synaptic connectivity over time. Patients who, due to neurological deficits or damage, are unable to remember, live in an endlessly present moment without the benefits that memory may bring to bear on the capacity to regulate affect arising out of current experience. Let's first review briefly the nature and making of memory. The asymmetries in the two hemispheres of the brain give rise to two very different systems for processing and recording different types of experience. One is known as explicit or declarative memory, which can be accessed and spoken about. The other is described as implicit, nondeclarative, or procedural memory and is not dependent upon conscious processes. Understanding the nature of these two systems is fundamental to our appreciation of the connection between relational and interpretational aspects of the therapeutic process. The earliest form of memory is unconscious, implicit, emotional, and inaccessible, arising out of right-hemisphere processing of early relational experience; it is online from birth. This memory system stores procedural information such as acquired skills, the "how to" of memory conditioned and emotional and unconscious responses that manifest in fundamental ways of moving through the world. This memory system also stores emotional memory, which derives from emotional responses to stimuli and is processed by the amygdala. Negative or traumatic feeling responses are particularly associated with the amygdala. Appreciating the existence of implicit memory allows the concept of the unconscious to include anatomical structures where emotional, affective, sometimes traumatic, presymbolic preverbal experiences are stored (Mancia, 2005, p. 83). LeDoux (2002) points out that many different systems in the brain engage in implicit learning. He notes that these are not specifically memory systems as such, but were designed for specific functions such as perceiving stimuli, controlling precise movements, and maintaining balance. He adds that "plasticity (the ability to change as a result of experience) is simply a feature of the neuronal structure of these systems" (p. 117).

Later memory is conscious, explicit, informational, and accessible, arising from predominantly left-hemisphere processing and online by the time a child is about 3 years of age. Explicit memory consists of episodic, personal, biographical memory—the "this is my life" type of memory—and semantic factual memory—the "what" of memory. Explicit memory content is processed by the hippocampus, which tags time and place to memory (the "where" and "when") ensuring the memory's accessibility to consciousness in an identifiable form. Once the hippocampus has consolidated the memory in the cortex, each individual element that comprises the memory is stored at the cortical site where it was originally received (Wilkinson, 2006a).

Retrieval

The retrieval of memories is "not the simple act of accessing a storehouse of ready-made photos in a stable neural album" (Young & Saver, 2001, p. 79). The different elements of a particular memory are "distributed widely across different parts of the brain, such that no single location contains a literal trace or engram that corresponds to a specific experience" (Schacter & Addis, 2007a, p. 774). Retrieval requires a complex assembling of these constituent elements that have been stored at the various cortical sites. When recall has taken place and its use is over for that occasion, then the memory is disassembled, so to speak, and stored again in its individual elements at the original cortical sites. Those elements remain ready to be reassembled should they be required, but with the overlay of the most recent experience of remembering. Synaptic plasticity plays a significant part in "the organizational basis of long-term memory, implicit and explicit" (Mancia, 2005, p. 86). The actual reexperiencing of the memory and the context in which that takes place will affect the process. A memory of fear is not necessarily permanent and can change when retrieved: "The reactivation of a consolidated [fear] memory can return it to a labile, supposedly protein synthesis-dependent state, a process that is referred to as reconsolidation" (Kindt et al., 2009, p. 1). The working through of fear memories in the safety of the therapeutic relationship may help to weaken their destructive power in just this way. It may be necessary to regulate the process of the return of memory, slowing it down and helping the patient toward self-regulation of affect, so that the trauma is processed in small manageable amounts.

In this realm it is not a question of true or false, belief or disbelief, but of respecting the emotional integrity of the process while appreciating that what is held in implicit memory is, by definition, unthinkable and therefore will not provide what may be thought of as accurate snapshots of a particular traumatic experience.

Memory and Affect Regulation in Therapy

Emergent Memory

A patient remembered vividly her "Bunnikins" plate from which, in her earliest years, she ate every day (Figure 2.2). In one session she seemingly recounted each detail of the picture and her memory of being told to "eat up, then you will be able to see the little rabbits" or "have another mouthful, then you will be able to see the pretty blue and white china on the dresser" or "where is Mrs. Rabbit? Can you find her?" She remembered that Mrs. Rabbit was bathing her little rabbits in a tin bath by the fire. They looked up into her face, enjoying the moment, just as the child must have looked up into her mother's face, enjoying the story of this moment in the little rabbits' life as she ate the inviting food provided for her. Another rabbit child was playing with a red and blue train. Above the window hung big bunches of bright orange carrots and white turnips, presumably to be eaten by the rabbit family at a later time. In the background was the dresser and on the shelves was a beautiful set of blue and white plates of different shapes and sizes. At one level a happy moment of family life was indissolubly linked to food forever for the patient who came to like nothing better than an informal meal with close friends.

After recounting this material in one session, the patient went home and looked again at the picture on the plate. The next day she commented that all was much as she had remembered, except for two rather significant differences: There were several rabbit children playing with toy horses, not one with a train, and the father rabbit was sitting peacefully close by reading his newspaper. The patient had one sibling, a younger brother who loved to play with his toy train and would usually have been "in the picture," in contrast, her father was often absent and when present had found it difficult to accept his eldest child. The patient's memory and telling of the story had accurately represented her own inner world experience, rather than the actuality of the picture on the plate. The original memory of the picture becomes overlaid with personal affective experiences with significant others, leading to a memory that privileges emotional truth over accurate physical detail.

How the therapist engages with the patient will contribute to the emergence of such memories. As aspects of earliest affective experiencing, the tone and musicality, the rhythm and lilt of the therapist's voice—the ability to speak in "pastel not primary" colors (Williams, 2004)—may help to access the patient's early experience. It is not only the words but also the right-hemisphere "processing of the 'music' behind our words"—the emotional right-brained engagement with the other—that enables the patient to explore traumatic early experience. Psychotherapy is not only the "talking cure" but perhaps rather the *communicating* cure (Schore & Schore, 2008, p. 14). Andrade (2005) suggests that often what is said is immaterial because "it is the affective content of the analyst's voice—not the semantic content—that has an impact on the patient's implicit memories" (Andrade, 2005, p. 683). I think this disregard of semantic content is to confuse, at least in part, the state of the baby mind where only implicit experiencing is possible, with the adult mind–brain, where both implicit and explicit memory reside. Furthermore, it is not only the voice but also the posture and especially the facial expression of the therapist that play a part in all this. Bucci (2001) argues that "subsymbolic indicators, such as vocal tone or body movement or reports of intense feelings, provide evidence that an intervention has connected to an emotion schema. . . . At some point, the analyst will call on verbal formulation . . . to test her understanding" (p. 65). Such work calls for "a profound commitment" by both and "a deep emotional involvement on the part of the therapist" (Schore & Schore, 2008, p. 16). Indeed, I would add a deep emotional involvement is needed by both, which is inevitably difficult to achieve adequately in a very limited number of sessions. When possible, I argue for treatment in depth over time, at least for those who, although significantly traumatized, reveal enough resilience to be able to make good use of such an approach.

Affect Regulation

Harriet, our little 4-year-old from the park, was fortunate in that therapy was arranged for her quickly, which enabled her to process much of her early trauma. Sadly for many that is not the case. Let us imagine for a moment that Harriet had not received help but had recently come into therapy some 20 years later, that difficult life events—such as the break up of a marriage, an incident of rape, or the loss of a child—have called forth her early experiences from the implicit memory store and they threaten to overwhelm again. Perhaps she finds herself easily upset, describing it in an initial interview as "crying with no reason," or alternatively increasingly worried by the fact that she finds herself inclined to switch off, drifting into states of "no think" and "no hear," so that her loved ones, friends, and work colleagues all begin to comment on how they are constantly having to try to regain her attention. She may need considerable help with affect regulation, and the therapist will see this focus as an integral aspect of the therapy. In an early session she may tell just how frightened she was of some of the films that she saw as a child. It might be that she remembers *Bambi*, and the hunter that killed the mother deer and left Bambi with the fierce stag father, or she might remember her horror in the *Wizard of Oz* when it became clear that the tin man hadn't got a heart. Slowly and painfully they begin to do some more work on the patient's story. It is not until much later in the therapy that Harriet recalls something of the incident in the park with its very close links to her forgotten early trauma. Patients with experiences such as Harriet's may struggle with affect regulation throughout their lives, especially at times of emotional stress. As adults it may be most helpful to reengage in shorter periods of supportive therapy during periods of major stress throughout their lifespan rather than assuming that one long period of therapy will resolve the problem forever (McQueen et al., 2008).

Therapists help patients such as Harriet learn to regulate their mood. As patient and therapist work, the therapist pays attention to changing levels of affect. "Like the securely attached mother, the empathic psychobiologically attuned clinician's regulation of the patient's affective-arousal states is critical to transforming the patient's insecure nonconscious internal working model that encodes strategies of affect regulation" (Schore, 2007a, p. 12). Regulatory processes are fast, often below levels of consciousness; they are intuitive, empathic responses to the other in the room. As he or she reflects on the session when it is over or in supervision, the therapist may ponder his or her own responses and wonder whether they were helpful to the patient or whether they were the effect of some unconscious defense. It is the continual integration of right-hemisphere responses with left-hemisphere understanding and discernment that enables effective affect regulation by the therapist. Eventually patients become able to internalize this affect regulation for their own well-being.

The therapist can utilize four broad foci for regulating affect in the therapy session: the body, words, timing, and the analytic frame.

• *The body as a regulator.* The therapist is aware not only of changes in mood communicated via words but also of mood changes revealed by fluctuations in the rhythm, lilt, and prosody of the voice; in breathing; skin tone/flushing; looking away, looking down, looking intently into the eyes of the therapist; turning away or turning toward the therapist; and in the tension or rigidity in the body versus states of floppiness. In response the therapist may lean forward and engage the patient's eyes to bring him or her back. Or the patient might find him- or herself leaning back and looking slightly away, unconsciously creating a degree of disengagement. If the patient becomes distressed and overaroused, it will be reflected immediately in her breathing; he or she may become breathless, may hold the breath, or may breathe too rapidly, which, if unattended, could result in a panic attack. If the therapist breathes slowly, calmly, and deliberately, the patient's breathing may soon follow the therapist's rhythm—such are the powers of mirroring, resonance, and empathy. Schore and Schore (2008) describe interactive psychobiological regulation as the fundamental purpose of nonconscious attachment dynamics and note that this regulation acts as an "essential promoter of the development and maintenance of synaptic connections during the establishment of functional circuits of the right brain" (p. 11).

• *Words as a regulator.* The therapist's words can draw the "switched off" patient back into the room and the therapeutic engagement. Sometimes as he or she reflects on her intuitive response to a particular patient, the therapist will notice that he or she used short sentences or brief open-ended questions. At other times he or she may have slowed her speech or modified the tone.

• *Timing as a regulator.* The therapist holds the stage of the session in mind, knowing that it is safest to deal with the most traumatic experience in the middle portion, so that the patient has time to recover and regulate his or her affect before leaving. If a patient has been unduly distressed, the therapist can become most active in helping him or her to regain equilibrium toward the end of the session, so that the patient leaves in a more regulated state of being. Simple remarks can help the patient to look around and refind familiar safe aspects of the room. The patient also may have found soothing inner images to hold on to that he or she can recreate to stabilize his or her mood.

• *The frame as a regulator.* As therapists we guarantee regular sessions that begin and end on time to provide continuity of time, space, and environment. We seek to provide a room that is not overstimulating, that is containing and protected from intrusion. Within the analytic frame we respect confidentiality and aim to work in a way that facilitates trust. We seek to behave in an absolutely predictable way around management of breaks, holidays, and fees. We regard boundaries as playing an essential part in the therapy itself.

Attachment and Its Effect on Affect Regulation in Adolescence

Goleman (1996) comments that "emotional intelligence is a master apti-tude, a capacity that profoundly affects all other abilities, either facili-tating or interfering with them" (p. 80). Emotional executive competence facilitates effective learning in every aspect of life and relationship. It is the socialization experiences of the early years and adolescence that play a vital role in the maturation of the orbitofrontal regions, the executive control centers of the brain. This control center of the brain, located in the cortex, the "thinking cap" of the brain (which is the latest part of the brain to develop in evolutionary terms and which is most highly devel-oped in humans), has direct connections to virtually every other part of the brain.

In the earliest years one of three problematic responses to relation-ship may develop and, in later years, will be clearly identifiable in adoles-cence. The teenager who is affected may well not realize it but will operate in a certain way with regard to others: as avoidant, ambivalent, or disorganized.

• *The avoidant adolescent.* If the adolescent could make a conscious statement about how he or she operates in relationships, it might be this: "I must avoid people's anger by avoiding knowledge of my own difficult feelings, pushing them down, switching them off." This pattern may lead to a distant, switched-off attitude to all that is offered by adults, in partic-ular. It is an attitude that may well be exacerbated in adolescence because of the natural urge toward separateness that is part of growing up. As such, it leads to a defended attitude toward the adult world and will interfere with emotional learning that requires cooperation with others.

• *The ambivalent adolescent.* This adolescent might say: "Sometimes people are okay, sometimes not; I must watch carefully and modify my mood and feelings to theirs." In adolescence some of young people become distant and avoid others, some become overanxious and clingy, overeager to please, unable to think and function independently, in their efforts to solve their dilemma of how to relate to others.

• *The disorganized adolescent.* This adolescent might say: "People are so unpredictable, I just don't know what to do for the best, whether to cling to others or to avoid them; I'm afraid all the time—sometimes I manage to pretend I am not, but it's there, deep down all the time." This last group of adolescents, who oscillate between clinging to and avoiding others, has the most complex response to relationship, these youngsters will find it most difficult to relax their guard enough to be able to relate empathically to others and to fully utilize learning opportunities. The plasticity of the brain may lead these young people into rapid dependence on alcohol, street drugs, or self-harm that may manifest in forms such as cutting. Alternatively, their anger may easily overwhelm them and lead to dysregulated behavior that results in antisocial activity.

These problematic attachment styles are not the problem of just a few of our young people. Holmes (1996) suggests that "in average populations about one-fifth of children are avoidant, one-sixth ambivalent, and one in twenty disorganized" in their attachment style (pp. 7–8). Without the provision of a different experience of relating made available in adequate therapy, these damaging patterns of attachment will become long-lasting, affecting the sense of self, in the deepest aspects of being, in a lasting way. Adolescence is further complicated by a second wave of nerve cell development, which results in the uneven development of emotional competence as emotional experience outpaces executive control. As the frontal cortex, responsible for reasoning and judgment, lags behind the limbic system in development, the availability of a good-enough parent or teacher who knows of when and how to say "no" may be of crucial importance in helping a young person to develop the internal ability to control impulsive behaviors. However, myelination of the axons is thought to increase at this time, making them into more effective transmitters that enable an increased capacity for communication and increased plasticity, which then permits rapid learning. Unfortunately, eating disorders, self-harming, and suicidal behaviors may emerge at this stage as the brain becomes as easily programmed to patterns of abuse as to patterns of achievement. Plasticity means that the young person very quickly becomes attached to the overwhelming pleasure that drug abuse seemingly brings.

If a different, more consistent experience of healthy relating is provided then these young people may be able to move into a "learned secure" attachment style. Schore and Schore (2008) note that providing experiences of secure attachment is the very heart of the therapeutic endeavor—"the essential matrix for creating a right brain that can regulate its own internal states and external relationships" (p. 17).

The Neurobiology of Attachment and Affect Regulation

Noriuchi et al. (2008), in an fMRI study of 13 mothers watching video clips of their own and other 16-month-old babies smiling and crying, found that a limited number of brain areas were specifically involved in recognition of their own infant, namely, the orbitofrontal cortex (OFC), the periaqueductal gray, the anterior insula, and the dorsal and ventrolateral parts of the putamen. They also demonstrated the strong and specific response of a mother's brain to her own infant's distress and the fact that a mother responds most strongly to her infant when it is in distress. A mother's own infant's distress cry activated multiple brain areas: the dorsal region of the OFC, the caudate nucleus, the right inferior frontal gyrus, prefrontal cortex (PFC), the dorsomedial prefrontal cortex (DPFC), the anterior cingulate, the posterior cingulate, the thalamus, the substantia nigra, and the posterior superior temporal sulcus.

A second study used fMRI scanning to explore the capacity of 16 mothers to understand and imitate their infant's facial communications, on the premise that in the their first year together, exchanges and communication between a mother and her infant are exclusively preverbal and are based on the mother's ability to understand her infant's needs and feelings in an empathic way (Lenzi et al., 2008). The mothers were scanned while watching and imitating faces of their own child and that of someone else's child. The researchers "found that the mirror neuron system, the insula and amygdala, were more active during emotional expressions, that this circuit is engaged to a greater extent when interacting with one's own child, and that it is correlated with maternal reflective function"; furthermore, "joy expressions evoked a response mainly in right limbic and paralimbic areas" and "ambiguous expressions elicited a response in left high-order cognitive and motor areas, which might reflect cognitive effort" (p. 1, 24) (Figure 2.3).

Panksepp (2008) argues that adequate early affective communication promotes the development of linguistic prosody within the developing right hemisphere. Here he echoes the work of Schore, who has long emphasized the key role of attachment communications between mother and infant in the development of the early maturing right hemisphere (Schore, 1994, 2003a, 2003b). He emphasizes that "the affective intensity of the emotions arises more from the lower subcortical reaches of the brain than the various conditional, secondary-process routes that enable control over emotional urges" (p. 48). He goes on to stress the central role of the right hemisphere in the early affective mother–infant interaction that allows "the programming of prosody," that is, "the lilting, sing-song emotional-communicative dance between mothers and infants, where high-pitched melodic 'motherese' prevails" (pp. 48–49), which, in turn, enables the development of language. Panksepp warns against the premature overlocalization of certain brain functions in certain brain areas. He also makes clear that no hard and fast boundaries can be discerned, for instance, in relation to the margins of the amygdala or indeed the boundaries of the limbic system. Panksepp prefers the use of terms such as the "extended amygdala" and the "extended limbic system."

Emde (1999), too, notes that the affective core depends on multiple experiences with significant others that become internalized in the course of early development. He acknowledges the importance of what Damasio (1994, 2003) conceptualizes as "background feelings"—that is, complex representations of current body states that are distributed over a number of cortical and subcortical brain locations. He comments: "Such feelings, Damasio emphasizes, contribute to our ongoing sense of identity, anchoring our 'illusory sense of sameness' in the midst of change" and adds that "since emotions are linked to specific relationship experiences in the past, they are likely to be activated by circumstances in the present that are similar" (Emde, 1999, p. 326).

The Effects of Trauma

It has become even clearer that early stress and maltreatment produce a cascade of events that have the potential to alter brain development in a

far-reaching manner that has consequences not only for current development but also for the later development of the slowly maturing brain.
Many studies have investigated the effects of trauma on the young developing brain and its implications for future mental well-being. Let's take a
bird's-eye look at some of the papers emanating from one researcher,
Teicher, undertaken with various colleagues. Teicher et al. (2002) studied
the developmental neurobiology of childhood stress and trauma and
noted that the first stage of the cascade of responses evoked by trauma
involves the stress-induced programming of the glucocorticoid, nora-
drenergic, and vasopressin–oxytocin systems to augment stress responses.
They concluded that these then affect neurogenesis, synaptic overproduc-
tion and pruning, and myelination during specific sensitive periods. Major
consequences include "reduced size of the mid-portions of the corpus
callosum, attenuated development of the left neocortex, hippocampus,
and amygdala," along with "abnormal frontotemporal electrical activity,
and reduced functional activity of the cerebellar vermis." They stressed
that such changes form the neurobiological framework through which
"early abuse increases the risk of developing posttraumatic stress disorder
(PTSD), depression, symptoms of attention-deficit/hyperactivity
disorder, borderline personality disorder, dissociative identity disorder,
and substance abuse" (Teicher et al., 2002, p. 397).

In a further study of the neurobiological consequences of early stress
and childhood maltreatment Teicher, et al. (2003) reported that "early
severe stress and maltreatment produces a cascade of neurobiological
events that have the potential to cause enduring changes in brain development." They stress that these changes occur on multiple levels, from
the neurohumoral (especially the HPA axis) to the structural and functional. They also stress that there are gender differences in vulnerability
and functional consequences (Teicher et al., 2003, p. 33).

Teicher, et al. (2004) explored the relation between childhood neglect
and reduced corpus callosum area. Magnetic resonance imaging (MRI)
scans were used to compare the corpus callosum area in 26 boys and 25
girls admitted for psychiatric evaluation (28 with abuse or neglect) with
115 healthy control subjects. Neglect was the strongest experiential
factor and was associated with a 15–18% reduction; sexual abuse seemed
to be the strongest factor associated with reduced corpus callosum area
in girls. Animal research has led to similar conclusions.

An overall view of research into the neurobiological and behavioral
consequences of exposure to childhood traumatic stress and its signifi-

cance for later development is offered by Teicher, et al. (2006). Emphasis is placed on the vulnerability and plasticity of the developing brain, which allow it to be sculpted by postnatal traumatic experience in far-reaching ways as the system attempts to adjust to what is perceived as a threatening, hostile environment. They conclude that "in essence, stress response systems are programmed by experience to respond more drastically to events in later life" (Teicher et al., 2006, p. 191). Alterations occur in the amygdala and other limbic regions as part of readying for the flight or fight response in the face of further threat.

Such stress-induced changes affect the trauma victim's capacity for engagement and affect regulation. Fonagy and Target (2008) point out the effect of early relational trauma on the child's attachment system: "Trauma normally causes a child to seek safety by gaining proximity to the attachment figure. This generates a characteristic dependency on the maltreating figure, with the real risk of an escalating sequence of further maltreatment, increased distress, and an even greater inner need for the attachment figure" (p. 27).

The more slowly developing left hemisphere is not left unscathed: "Diminished left hemisphere maturation, reduced corpus callosum size and attenuated left hemisphere integration may substantially increase an individual's capacity to react rapidly and to shift into an angry aggressive state" (Teicher et al., 2006, p. 202). Lastly, Teicher et al. (2006) emphasize the "enduring alterations that occur in messenger RNA levels for vasopressin and oxytocin . . . [that] may predispose to patterns of sexual behavior and mating practices that foster reproductive success in a malevolent world" (p. 203). Indeed, overall, such hair-trigger reactions equip the individual with capacities necessary for survival in a hostile world. However, such reactions do not equip the individual for intimate relating in a more secure environment.

Other researchers reached similar conclusions. Shin et al. (2006) emphasize that amygdala responsivity is heightened and positively associated with symptom severity in PTSD. However, the medial prefrontal cortex is reported to be volumetrically smaller and hyporesponsive during symptomatic states, whereas medial prefrontal cortex responsivity is inversely associated with PTSD symptom severity. They summarize that "the reviewed research suggests diminished volumes, neuronal integrity, and functional integrity of the hippocampus in PTSD" (p. 67).

In a recent and significant study researchers (Heim et al., 2008) explored the neurohormonal consequences of childhood abuse in adult

men and found that early emotional distress can have long-lasting consequences on the emotional well-being of such victims. They recruited 49
healthy, medication-free men, ages 18–60 years, without mania,
psychosis, active substance abuse, or eating disorder, and four study
groups of normal subjects: (1) those with no childhood abuse history or
psychiatric disorder (2) those with childhood abuse histories without
current major depression (3) those with childhood abuse histories with
current major depression, and (4) those with current major depression
and no childhood abuse history.

When tested, men with childhood abuse histories exhibited increases
in adrenocorticotropic hormone (ACTH) and cortisol responses to
dexamethasone/ corticotrophin releasing factor (CRF) compared with
nonabused men, and abused men with current major depression showed
increased responsiveness compared with control subjects and depressed
men without childhood abuse experience. The researchers concluded
that childhood trauma increases HPA axis activity and is a risk factor for
depression later in life.

Schore (2003a) points out that trauma in early life results in "permanent alterations in opiate, corticosteroid, corticotropin releasing factor,
dopamine, noradrenaline and serotonin receptors" (p. 290). He notes
that such changes may have a permanent effect on physiological reactivity in the limbic system and stresses that "elevated corticotrophin
releasing factor is known to initiate seizure activity in the developing
brain" (p. 290). He concludes that this circuit hyperactivity may continue
to give rise to psychogenic nonepileptic seizures, or partial seizures.

Panksepp makes a further point, one that is in a sense more fundamental, relating as it does to the earliest interaction between mother and
child. He argues that when right-hemisphere prosodic and reality testing
functions are damaged, the left hemisphere's story lines are affected. He
suggests that the story lines become "more superficial and disconnected
from the deep affective needs and life-stories of people" and that left-
hemispheric propositional language is compromised when it becomes
"decoupled from affective values" (Panksepp, 2008, p. 50). Thus early
healthy right-brain to right-brain relating is essential to the development
of sound language, reasoning, and coherent narrative in the left. This point
makes an even stronger case for the fundamental importance of a healthy
early prosodic relationship between mother and child out of which all
higher functioning ultimately emerges. Teicher et al. (2006) cite research
that indicates that young adults who were exposed to early and severe

parental verbal abuse had significant and selective reduction (15%) of gray matter volume (GMV) in the right superior temporal gyrus, an area believed to be a key anatomical substrate for speech, language and communication (Teicher et al., 2006, p. 196). Gray matter areas are "relatively enriched in nerve cell bodies" (Crossman and Neary, 2000, p. 4).

Panksepp (2008) speculates that the left hemisphere may mediate the expression of defense mechanisms more than the right, especially in those defensive processes that use words to manipulate and control others. He goes so far as to conclude that healthy right-hemisphere functioning is absolutely essential to the development of healthy left-hemisphere functioning, commenting that "when the left hemisphere is less grounded in subcortical/right hemispheric emotional 'soil' it becomes more adept at self-serving rationalizations" (p. 50). He goes on to say that "this emerging understanding of higher brain development, whereby most cortical functions are epigenetically promoted by powerful subcortical processes, is rapidly approaching an established fact" (p. 52). I find in this perspective a confirmation of my argument that for therapy to produce effective integrated functioning of the whole mind–brain–body being it must be right-brained, relational, and emotionally engaged rather than merely left-brained, interpretational, and emotionally distant (see Chapter 5). Nowhere is this truer than in the case of rather schizoid patients who use left-brain intellectual functioning as a defense against affective engagement with life.

Case Example: Bill

In his late 40s, Bill was referred to me by the psychiatrist of the emergency inpatient psychiatric unit to which he had been admitted when he suffered what appeared to be a breakdown when his wife left after 20 years of marriage. She had become unable to tolerate his controlling behavior, which had reached into every aspect of their life together, and into his daughter's life as well. When his wife and daughter left, he described himself as initially unable to stop crying and completely at a loss as to how he was going to manage even the simplest aspects of living alone.

One of Bill's earliest memories was of wanting to go to the party of the child who lived a few doors down the road. He thought he was about 5 years old. He remembered that he was dressed in his best clothes and when the time came, he set off excitedly with his mother. However, when the door was opened and he went to step inside his mother gripped him tightly by the hand. She took the present out of his other hand and said to the other child's mother, "I'd better give this to you now. I know he won't stay—he's far too shy." He felt his face change color and his heart sink as he thought to himself "Maybe I won't manage." Only a moment later, it seemed, he found he was leaving with his mother. On another occasion, watching a Punch and Judy show with his grandfather, he was frightened by the shouting and violence that occurred between the two puppets, and only in therapy did he realize that this reminded him of the fright he felt on the rare occasions when his parents quarreled.

These early memories, recalled in therapy, seemed to encapsulate his experience with his parents and demonstrated how the intersubjective affects the intrasubjective, which then affects the intersubjective. It appeared that his parents, especially his mother, had been unable to help Bill regulate his emotional response to fear in a way that would have helped him to develop an ability to go out into the world with confidence. Only in therapy was he able to perceive how much his mother lacked confidence and kept herself and him within the four walls of their home. His father was not able to help him build his confidence either. If he got less than full marks for a test, there would be no pleasure in what his son had achieved, just a postmortem over his shortcomings—in particular, over the pieces of knowledge that he had not retained.

In secondary school Bill experienced some bullying. When he tried to speak to his mother about what was happening, she replied dismissively, "All boys get bullied at school—often much worse things happen to them." He went away even more fearful of what the "worse things" still to come might be, and feeling totally alone. He could not internalize a feeling of confidence and empowerment that would have helped him to cope in difficult moments because his parents were not able to model those attributes. As an adult, in reaction to his early experience, Bill set out to try to become invulnerable. He would be master of all available knowledge. Much later in therapy he was able to realize that both his parents had feared the world and kept it at arm's length as far as possible.

Bill became an information technology (I.T.) expert in an industry where I.T. skills, combined with specialist knowledge of the technical base used by his particular industry, were at a premium. He had made himself virtually indispensable in the office because every member of staff knew that, when in doubt, he or she could ask Bill and he would know. He explained that he felt safe only when he was in possession of every scrap of knowledge concerning his work and the world in general. That was the only way he felt he could protect himself from making a mistake, from being found wanting in some respect. He had little or no awareness of the power and indeed control that he exerted through this stance. Over the years that we worked together, it became clear just how much he was valued in his workplace, and he began to internalize that valuation. It was still difficult for him to have any sense of being in control.

He remained an isolated man, often fearing rejection and retreating from relationship. However, what was apparent was that colleagues liked and valued him and on occasion sought out his company. Very gradually he became more able to notice and appreciate this positive attention and then to accept invitations to social gatherings. A highpoint came when he arrived at therapy announcing that he would be away for two weeks because he was going on holiday with friends from the office.

Conclusion

Appropriate affect regulation may remain tantalizingly out of reach for some patients, who may face the condemnation of "always overreacting" or being "far too sensitive for your own good" or "getting uptight far too easily" or "sleeping around." These are all expressions that patients have ruefully brought to therapy as they struggled to deal with their vulnerability to intense and immediate hyperarousal in the face of mild stressors. It is the reaction born of early trauma that gives rise to negative transference reactions, even in the benign therapeutic setting. Such reactions may gradually be identified as belonging to the patient's past, which has shaped the brain–mind body to respond as if to a hostile world. Such extensive change argues for relational therapy conducted over a significant period of time, therapy that is long enough and engaged enough to permit the internalizing of a very different experience to the early trauma that established such difficulties. It will be a therapy that permits the patient to experience sensitive regulation by another as a bridge to the difficult task of self-regulation.

3

Attunement:
Mirroring and Empathy

ATTUNEMENT—BEING AWARE OF AND RESPONSIVE TO ANOTHER—is absolutely fundamental to meaningful human interaction and therefore also to the therapeutic process. Perception and emotional learning in the area of attunement arise out of earliest relating to another. The human being, in common with other primates, demonstrates a capacity and facility for this from the earliest days of life.

Interest has snowballed in the role of attunement in the therapeutic process; research in the field has been stimulated by a number of studies that concluded that it was the quality of the relationship between therapist and client, rather than the theoretical orientation, that brought about a successful therapeutic outcome (see Chapter 1). McCluskey et al. (1997) explored the part played by attunement, in particular, in adult psychotherapy. In a study that involved the rating of therapists as attuned or nonattuned on the basis of clinical extracts, the rating was carried out first by senior clinicians and then by trainees. From the results it became clear that four primary characteristics were identifiable in each of the categories of attuned and nonattuned. The descriptors of the attuned therapists were "*engrossed, modulates response, provides input, and facilitates exploration*" (McCluskey et al., 1997, p. 1,268, emphasis in original). These researchers concluded that further research might enable the development of more appropriate training programs for therapists.

Therapeutic Attunement

Driver (2006) identifies the fundamental issues related to attunement that I seek to address in my work, namely:

How do we understand and touch the deep structures of the mind which are formed of implicit and embodied memory and which have formed patterns in the mind from early infancy but are unavailable to conscious memory especially in patients with early relational trauma? What relational dynamics do we need to consider, such as affective attunement and empathy, in relation to the restructuring of the connections of mind? (p. 5)

I have come to understand the therapist's mind–brain–body attunement to the patient's mind–brain–body being to be something that is fundamental to the process of changing minds through therapy.

The capacity for empathy is described by Fonagy et al. (2004) as arising in the second year of life. They make it clear that, in early development, healthy attunement consists of the mother mirroring the baby's affect in such a way that the baby is reassured and calmed. This process is fundamental to the baby's ability to develop self-regulation and a healthy sense of self. Fonagy et al. suggest that "affect expressions by the parent that are not contingent on the infant's affect will undermine the appropriate labeling of internal states, which may, in turn, remain confusing, experienced as unsymbolized, and hard to regulate" (p. 9). In response to repeated experiences of the mother's attunement, the baby in turn develops a capacity for awareness of and sensitivity to the other. Thus attunement and empathy are two sides of the same coin. It is the therapist's capacity for empathy—acquired through his or her experience of being related to in an attuned way—that enables him or her to attune, that is to respond empathically, to the patient.

Stern's (1985) work on attunement and misattunement in mother-baby interactions confirms earlier research findings that mothers naturally match and modulate their babies' affect, but that in moments of misattunement the mother may become the unknown, or the stranger, and the child will experience himself as deficient. Researchers understand such experiences of misattunement to be shame experiences. They warn that "unrepaired shame experiences result in a self defined in shame" (Spiegel et al., 2000, p. 25), a self that becomes focused on the needs of the other, a self preoccupied with feelings of shame. If such misattunement goes unrepaired then they suggest that the false self comes to be born. However, in good-enough circumstances, where an experience of misattunement is something that the parent addresses through empathic reengagement with the child, the self "developing within mutual empathic attunement and the experience of repaired misattunement will develop with integrity and a reliable capacity to accurately read the interpersonal environments" (Spiegel et al., 2000, p. 25).

While attunement offers opportunities for effective engagement in the therapeutic process, misattunement—with the opportunities it offers for effective repair—may be even more vital to equip the patient who has experienced early relational trauma adequately for the vicissitudes of relating in everyday life. Spiegel et al. (2000) noted that while empathic attunement gives rise to positive emotions and states of joy and excitement, misattunement has exactly the opposite effect. Repair is therefore a key concept for the working through of experiences of rupture that occur in therapy. Fonagy et al. (2004) suggest that psychotherapy with these patients will seek to "regenerate the connection between the consciousness of an affect state and its experience at the constitutional level" (p.14), thus developing the capacity to become aware of feelings and to make meaning out of bodily emotional experience.

As I consider how attunement actually occurs I am aware of the growing number of researchers who show substantial interest in how the neurobiology of emotional body language affects emotional understanding of the other and influences decision making. Schore (2008b) stresses how much more than words is involved in therapy and endorses the view of Hutterer and Liss (2006) who emphasize the need for nonverbal variables such as tone, tempo, rhythm, timbre, prosody, and amplitude of speech, as well as body signals, to be considered as crucial aspects of the therapist's interaction with the patient.

In Galton's collection of essays concerning touch in the psychoanalytic space, I was struck by the number of clinicians who did not use touch routinely but who spoke of definitive moments of meeting with patients that involved touch. Those definitive moments enabled patients to deal more effectively with poor early experience, acting as a "bridge between 'somatic' and 'psychic' modes of experience" (Totton, 2006, p. 160). Totton points out that touch enables us to reach back into the "infant world of the patient in very powerfully effective ways" but also urges caution because "the passage through the Oedipal field takes up and transforms infant eroticism into adult sexuality" (p. 159).

What is brought home to me as I engage with the varied experience of a wide range of practitioners is that we have to consider the unique multilayered developmental experience that each patient brings to the relationship, and how that is affecting, and being experienced in, the current therapeutic relationship.

Both therapist and patient have undergone a series of attachment experiences, past and current, that affect the capacity for attunement that they bring to the therapeutic relationship. In each, autoassociative pattern-matching processes will take place beneath the level of conscious awareness. These patterns in the mind–brain develop from an individual's earlier experience. The patterning, discussed more fully in Chapter 5, dictates the individual's expectations of how relationships with others will be. As the work together progresses, both will also be affected by any significant changes in their current attachment experiences caused by stress, loss, or positive occurrences. The therapist's ability to do this work successfully will depend very much on his or her capacity for empathy. In order to develop this ability, therapists must be aware of their own early and current attachment styles and the way these aspects of their inner world affect their capacity for attunement to each particular patient at any particular time. For example, therapists whose early attachment style was avoidant and whose current personal circumstances have suddenly plunged them into emotional pain may find themselves wishing to avoid the dependency needs of the baby part of an adult patient who comes to a session in a state of distress and who presents in a regressed state (Wilkinson, 2007b). They must also be wary of the hidden hazard of secondary traumatization that may afflict the therapist faced with very severe trauma in the patient's material through the mechanism of empathy (see also Chapter 9).

Case Example: Steve

When Steve, a man in his 40s, called to make an appointment, I encountered a seemingly very experienced and articulate patient. While we only spoke briefly it quickly became clear that he had had therapy from an analyst in a school of analysis very different from that to which I belonged and that he was used to working with his inner world in a very different way from the way I worked. While I thought in developmental and relational terms informed by attachment theory, my new patient thought and talked in mythological terms which at first I found quite difficult to relate to and which left me feeling inadequate. As I sought to attune to my would-be patient, my countertransference was to feel small and helpless in the face of the archetypes, an inner feeling that actually deeply echoed my patient's inner sense of a small and helpless self that had been almost overwhelmed by life-threatening earliest experience.

The first thing I was aware of when Steve arrived for his first session was of this very large man who was rubbing his hand slowly but firmly over his close shaven head as he walked toward me. Was he caressing it, rubbing the thinking cap of his brain or comforting some old injury, I pondered? While there was no visible damage of significance, I found myself wondering whether he had been the victim of a car accident. My engagement with the gesture, made first as he passed the window on his way into the room and then as he sat talking, was immediate and intense. Little did I know how symbolic a gesture it was, containing reference to both early and current experience. In the first session I felt sometimes as if I was with a newborn baby; in later sessions I would sometimes see a willful toddler or a confused and acting-out adolescent; and much of the time I was in the presence of a sensitive and caring man.

Soon I learned that Steve's arrival into the world had been most hazardous for both him and his mother. He recounted that his final forceps-assisted emergence into the world had damaged and deformed his head so badly that his mother had not been allowed to see him until he was 4 days old. He had been told this along with the fact that he had not been expected to survive. The utter loneliness and desolation of his earliest experience lying in an incubator rather than cradled in his mother's arms was something to which he returned many, many, many times. I was often filled with a sense of utter desolation just at the moment before he would begin to speak afresh about his earliest hours and days of life, but perhaps the experience weighed most heavily on me that first afternoon. Sometimes in our early sessions it seemed like Steve was hanging on to me, for grim death, just with his eyes. I guess that life-giving eye-contact with nurses, when he fought to stay alive, whose eyes expressed care and concern arising out of an understanding of something of his very earliest distress, was being reexperienced by us both in the room. As I sought to attune to him in his distress, I wondered about the mother who had not been there for him, and a system that had not allowed, or indeed enabled, her to be with her baby in his earliest hours of pain and distress.

Steve was a survivor; he had survived those early days of isolation, alienation, and despair, and he had survived unhappy experiences of bullying at school, the reason for which he did not understand. His parents proved unable to help him deal with, or understand, the bullying. His need for attunement, which went for the most part unmet, left him feeling shamed and vulnerable to bullying from outside, which matched the condemnatory voices that clamored from within. He and his parents (he had no siblings) lived in a rather barren, isolated, rural area until he was 11 years old. He survived the loneliness of this isolation by turning to animals for comfort, for example, riding for miles alone on his horse. Later came the greater loneliness of an inner-city secondary school where he felt out of place, a misfit who did not know what "streetwise" meant. He felt frequently let down by his rather absent father, who was an ex-army officer and a successful businessman, and whose interaction with his son seemed to be as if with a young and rather recalcitrant subordinate. However, Steve felt supported and encouraged by his grandfather and his grandmother who, in spite of the generation gap, were much more aware of how he felt. He went to live with them while he studied for his first degree.

He went on to have a successful career in the law, which involved prosecuting men in positions of power (fathers, bullies) who failed to act as they should. He became the attacker who could bully and shame the bully. That way he could for a while escape knowledge of the helpless, hurting little one within. Fonagy et al. (2004) observed that many patients who have experienced early relational trauma develop a survival strategy in which they use "the alien, dissociated part of the self to contain the image of the aggressor and the unthinkable affect" (p.13). After working with a therapist whom he described as a rather gentle man, he was able to shift to a career that had a more nurturing component to it and that required and used his new-found capacity for control rather than bullying and dominance. In his (Jungian) terms, the opposites had begun to come together in him in a wholesome way. He married and felt more settled. His new career flourished and he managed to develop it in ways that were satisfying to him. His mother remained, as she had been from the beginning, a shadowy figure. His early therapy had enabled him to deal with some of his pain by providing a secure relationship, but a curiously impersonal quality clung to the way in which he talked to me of archetype and myth; somehow it felt as if life had barely begun to be a human existence for him.

Yet there was a sense in which I felt a larger-than-life quality in this man, a quality that I felt might threaten to overwhelm both of us. At these times I was aware of the need to remain separate rather than to allow his regressive state to overwhelm the two of us. At such moments I felt a need to think about the continuum of need from attunement to detachment. When he went to sit on the floor, I asked him to sit on the chair; when he moved the chair in a way that blocked the door, I asked him to move it back. I was surprised at my own directiveness. Internally I questioned myself about my defenses. What was I defending against? What was going on? In the first instance I felt he was not yet ready to confront his infant self so directly; in the second I was simply not comfortable that the route out of the room for either of us was blocked.

A breakthrough came when Steve arrived with a pen-and-ink drawing (Figure 3.1) he'd done at home. In a way it seems that he was attempting a symbolic reconciliation of his objective understanding of the brain with his subjective experience of early birth and postbirth trauma and how his early experience had determined his sense of self and his journey through life. The drawing was a line drawing done on brown paper. He described the paper as fibrous and said he had chosen it for that quality. It seemed that somehow the texture made the paper feel alive, in some way related to the fiber of the human body, in particular, his head. He felt that, in some way, the drawing reflected his head. He began to talk about the drawing in a strangely inarticulate way for a man who had earned a living through the skillful use of words for much of his life. The drawing appeared to be an attempt to reconcile what had happened to him with the life he had subsequently lived. He had written:

- My inner landscape is changing . . . the making of mankind
- Head games . . . head injuries . . . where do they come from? . . . A man? . . . The birth canal? A doctor?
- The top of my head feels vulnerable . . . Ow! Ow! Ow! . . . Cover your head
- Careful—careful—burning down the house, but I'm scared of fire. I burnt myself trying to light the heater.

The drawing represented his life's journey, my patient slowly explained. As I looked at it I was struck by its uncanny resemblance to a brain. I said, "In some ways it reminds me of a brain." He looked and agreed with surprise that that was indeed just what it looked like. He felt that the drawing was somewhat like a map with contour lines but that it was also very much in the shape of a brain, with something being pulled off at the top. He brought a drawing of the brain in a subsequent session and we looked at the similarities that he saw between his drawing and the illustration.

Hirao, Naka, et al. (2008) explore the use of sandplay therapy, that is, the use of a sandtray with figures and objects with which a patient may express him- or herself, as one possible nonverbal clinical method of helping patients to integrate objective and subjective experience. In the example they offer, they combine neuroimaging and images from sandplay therapy to explore the objective and subjective view of a male patient's self in conflict following the onset of nonfluent aphasia. They chart his recovery through the series of images that he makes and in a process they call "mind-imaging." It seemed to me that a rather similar process of mind-imaging occurred for Steve when he unwittingly made an image of the brain that had references all over it of the painful journey that had been his early experience of life. Interestingly, Steve chose to call this drawing The Sandpit; perhaps he had devised his own version of the sandtray experience!

In looking at his representation of his mind–brain he found himself beginning to be able to remember more detail of his mother's account of his very early days of life. He told me that his mother had not been allowed to see him for the first 4 days of his life and that the staff had kept saying to her "We're praying for him" when she asked to see her baby. His fantasy was that he had been appallingly bruised, that his mother must have felt that she had given birth to a monster, and that he had been that monstrous baby. I made an intervention that spoke of the effect that such an early, painful experience must have had on his life's journey. From that moment the quality of our work changed—the focus became relational. Now there could be a "good enough" mother in the room, one who had been able to look at and understand what his hurt head symbolized, that is, the traumatic trajectory of the development of his very early mind. He struggled with issues of blame for his suffering. As I sought to work in an attuned way I felt as if I suddenly caught sight of the small boy who somehow thought what had happened was his fault and who feared his own destructive rage. Just as the corpus callosum links the two hemispheres of the brain, so as my patient looked at his image and the representation of the human brain that he had found he became able to begin to make links between his affective experience (the domain of the right hemisphere) and his capacity to think about his early experience (the task of the left). He spoke about the links between affective and cognitive experiencing and commented that it would be helpful to identify the corpus callosum on the illustration.

The therapy seemed to enrich Steve's understanding of his inner self states, his inner attachments, and his attachments in the wider world. What seemed quite extraordinary about him was not only his ability to allow me to help him with some of his difficult encounters with the parental figures that he came across in his world of work, but also his increasing ability to identify, care for, and contain more primitive self states within his inner world. He would speak of "the little fellow," say "He's been having a hard time," and then make a gesture such as a Mum might make as she sits her baby on her lap to burp him. He would speak of the teenager within and the way in which he had helped and managed that part of himself that might have turned to alcohol as a way of escape. As I worked with him I was aware that I always had to have the very young parts of him in mind, even though I might be having a very erudite discussion with a very grown-up part of him. I remained impressed by his capacity to parent these needy parts of himself and finally came to wonder whether my attuned way of working had enabled him to allow them into mind in such a nurturing way.

During his time in therapy with me he studied for a higher degree and achieved distinction at every stage. His determination to overcome all difficulties was impressive. It was as if being "determined" was determined in him by his earliest experience. I don't understand yet quite how that determination comes about with such difficult early experience, although I have seen it in several patients with early relational trauma, where the very issue of survival has been in question. It may be that determination is a way of escape, a survival strategy. I find myself wondering about the neural circuits of survival. Steve's determination may have been a useful by-product of the hypervigilance that is occasioned by such trauma. It may have been the process of pattern completion at work, of locking on to the familiar in the face of uncertain stimuli. Maybe there was an echo of the way in which some, despite his trauma, had fought very hard for his life at the very beginning. As I reflected on our experience together I realized that:

For the patient:
- Attunement from therapist overcomes isolation.
- Attunement from therapist provides a route to greater awareness of earlier painful states.
- Attunement from therapist leads to containment of difficult early feelings.

- Attunement from therapist and with therapist leads to greater attunement to changing inner self states.
- Attunement from therapist enables maturational processes.

For the therapist:
- Attunement requires attention to the separation–attachment continuum.
- Attunement requires awareness of the need for affective engagement or disengagement.
- Attunement requires the ability to catch fleeting emotional states in the other; an openness to allow experiences, as yet unconscious, belonging to the other, to be known through one's own experience; a knowing of the other not only from outside (observation) but from inside (countertransference) as well.
- Attunement requires an opening of the self to the self of the other.

Neurological Substrates of Attunement

Early attunement from mother to baby has been widely studied. Lenzi et al. (2008) undertook an fMRI study of 16 mothers with babies between 6 and 12 months of age, the stage when exchanges and communication between a mother and her infant are exclusively preverbal and are based on the mother's ability to understand her infant's needs and feelings. The mothers underwent fMRI scanning while observing and imitating pictures of their child's face and the face of someone else's child. The researchers discovered that "the mirror neuron system, the insula and amygdala were all more active during emotional expressions, that this circuit was engaged to a greater extent when interacting with one's own child, and that it is correlated with maternal reflective function (a measure of empathy)" (p. 1124). When the researchers compared single emotions with each other, they found that joy expressions evoked a response mainly in right limbic and paralimbic areas, suggesting an empathic response characteristic of maternal reflectiveness or attunement, but that ambiguous expressions elicited a response in left high order cognitive and motor areas, which might reflect the greater cognitive effort involved in recording expression that is less easy to read. Attunement will be not only to mind but also to facial and bodily expressions. Emotional communication depends as much on posture, gesture, movement, facial expressions, tone, syntax, rhythm of speech, and the pauses and silences that punctuate it as on verbalization itself (Jacobs, 2005). From the earliest days the young mind appears to be aware of the human body just as it is of the human face. De Gelder (2006) reports research indicating that "three-month-old human infants can discriminate point-light displays of human movement from random patterns" (Bertenthal et al., 1987) and at the same age infants presented with distorted bodies react significantly in areas of "brain potential that is typically evoked by the sight of faces and bodies" (Gliga & Dehaene-Lambertz, 2005).

Such attunement occurs rapidly at levels that are both conscious and unconscious. In the first minutes of life infants are attracted by face patterns; by two months they are able to recognize their mother's face among others (Morton & Johnson, 1991). Martin et al. (as cited in Harrison et al., 2007) found that individuals who score highly on scales that rate social empathy need less time to identify emotional expressions even when seen very briefly. Both right and left amygdala show greater activity in response to faces with big rather than small pupils, and researchers in the area conclude that "amygdala sensitivity to pupil dilation is usefully conceptualized as an alerting response to the wide range of biological outcomes that this signal can predict" (Demos et al., 2008, p. 2,732). The amygdala plays a central role in this area and is vital to the processing of threatening faces.

Davis and Hadiks (as cited in McCluskey et al., 1997) set out to explore whether nonverbal behaviors were indicative of changing states of mind in therapy and concluded that body movement patterns at levels below the threshold of consciousness were indicative of intrapsychic and interpsychic changes during the therapeutic session. Concerning emotional body language, de Gelder (2006) posits a two-system model of attunement: a rapid reflex-like system that functions from subcortical structures involving the superior colliculus, pulvinar, striatum and amygdala, and a second system consisting of a cortical network involving "the fronto-parietal motor system, and connectivity between the amygdala and the ventromedial prefrontal cortex" (de Gelder, 2006, p. 247). Again the amygdala plays a major part in such processing, as it has reciprocal connections to both cortical and subcortical structures and, as such, acts as the crossroads in the interactions emanating from these structures.

Cozolino (2008) also stresses the integrative role of the insula, blending outer and inner sensation and linking cortical, limbic, and visceral experience. The right insula becomes activated when a face is judged to be a threat; it also becomes activated in relation to the experiencing of emotions. Both the insula and the anterior cingulate become activated when we experience pain or see others in pain (Cozolino, 2008). Again, the involvement of structures within the right hemisphere is seen to be crucial in the processing of painful emotion in relation to self and other. Because the right orbitofrontal cortex controls the regulation of emotional and bodily feelings, it has become known as the emotional executive of the brain, acting as it does "in concert with the amygdala and somatosensory cortex" (de Gelder, 2006, p. 244).

The role of mirror neurons in the realm of empathy and attunement is much debated currently. It was established in the 1990s, "the decade of the brain," that action observation involves neural regions in the observer similar to those engaged in by the active participant during actual action sequences. A new group of neurons, described as "mirror" neurons, were discovered in the ventral premotor cortex of the macaque monkey. It was observed that these neurons are activated when a monkey intentionally performs hand and/or mouth acts and that the same neurons also become activated in the brain of a monkey observer as it passively watches this event. Further work on parietal mirror neurons indicates that single motor acts depend on each other, combining to form "pre-wired intentional chains, in which each motor act is facilitated by the previously executed one" (Gallese, 2007, p. 62). Some argue that mirror neurons play a part in the perception of emotion as well as action. Cozolino (2006) notes that "mirror neurons lie at the crossroads of the processing of inner and outer experience [and are] most likely involved in . . . the evolution of gestural communication . . . and empathy" (p. 187).

Harrison et al. (2006) point out that until recently empathy research had not identified convincing neurobiological substrates. They summarize recent developments, stressing that discovery of mirror neurons within the premotor cortex has provided a potential neural mechanism that mediates how we understand other people's actions and intentions, thus providing a neurological basis for intentionality. They note concurrent advances that also take in the realm of feelings and emotions and observe that together these offer "a common neural representation for the perception of actions and feelings in others and their experience in self [and] basis for a neuroscientific account of intersubjectivity" (p. 5).

Many questions are being posed that may point to directions for fruitful future research. Hart (2008), writing as a clinician, is exploring whether "the recruiting of mirror neurons in the service of the devel-

oping processes of identification and empathy" is what actually underpins an attuned approach to working with traumatized and developmen-
tally delayed children (p. 259). Recent research data suggest that autism
is associated with an impairment of a basic automatic social–emotional
process. It was found that autistic participants did not demonstrate the
ability to mimic facial expressions automatically, whereas the control
group of typically developing participants did. However, both groups
showed evidence of successful voluntary mimicry. The researchers
concluded that in development, such a mimicry deficit could impair a
child's ability to grasp others' emotions. If such a deficit occurred early,
it could impair the child's ability to form self–other correspondences,
affecting the sense of intersubjectivity and emotional correspondence so
fundamental to a developing capacity for understanding other minds,
perhaps even contributing significantly to the development of autism
(McIntosh et al., 2006). If this is the case it has profound implications for
the study of attachment and affect regulation in children deemed to be
on the autistic spectrum. As a result of a large-scale study of young children on the autistic spectrum, Greenspan (2000) observed that
connecting affect to sequencing involves left and right-hemisphere
connectivity and questioned whether between the ages of 12 and 30
months it may become possible to identify a particular metabolic or
neurotransmitter system that plays a critical role in integrating affect or
intent and sequencing functions.

Javanbakht and Ragan (2008) draw attention to the work of those who
suggest that "frontoparietal and frontotemporal mirror neurons function
as a bridge between self and others" and understand this mechanism as a
possible substrate for the recognition of the intention and affect of the
other (p. 260). De Gelder (2006, p. 244) points out that research into
autism has demonstrated that people with the condition "show less
activity in the mirror neuron system when passively observing or actively
imitating facial expressions, consistent with reduced cortical thickness in
mirror neuron brain areas," which might point to a key role for mirror
neurons in the processing of emotion. However, she strikes a cautionary
note by observing that the reduced activity in the mirror neuron system
might be caused by a deficit in the amygdala itself rather than in the
mirror neurons primarily. The neurological substrates of attunement and
empathy are explored further in Chapters 4 and 9.

Pattern completion is the autoassociative mechanism by which we lock
on to familiar aspects of new experience and eliminate difference as

seemingly irrelevant, in order to make best sense of the new in relation to past experience. The patterns in the mind that have developed as a result of early and subsequent experience and are stored in implicit memory, are discussed more fully in the next chapter in relation to the transference and countertransference, both of which (but especially the latter) may be understood as aspects of attunement.

Case Example: Marie

Imagine for a moment a patient, whom we will call Marie, who recently shared a traumatic experience of attunement from her childhood, which had continued to affect her bodily experience well into her therapy. An empathic therapist enabled Marie to feel secure enough in the relationship to explore the way in which she had become locked into an unconscious identification with a traumatic moment in the life of her young sister. She told her therapist that as a 10-year-old she had often been left with the responsibility of caring for her two younger sisters while her parents were at work. The children were allowed a great deal of freedom and spent much of the time swimming in a natural harbor. Marie was a strong swimmer and so was always charged with the responsibility of watching the other two. She remembered that on one occasion she was standing in the sea and watching them as they bobbed up and down, playing in the waves, some distance away in what was a seemingly safe situation. Suddenly she noticed something odd; one sister was now also watching as the other continued to seemingly bob up and down but disappeared into the water for longer and longer each time. As she retold the incident in therapy it was as if her memory cut off abruptly at this point for a moment or two, but then the scene she was recounting moved to a fully clothed man suddenly diving into the water near her sisters. Now there was another blank and her little sister was lying on the side and the man was thumping her chest. The scene changed again and the man was shaking Marie by the shoulders, shouting loudly "Don't you know about cramp, surely you know about cramp!" She did not know what *cramp* was.

As she recounted this incident she remembered with distress that she had felt that she was castigated and punished by her parents because she had failed to take care of her sisters properly, and a sense of deep shame had lingered until she was able to begin to work with the experience in therapy. She did not go into the water again until she became an adult. Nobody noticed that as a result of the aftermath of their swim, she had actually become terrified of going into the water, especially if the sea had "white horses." Much later she took swimming lessons to try to overcome her fear and after several lessons her coach became aware that she was not actually breathing at all as she tried to swim. In therapy she gradually realized that without knowing it, she was locked in an unconscious identification with her sister who had breathed in while under water and who had nearly drowned because of it. Her body had remained in a time warp of memory; her very attunement with her sister had left her traumatized. Woodhead (2004) comments that such a pattern formed out of a particularly traumatic experience of relating to another is "likely to be played out, outside of awareness, throughout her lifetime" (p. 146). Marie remained unable to break the spell until she gained insight, born of her transference experience in the consulting room, that enabled her to think about what had happened an how she had responded. She also became aware that she was trying to find a way to take care of her therapist just as she had sought to take care of her sisters and continued to do with others who mattered to her. Such thinking becomes possible within the context of an attuned relationship that offers new experiences and expectations of relating and thus enables new patterns to form within implicit memory.

Attunement in Relation to the Whole Mind–Brain–Body Being

Finally, I would like to reemphasize that attunement concerns the whole mind–brain–body being of the twosome in the therapeutic session. Sometimes the therapist will experience attunement primarily to emotional feelings emanating from the patient; at other times attunement to bodily states, as yet unrecognized by the patient, may be crucial for the work. Three times in 25 years I have worked with patients with serious, previously undiagnosed medical conditions, and all made good use of supportive psychotherapy. The following material is a composite based on work with all three of these patients. It is interesting to speculate how much my growing experience enabled an unconscious pattern-making process to occur, which I was able to "lock onto" at an unconscious level and which called forth the questions that helped us to bear soma (in this case, the brain–body) in mind as well as psyche.

Case Example: Lindsey

The patient, whom I will call Lindsey, was referred by her family doctor for depression that was keeping her out of work. As we spoke together I held in mind the series of questions that I ask myself about the patient and some of which I sometimes ask the patient directly (outlined in Chapter 1). Lindsey had recently become engaged, and the doctor wondered if this had awoken early difficulties of which the patient was unaware. Significantly she had also complained of some physical problems, and the doctor had already sent her for investigations, but no medical problem was identified. She was a very bright, scientifically trained professional woman, who was increasingly experiencing bouts of depression; she also complained of increasingly severe headaches. When asked to say more about the headaches, it became clear that sometimes they interfered significantly with her capacity to work, and although she had only recently stopped working she had self-medicated the headaches for a long time. As I heard this, I made a mental note to pay attention to the possibility of physical illness while also noting the need to try to understand the meaning that was attached to these headaches for my patient.

Lindsey moved on to explain that she had had a difficult relationship with her father all of her life; he had been dominant, demanding, scathing, and controlling. Nevertheless Lindsey had a significant degree of resilience, having done well at school and university and having entered successfully into her chosen career. For the most part she seemed to cope well socially and professionally but was having understandable concerns about what might be happening to her. I found a sense of unease within me that I couldn't quite identify. The patient came for her fourth appointment and complained of more severe depression, accompanied by suicidal ideation. Something resonated deep inside me, and I found myself listening, with serious concern, to the patient's description of how she had been feeing physically, feelings that she associated with her depression. I asked, "Is the increase in depression and headache related to your menstrual cycle?" She replied, "Oh, I don't have periods, I haven't had a period for years now." Having ascertained that this amenorrhea was not because of any contraceptive choice she had made, I said firmly to this scientifically educated, young woman, "Then that is something you must go and talk to your doctor about. Will you do that before you come back to see me next week?" This step led to diagnosis and treatment of her hitherto unsuspected but serious physical problem.

Our work together had begun with an attuned awareness inside me of deep unease, which ultimately reflected my patient's inner experience of dis-ease. As one thinks about the patient as a mind–brain–body being it becomes increasingly clear how mind–brain and body are intimately and inextricably linked. As we worked together on her early trauma, the development of my capacity to experience the other in an empathic way was at the heart of our work. We sought to find each other and to work together in the today, seeking to manage her depression, her difficult current life experience, the issues around medical and surgical options for her further treatment, and her hopes and fears around pregnancy and ultimately about becoming a mother herself. It seems that in those early sessions I was becoming deeply attuned to my patient's inner being and was therefore able to sense in a right-brained empathic manner, through the countertransference, the level of deep malaise that she was experiencing.

Conclusion

While further research is needed to clarify the role of mirror neurons in the empathic process, the central role of attunement, achieved through the mechanisms of mirroring, resonance, and empathy is clear. The work with these patients brought home to me the need for attunement and the knowledge that such attunement will be to body as well as to mind. The working through of the insights that are made possible by such attunement is underpinned by right and left brain processing, by the capacity to feel with another while remaining able to think.

4

Patterns That Persist:
Transference and Countertransference

THE SELF IS FUNDAMENTALLY ASSOCIATIVE and its development relational, thus mechanisms such as transference (whereby past experience of relating is transferred on to new relationships), and countertransference (where the therapist intuits within his or her self something of the patient's transference process), are inevitably rooted in the very earliest experience of mind. Implicit memory is the source of the deeply founded ways of being and behaving that govern an individual life and the ways that person seeks to relate to others. Lichtenberg (2004) notes that in infancy "experiences are categorized and generalized into maps of feeling states or very basic affect stories" (p.137). These early established maps or neural networks are held in the implicit memory store of the early developing right hemisphere.

As we have seen in chapter 2, the interactions that occur between mothers and babies have been closely studied and basic types of attachment have been identified. These are then manifest in patients' ways of being, feeling, and behaving in the consulting room. Through the transference/countertransference experience the therapist can become aware of the nature of a patient's earliest attachment pattern. Part of the task of the therapy will be to help that patient explore and become aware of his or her early attachment style and become able to look at the way this may be mirrored in his or her current relationships.

Unconscious or implicit aspects as well as conscious, explicit aspects of experiencing together play a fundamental part in the therapeutic relationship. Interactions in the consulting room express affective experience arising from implicit early memory; such interactions occur because of the affective reexperiencing that occurs within the transference. Through the transference relationship with the analyst, the patient is able to explore his or her own deeply established patterns of reacting to another, patterns which are formed by earlier experience. Through the countertransference the therapist is first able to live them with the patient, then through the therapeutic process to examine these recurring patterns with the patient. Acute attention to the unique interactive experience between therapist and client is crucial for understanding the underlying patterns in the individual patient's mind that affects his or her understanding of relationships. The processes of patterning and pattern completion are fundamental to the way in which we use the past to help us to integrate new experience and to predict future experience. Although they have been studied most thoroughly in the sensory modalities, some researchers are now concentrating on thalamo-cortical pattern-completion and others on hippocampal systems of pattern-completion. Hershberg (2008) notes that "These organizing patterns are developed in relational contexts, through lived experience, and are experienced at implicit and explicit levels of awareness" (p. 28). Javanbakht and Ragan (2008) suggest that these kinds of processes may "occur with conceptual and affective patterns of relatedness" and understand them as vital tools for understanding transference and countertransference experience (p. 259).

Such patterning, both explicit and implicit, is perhaps more common in life that we realize. "Pass it on to the next generation" is a characteristic remark that I remember my maternal grandmother making when I would thank her for some thoughtful gift or treat. I remember with great clarity the first time she said this to me, on our return from my first holiday abroad. It was 1953, the postwar period of austerity when people in England still rarely had the luxury of a trip to Europe. From my early childhood my grandmother had nurtured in me an understanding of the wider world and the viewpoints of a wide range of peoples. Some of the first stories that she told me were of her childhood spent in India. One of the first books she read to me was about the Kon-Tiki expedition, and another was about Scott of the Antarctic; *National Geographic* magazines abounded in her otherwise spare home. It came as no surprise that this grand old lady, then living in relative poverty, chose to use the proceeds of an insurance policy that had matured to take my aunt, my cousin, and myself to Switzerland, a country she had visited many times as a young woman, had come to love, and wanted to share with us. It was a wonderful holiday, full of new sights, sounds, and ways of being. It gave me a love of travel and of Switzerland that has remained throughout my life. The way of being with another, as my grandmother was with us, might be said to encourage a quality of mindful awareness of the being and needs of another. In turn I have taken two generations of young family members to Switzerland for their first holidays abroad, telling them the adage of their great-grandmother and great-great-grandmother, respectively, as I did so.

So much that matters, that is of special value, and indeed that contributes to the essence of who we are, is passed from generation to generation, not in an explicit way, as this principle of generous living was, but at an implicit level. Both my mother and grandmother were born in India; both loved their *ayahs* (nurses) very much and always spoke of them with great affection. When my mother was with her sisters or her mother, they would talk together in a certain way that I have also taken in "with my mother's milk." On my first visit to India, several years ago now, I sat idly on a low wall enjoying the beautiful garden of a palace while my friend lingered to take some photographs. I watched as a group of Indian women, dressed in colorful saris, sitting close to me, talked together. The moment was full of color and the musicality of the women's voices. As I watched I suddenly realized that I was seeing and hearing women talking in exactly the way my grandmother did with her daughters and, indeed, most surprisingly to me, how I can often be with friends in moments of enthusiasm, friends who do not necessarily communicate in the same style themselves but who greet it in me with warmth. In short, I recognized a fundamental way of being and relating that my most English grandmother and mother had both acquired in the nursery from their much-loved *ayahs* who were their primary caretakers, and that I, in turn, had acquired from them.

The inferior colliculus (where the imprint of the mother's or primary caretaker's voice is thought to be stored) is also close to the zones of convergence that receive and integrate inputs from many different brain areas and produce a "virtual map" of the inner and outer being. It may be that our very being is in part sculpted by our earliest experiences of our mother's voice and the voices of the loved ones who sculpted her very being; indeed, within our very makeup are voices from the far past echoing down the generations in this very particular way. What I saw and recognized so vividly and celebrated on this occasion were happy voices, but what about those whose earliest encounters were with frightening, hostile, or disinterested voices?

The Realm of the Implicit

Now I want to turn specifically to the transgenerational transmission of ways of being and behaving, and, in particular, to a sadder aspect of what a child may take in "with his or her mother's milk"----the transgenerational transmission of trauma. We will bear in mind its effect on the individual's extrapolation of how future relationships may be and how this may be explored in the consulting room. Bromberg (2006) comments that developmental trauma matters so much because "it shapes the attachment patterns that establish what is to become a stable or unstable core self" (p. 6). Bromberg warns that unintegrated affect from psychic trauma, "threatens to disorganize the internal template on which one's experience of self-coherence, self-cohesiveness, and self-continuity depends. . . . The unprocessed 'not-me' experience held by a dissociated self state as an affective memory without an autobiographical memory of its origin 'haunts' the self" (p. 689).

Stein (2006) emphasizes that the quality of containment offered to the baby is "highly dependent upon the attitudes and resources that happen to be available to the adult caregivers" and is also "crucially dependent on their emotional stability and maturity"(p. 201). Early traumatic interpersonal experience affects what is available to be encoded, as well as the processes of encoding and recall of the memories associated with it. The earlier in life and the more sustained the traumatic experience the more likely it is to be held in the realm of the implicit. Jung explains that affectively toned memory images are lost to consciousness and form an *"unconscious* layer of psychic happenings" (Jung, 1951, par. 231, emphasis in the original). Such experience becomes encoded in implicit memory, unavailable to the conscious mind. Implicit or procedural memories are readily acquired without intention and remain in the mind but without entering conscious awareness; thus they can be understood as underlying patterns of being and behaving, which, although outside conscious awareness, nevertheless affect our ways of being and behaving thereafter.

The actual hardwiring of the emotion-processing circuits of the baby's developing right hemisphere, which are dominant for the sense of self, is determined by "implicit intersubjective affective transactions embedded in the attachment relationship with the mother" (Schore & Schore, 2008, p. 12). Woodhead (2009) points out that, in parent-infant psychotherapy, where the therapist works with both mother and child to help to redress very early relational trauma, "neuroaffective touch and holding may form an important tool to bring about change" (p. 145) and to allow the development of new more benign patterns of being in the infant. She suggests that this "facilitates the emergence of the infant self" (p. 145). Watt (2003) emphasizes that children who grow up with trauma at the heart of their experience will go down what is "not just a bad psychological pathway but a bad neurological pathway" (as cited in Schore & Schore, 2008, p. 12). Experience of actual trauma retained in implicit memory is known yet inaccessible to thought; as such it hardwires what become the deeply held ways of being and behaving that set the scene for the transference that will be experienced later in analytic work.

The limbic system as a whole plays a significant part in processing and enabling our response to trauma, a response that originates from rapid processing of danger signals with immediate effects on body and emotions. Our initial response is so fast that only later does information reach the cerebral cortex, where it can be recognized, felt, and pondered. Modell (2005) draws our attention to the ancient association between motility and emotion:

> The limbic system appears to be present only in those animals who are motile, which suggests that the origin of emotions may be related to the need for the individual animal to mobilize bodily responses as a whole, to respond to the requirements for homeostasis that provides the appropriate internal signals that mobilize the individual to either fight or flee. . . . Emotions or protoemotions—internal signals that monitor homeostasis—existed for millions of years before the advent of consciousness and feelings. (p. 39)

Considerable interest has also focused on what has come to be known as the default system. Particular regions, including the posterior cingulate cortex and ventral anterior cingulate cortex, are thought to constitute a network whose activity is ongoing during resting states and suspended during tasks that require active cognitive processing. Greicius et al. (2003) remark:

> Taken together our results demonstrate that a distinct set of brain regions, whose activity decreases during cognitive tasks compared with baseline states, shows significant functional connectivity during the resting state, thus providing the most compelling

evidence . . . for the existence of a cohesive, tonically active, default mode network. (p. 256)

Although some have argued that the notion is valueless (Morcom & Fletcher, 2006), functional brain imaging studies have nevertheless yielded a considerable amount of research evidence (Gusnard et al., 2001; Greicius et al., 2003; Raichle & Snyder, 2007) indicating that this default network is active in the task of sorting and storing memories, thereby helping to create a narrative of the past that may be used to inform future thinking. Both self-referential mental activity and emotional processing may represent elements of the default state (Gusnard et al., 2001, p. 4,259). Raichle and Snyder (2007) comment: "Intrinsic activity instantiates the maintenance of information for interpreting, responding to and even *predicting* environmental demands" (2007, p. 9, emphasis in the original).

Bar-Yam (1993) suggests that the temporary subdivisions that occur in the brain during sleep also enable a selective relearning process to take place that, in turn, permits the development of these predictive patterns in the mind. The fundamental motivation for such subdivision of the brain is the need to generalize patterns that may recur in life by identifying those aspects of the day's experience that may recur in other contexts. Here we have the grounding for the experience of the unconscious patterns that occur in the transference and countertransference.

The realm of the implicit, as the resting place of emotional experience, especially early emotional experience, gives rise to much that we experience in the transference and countertransference. It also produces the trigger responses that engender intense transference behaviors. It is from the realm of the implicit that such mechanisms of projection arise and become manifest in therapy. Fowler et al. (1996) note that "viewing projective data as a communication to an 'other' has broadened the interest of researchers" and assert that this approach "shifts the primary focus from assessing a one-person psychology to the assessment of a two-person interactive paradigm of transference and countertransference" (Fowler et al., 1996, p. 400). Schore emphasizes the importance of the capacity to "feel the emotional processes both between and deep within each member of the therapeutic dyad" (Schore, 2007b, p. 754). Schore and Schore (2008) stress the value of focusing treatment on "the affective dynamics of right brain insecure internal working models that are activated within the therapeutic alliance" (p. 10).

The Impact of Trauma

As danger threatens a young brain–mind–body being, the brain's initial response takes place in the brainstem, midbrain, and thalamus long before it gets to the cortex, where it can be thought about. In the face of such threat an infant's body immediately responds in an intensely aroused way. When this response is to no avail, a sense of hopelessness and helplessness overwhelms the baby, his or her systems shut down, and the dissociative response reigns supreme as a last ditch attempt to conserve life in the face of overwhelming trauma. Janet (1889), Jung (1912, 1928, 1934a), Schore (1994, 2003a, 2003b), Cozolino (2002, 2006), and many others acknowledge that when, in Bromberg's (2006) words, "a chaotic and terrifying flooding of affect . . . can threaten to overwhelm sanity and imperil psychological survival, the mind's normal capacity for dissociation is typically enlisted as a primary defense" (p. 33).

The Dissociative Continuum

The mind's normal capacity for dissociation, and the continuum that runs between normal and pathological use of the dissociative strategy as a young person responds to varying degrees of trauma, has been brought home to me by several patients. The continuum ranges from the kind of dissociation in which we all engage when we concentrate so hard on one thing that our awareness of what is happening around us is diminished, through to the extreme end of the pathological defense which is resorted to initially in the face of overwhelming trauma and then becomes a habitual response, a way of escaping from the immediate that may be resorted to unconsciously in a wide range of circumstances.

At the normal end of the continuum might be:

• The rather lonely boy who, in therapy as an adult, explains that he always made up stories in which he was the hero at the times when he felt particularly alone. The habit of retreating into this other world where he was special and surrounded by friends had gradually spread into much of the time when he was alone and had spare time to think. The time during which he traveled to and from school had become a regular period of retreat from reality to the world of make-believe. He might go on to tell that although he had a lively social life and was well liked in adulthood, the habit of entering another world still persisted, especially on the long solitary drives in the car that business trips required. In times of difficulty it might become something of a consolation. In therapy such a patient might become able to think about this habit and decide to make sure it did not dominate his or her life in an unhelpful way.

A little further along the continuum may be:

• A patient who reports that in her childhood, as she became ever more deeply aware of the unhappiness that reigned in her home because of the difficulties that each parent had with the other, she would retreat from the parental quarreling by going into another downstairs room. In that room there was a standard floor lamp, which had seemed to her to be very old and which she felt might have been in the house for a long time. She had thought to herself "Happy people must have lived here once—maybe if I stand on the base of the lamp and cling tightly to it, I will be able to get back in time to them." She would step up onto the base, curling her toes around the slippery curved surface, cling tightly to the lamp, shut her eyes, and imagine flying back in time. Later, in therapy, she explained rather ruefully that she felt she must have had in her mind a rather mixed-up version of a magic carpet and Aladdin's lamp. She concluded: "It was a rather unsuccessful attempt to do what Harry Potter was able to do when he found Platform 9 and three-quarters and could enter another world" (Rowling, 1997).

Much further along the dissociative continuum would be:

• A 12-year-old girl poised between latency and adolescence, with a much more fragmented internal world who spoke of her regular retreat to the world of Doctor Who, where she felt protected and safe in a way that was not her experience in the real world. She told of hiding behind the sofa, timidly peeking out from time to time to watch the world of Doctor Who (which unknown to her, mirrored her frightening and fragmented intrasubjective reality formed from the scary world that she had known as a very young child). In therapy she recounted that she had heard the Doctor say to her "If you are frightened in your world, come into ours and I will protect you." For much of the time this girl was living in this other world of which she spoke as "in pretend." Her use of this phrase indicated that there was the possibility of helping her to distinguish between "in real" and "in pretend" and over time enabling her to feel more comfortable in the world of reality. My first step toward facilitating this shift was to quietly underline her first use of the word *pretend* simply by repeating "in pretend?" with a slightly questioning note in my voice. When she was not taking part in adventures with the Doctor, then she might find that she had, in imagination, cast herself as the principal boy in pantomime. British children are often taken to the pantomime at Christmas. The story (usually a fairy tale) centers not only on the heroine but also on the hero (e.g., Prince Charming or Aladdin) who is always played by a woman dressed as a man. This role offered a retreat into a world where she did not have to be a girl; as principal boy she escaped in imagination to a safer role where she would no longer have to contend with the possibility of sexual abuse.

The imaginary material from these patients demonstrates how both in the immediate aftermath of adverse experience and later in childhood the dissociative response becomes the default mode for dealing with life. Although some of the material here may seem almost delusional in quality the defense operating in each case was primarily dissociative— that is, an attempt to escape where there is no escape. Schore (2007) cites Allen and Coyne's conclusion that while such patients may have originally "used dissociation to cope with traumatic events, they subsequently dissociate to defend against a broad range of daily stressors . . . pervasively undermining the continuity of their experience" (p. 759). This defense may manifest itself in the consulting room in the most hidden, subtle ways: the averting of the gaze, the turning of the head, the momentary closing of the eyes, a glazed look manifest in an otherwise usually alert and engaged patient, the dulling of mind—and not only the patient's mind but also that of the therapist, caught in a transferential experience of the dissociated state.

Kradin (2007) has made an interesting exploration of the effect on development of being constantly subjected to interactions that lack adequate information from the caregiver. Kradin believes that such experiences are revealed through the projected complexes that become manifest in the consulting room. He has focused attention on those projections that indicate lifelong styles of response to early informational absences. He points out that "when an early caregiver fails to provide adequate information of either a factual or affective nature . . . [or is physically absent it] can potentially lead to the development of crude parental imagos that the psyche will attempt to flesh out with archetypal images" (2007, p. 3). Here Kradin offers a key to understanding the effect on a child's development of what must be understood as an affective lack, as only the right hemisphere, which deals with affective rather than factual information, is fully online at this early stage. The dominance of archetypal imagery in the absence of a good-enough experience of the human can be seen in material that emerges from many patients, such as Holly's illustrations of her journey (see paintings in Chapters 5 and 11) and Clare's comments concerning her inner world experience (Chapter 3). In considering a patient's response to such informational deficits, one must bear in mind that pattern completion comes into play when information arriving in the present is vague. How difficult this must be when there are early informational deficits that have given rise to inadequate and incomplete patterns of reference in the mind.

It is no surprise that intrapsychic experience that arises out of such interpsychic lacunas gives rise to uncertainty about how the other person actually is, and results in the transferring onto others characteristics of distance and disinterest, as well as sometimes more scary feelings that may have rushed in to fill the inner void.

Those adult patients whose early experience was dominated by fear, anger, and abuse tend to transfer the patterns of expectation of the other that have been formed in response to that poor early experience onto the therapist. The expectation may be of anger, cruelty, or rejection. This will happen especially at moments of uncertainty and is often described as "negative transference." The emotions may indeed be negative, but they inform the therapist about the patient's inner world in a powerful way. Their emergence gives the therapeutic dyad a chance to explore them and ultimately, through different experiencing of the other in the consulting room, a different expectation of the relationship may be forged. The therapist must take care to regulate the patient's level of arousal and, through relating in a different way as well as offering interpretation, help the patient to modify the expectation of relationship.

In turn the therapist may find that he or she feels that he or she is being cruel and abusive or disinterested and switched-off. The therapist will ask him- or herself "Is this my stuff?" and indeed sometimes that may be the case. Further self-questioning along the lines of "But why with this patient? Why now?" may lead to fresh insight about the patient, a modified way of being with the patient, and will keep the work on track.

At this point I will look at the neurological substrates which underpin these processes and then close with case examples and some technical considerations that are helpful to keep in mind.

Neurological Substrates of the Transference

The right hemisphere is equipped to enable us to perceive different qualities in experience, particularly frightening experience, and to react accordingly. Therefore it must hold the key to the modification, even the resolution, of transference phenomena. The right hemisphere, it has been found, is "particularly sensitive to the affective semantic content of emotional stimuli" (Atchley et al., 2007, p. 145); that is, the right hemisphere plays a key role in processing early emotional experience and in determining the patterns of response to others that will arise out of such experience and that will be transferred to all subsequent relationships that stimulate similar feelings in any way. The right posterior association cortex also plays a particular role in "processing novel input, guiding reactions to emergencies, and anticipating consequences" (Schutz, 2005, p. 11). Panksepp (2008) notes that the affective "intensity of fear emerges from convergence on central nuclei of the amygdala." In contrast, corticomedial regions of the amygdala "promote aggression and sexuality" (p. 48).

The sophisticated response system of the right brain's for dealing with threat and negative emotions such as hostility, dread, and fear means that "such emotion interrupts other, ongoing activities . . . and seizes the whole brain's focus . . . compelling the mind to handle urgent matters without delay" (Schutz, 2005, p. 15). Schutz explains that the "most complex imagery of prediction and anticipation of what might come to be is also the product of right-brain activity. . . . The right posterior cortex not only previews failures and disasters but feels their emotional impact in advance, stiffening resolve to avoid them" (p. 16). Some of the intensity of felt experience in the therapeutic transference may reflect these aspects of right-brain activity.

Schore stresses the central role of the right hemisphere, especially the prefrontal cortex and limbic areas, in the dissociative response (Schore, 1994, 2003a, 2003b, 2007a, 2007b) and notes the dense reciprocal interconnections "with emotion processing limbic regions as well as subcortical areas that generate both the arousal and autonomic bodily based aspect of emotions" (2007a, p. 760). He summarizes with great clarity the conclusions of a mass of research that indicates that "the infant's psychobiological reaction to trauma is composed of two separate response patterns—hyperarousal and dissociation," which depend on "two parasympathetic vagal systems in the brainstem medulla" (2007a, p. 757). The ventral vagal complex rapidly enables fluid engagement and disengagement with the social environment and rapid response to pain, in contrast the dorsal vagal complex, which is "associated with intense emotional states and immobilization and is responsible for the severe hypoarousal and pain blunting of dissociation" (2007a, p. 758). He draws attention to Porges's (1997) work, which describes the prolonged and involuntary nature of the dorsal vagal response and links this to the gaps in patients' ongoing experience of reality at such times (Schore, 2007a).

Schutz (2005) notes that the right posterior association cortex is larger in the right hemisphere than in the left, with "denser association fibers . . . greater interconnection of neural columns (identified in the temporal lobe) . . . and larger integrative structures" (p. 13). He observes that "right-brain problem-solving generates a matrix of alternative solutions, as contrasted with the left brain's single solution of best fit" (p. 13). I remember, as a trainee, being struck by Klein's (1975) capacity to wonder with her young patient, Richard, in a sensitive way about a number of possibilities of emotional meaning in what they were experiencing together. The right brain specializes in the processing of negative stimuli and is at work in situations where the negative transference predominates (Kimura, 2004; Sato & Aoki, 2006). To respond by using its capacity for examining alternative solutions in the way Klein advocated is therefore likely to be more effective than any head-on or either/or approach to a particular manifestation of the negative transference.

Imprinted patterns of neural excitation give rise to ways of being and behaving in the present in anticipation of future happenings based on past experience. Bar-Yam (1993) summarizes:

> In theoretical models an imprinted pattern of neural excitations can be recovered if a sufficiently large part of the pattern is re-imposed on the neurons. Evolving the activity pattern then causes the complete original imprinted pattern to be recovered. This is an associative memory which associates the restored pattern to the part-of-it that was imposed. Such neural networks are also considered to be capable of generalization. This capability arises because the region of "possible experiences" near a particular memory evolves by neural dynamics to the memory. (p. 2)

Perhaps we have here a description that can be helpful in thinking about the process of first experiencing and then understanding elements of the transference, as it arises in response to emotional exchanges that in some way trigger implicit memory of earlier traumatic experience.

Pally (2007) describes such patterns as the product of the predicting brain; she suggests that at a nonconscious level the brain "predicts what is most likely to happen and sets in motion perceptions, emotions, behaviors and interpersonal responses best adapted to what is expected" (p. 861). In life this can lead to a bringing about of what is most feared, as the person who adopts a response in anticipation of being hurt may bring about just that. In therapy the therapist must identify the feared response and seek to avoid responding in that way. Over time he or she may help the patient to identify and abandon, rather than continue to repeat, such maladaptive reactions. Pally (2007) gives weight to the cognitive as the curative element, whereas Schore favors the role of relational-emotional contact in the therapeutic dyad as the crucial factor in achieving lasting change (Schore, 1994, 2003a, 2003b, 2007a, 2007b).

Neurological Substrates of the Countertransference

Although still speculative and as yet poorly understood, it appears that a body of evidence may now be emerging that establishes a neural basis for empathy in that the perception of emotion in another activates the neural mechanisms responsible for the generation of emotions. If this should prove to be the case, it will provide an understanding of the depths of the transference–countertransference process and will establish an indissoluble link between those processes and the development of mind.

The countertransference is a very particular form of musing about one's own body–brain–mind response as part of the experience of being with the patient; it is a musing that brings creative knowledge of oneself and the other via the unconscious communication of self states and relational patterns from the patient to the therapist. These states are absorbed by the therapist at the level of the implicit, below the threshold of consciousness. Perry (1997), following Samuels (1985), suggests that both therapist and patient "contribute to and are part of a shared imaginal realm, in which bodily responses, feelings and phantasies can be viewed imagistically" (p. 160). Many describe the countertransference experience as being rooted in bodily experience; Sidoli (2000) described her experience of countertransference in the following way:

> The analyst must pay a great deal of attention to the subliminal messages conveyed by the body. The unintegrated emotional fragments are located in the body. Thus one must listen with a

"third ear" and observe with a "third eye." . . . My countertransference with these patients is rooted . . . most of all in my experience of observing young infants and their nonverbal way of
relating. . . .I have to make my way toward making the hopeless
infant inside the patient trust. . . . When the attachment sets in,
the patient will slowly use me to make up for the mirroring experience he or she missed. (p. 102)

Modifying Past Patterning

Case Example: Jill

Jill, a woman in her forties, whom I describe more fully in Chapter 6, had
an effective, well-adapted coping self that stood her in good stead in most
situations, most of the time. The often unpredictable, impulse-driven
behavior of her alcoholic mother and resentment of her very existence
that emanated from her stepfather together combined to provide a
particularly acute state of what Kradin (2007, p. 3) terms "informational
absence." These parenting failures persisted throughout her childhood
and into adolescence, which, although it might have offered a second
chance to experience a meaningful affective relationship with either
parent, passed without much change in either's parenting style. The
intense affective informational absence that resulted was partly modified
by an aunt's warmer way of relating and attempts to explain factually the
parents' shortcomings. This information enabled the patient to develop
enough resilience and intellectual understanding of her dilemma so as
not to be destroyed completely, though she used the mechanism of
projection defensively, in a rather rigid and inflexible way, particularly
the projection of her own destructive anger. This could affect her transference to me at difficult moments in the therapy.

Transference phenomena are perhaps seen most clearly when they are
manifest in the consulting room; that is, when difficult feelings which are
the product of poor early relational experiences get transferred onto the
therapist. With time and patience such feelings may be recognized,
understood, and worked though so that it becomes more possible for the
patient to relate to others in a different way. However the patterns that
build in the mind of how relationships with others develop will also get
transferred onto others; they may become manifest in relations with

friends, family members, or co-workers. It may take very little to trigger such transference phenomena in someone whose early experience has been full of fear and uncertainty.

Hidden deep within Jill, unknown to her for much of the time, was a much younger hurt and frightened aspect of herself that was evoked when, as an adult functioning well in the workplace, she hit a difficult patch. As she told me the story she looked at me in a defensive way as if she was sure I would criticize her. It felt as if a senior colleague were pulling out the rug from beneath her feet, in a way that posed a very serious threat to her continued well-being and success at work. Jill told how she had gone home from work the previous evening uncertain of how the situation would develop. As she thought about it at home, she suddenly felt herself becoming overwhelmed by an anxiety that developed into a full-blown panic attack accompanied by a sudden and very vivid memory of an occasion from the eighth summer of her life. She had been out with young friends, unaccompanied by any adults. They had chosen to walk into the bottom of an old quarry, knowing that they would have fun, climbing up the steep side of it. Jill was overwhelmed by a sudden and intense flashback of how when she was halfway up this climb, she had suddenly found that her feet were slipping; she had felt the soil surface slipping away beneath her feet. She had made an abortive attempt to grab at some low-growing bush as she began to slip and slide. The memory was so vivid she felt that she was actually reliving the experience again. Somehow she had managed to save herself by clinging to a ledge with her legs trembling, until she became calm enough to finish the ascent. She never climbed that quarry again.

Although the incident had seemed long forgotten, if remembered at all, the actual moment of slipping had returned, as if it were happening to her all over again in an intensely vivid way, even as she retold it in the consulting room. She felt that she had been very lucky to have managed to save herself from what would have been a very dangerous fall from a considerable height. After we had worked on lowering her level of arousal, grounding her in the room and in the present (see Chapter 2 for a fuller explanation of this process), we were able to speak briefly about the way the brain remembers previous danger, stores such experience implicitly as "the old present," is able to recognize similarities in contemporary experience, and then pattern-matches in a rather general way in an effort to protect from further distress. We went on to make the links to her workplace, her difficult early experience, and her fears that I would not understand but would blame her. We discussed how frightening the situation there felt, how it mirrored some of her very painful early experience as a child. I then asked about strategies that might help her to manage the work situation. She became much more able to think about what steps she might be able to take to deal with the current threat to her well-being once she had laid to rest the ghosts from the past. Such unresolved traumatic transference experience poses a constant challenge for the therapist when, through enactments in the therapy, the dynamics are replayed again and again, not in the workplace as on this occasion, but in the therapy itself, as the patient unconsciously seeks an experience not only of the rupture, undergone so frequently in childhood, but also a new experience of healthy repair.

Kradin's Patient B.: Using the Reality of the Analyst to Compensate for Early Patterning

Kradin (2007) describes a patient, B., whose parents alternated between unwelcome impingement and emotional abandonment. Kradin highlights one of the limitations of working in a psychoanalytically abstinent way (i.e.,) with such patients. He suggests that although abstinence may foster projections, it may also unwittingly contribute to the "domain of informational absence" (Kradin 2007, p. 4). He realized that such a stance for this patient, although it might be *operationally* neutral, was not *analytically* so, understanding that it was "too close to the informational void that [the patient] had experienced with his father" (p. 5). He began to work cautiously in a way that allowed his patient to have more sense of an actual person in the room. Cozolino (2002) also stresses the difficulty that working in a silent, abstinent way poses for such patients, pointing out that "silence is an ambiguous stimulus that activates systems of implicit memory" (p. 99). Kradin (2007, p. 5) concludes: "Once B. realized that I was a person in my own right, his reliance on transference projections diminished." Kradin makes clear that an abstinent evoking of projections accompanied by a left-brained interpretational approach is not only an inadequate way of working on this occasion but also actually unhelpful for such patients whose early affective distress is enacted again in the room. The rough pattern matching that goes on in the brain–mind can become particularly intense as a patient relives traumatic experience.

"A kind of novelty that is useful, valuable and generative" (Stokes, 1999) and a kind of unfocused attention (Mendelsohn, 1976) seem to me to be the hallmarks of creative countertransference experience.

Concerning the process of creative thinking, in particular, it has been argued that the right hemisphere:

- Operates in a more "free-associative, primary process manner, typically observed in states of dreaming or reverie" (Grabner et al., 2007, p. 228).
- Works "in a more parallel or holistic processing mode, in contrast to the sequential, logic-analytical processing mode commonly assigned to the left hemisphere" (Grabner et al., 2007, p. 227). (It is this holistic processing mode that I believe enables the experience that we describe as the countertransference.)
- Has an increase in its alpha power in the subjective experience of insight (Jung-Beeman et al., 2004; Bowden et al., 2005; Grabner et al., 2007).

Gallese's work, although speculative as yet, emphasizes our capacity to directly understand the inner world of others without recourse to complex sophisticated mentalizing abilities. He suggests that such direct understanding is arrived at by means of an "embodied simulation" mechanism resulting in the activation of chains of related neurons that enable not only low-level mechanisms such as empathy but also "more sophisticated aspects—like the attribution of mental states to others." He further suggests that "this mechanism enables *attentional attunement* with the observed agent" (Gallese, 2007, p. 661, emphasis added).

Carr et al. (2003) explain empathy as arising from a mechanism of action representation that enables emotional understanding. They stress the role of the inferior frontal cortex because of the role of empathy in understanding the goals of the other. They also observe the part played by activity in the amygdala in the right hemisphere (rather than the left amygdala) in the imitation of facial expressions. I have come to think of the bodily experiencing that occurs as part of countertransference phenomena as embodied empathy.

Pally (2007) emphasizes the way in which nonconscious brain predictions that arise from earlier experience actually alter brain activity and suggests that this process offers a biological mechanism by which the unconscious repetition of transference phenomena occurs. It is just this activity that I believe is picked up in the rapid processing that occurs at levels below consciousness that we have come to describe as countertransference. Cowan and Kandel argue that affective arousal increases neurotransmitter activity, which in turn fosters neural learning and development (as cited in Ginot 2007). Pally (2007) stresses the involuntary nature of nonconscious responses and emphasizes the importance of conscious self-reflection as an agent of therapeutic change; indeed interpretations, arising out of both transference and countertransference experience, have their part to play in effecting change.

In a groundbreaking summary of the literature concerning therapeutic change, Schore (2007a) emphasizes that for patients who have experienced early relational trauma, affective processes that lie beneath levels of conscious awareness are of critical importance and occur through the "ultra-rapid transactions of nonverbal facial expressions, gestures and prosody between the patient's and therapist's right brains" (p. 8). Schore also draws our attention to work that shows that only the right hemisphere, and not the left, is attentive to, and dominant in processing, negative emotional stimuli (Kimura et al., 2004; Sato & Aoki, 2006). Much of transference and countertransference phenomena is concerned with negative emotion, as the predictive patterns established in the mind–brain are patterns established in response to earlier trauma.

Apparent Absence of Empathic Countertransference

Early notions of lack of empathic countertransference were attributed to the intrusion of the analyst's own concerns, sometimes as a defensive strategy against overintrusion by the patient or otherwise unbearable states of mind evoked by the patient. However, sometimes sleepiness or mind-wandering states may be dissociative effects induced in the therapist by the patient, and as such are an informative countertransferential response that may mirror dissociative states of mind that threaten to overtake the patient. I have often found that to ask myself "Why this state of mind with this patient at this moment?" can be extremely informative. For instance, one young female patient might have experienced early relational trauma in the form of hospitalization without her mother at 2 weeks old, which was then followed by removal from mother to be with a foster carer from 3 months to 18 months old, and then by a return to mother and total loss of the foster carer to whom she would by that time have become very attached. In the consulting room it might appear that this patient had dealt with the most painful moments of her early experience by disengaging, by blotting out what would have otherwise been unbearable feelings and retreating into almost completely switched-off states. Perhaps there would be moments in the consulting room when, without knowing why, I would find myself increasingly switched off and struggling to remain alert and engaged. Eventually I might learn that at these times it helped to say something open-ended along the lines of "I think there's something quite difficult around." My patient might then be able to get into touch with some new aspect of this painful, well-nigh unbearable, early experience.

Ginot (2007) argues that complex "mutually reactivated dissociated memories and self-states" can occur, containing within them "entangled implicit relational schemas," and giving rise to enactments in the consulting room (p. 318)—perhaps better termed *reenactments*—because they arise out of the entanglement of the past experience of both members of the therapeutic couple. Ginot values such occurrences as providing a unique understanding of the patient's relational patterns, held in dissociated self states that result from early relational trauma and that, as such, cannot yet be verbalized. Stern (2008) regards enactments as an essential, indeed the *only* means, of encountering dissociated aspects of the patient. For him the value of enactment lies in the opportunity it offers to "understand the unconscious impact of the patient on him, and then to use his knowledge of this impact, and of his own disequilibrium, to grasp parts of the patient's experience that the patient has no way to put into words" (p. 402). Here it becomes clear that affective attunement based on empathic countertransference is the only medium that will enable understanding in the therapist and may lead to change in the patient's mind.

A useful distinction is drawn between *enactment* and *acting out* by reference to Lebovici's definition in which enactment is understood as something "achieved in a truly extraordinary moment in which the analyst feels in his own body an act which remains experienced and not acted out" (as cited in Zanocco et al., 2006, p. 148). Enactment concerns just these primitive elements of experience that have not yet entered the conscious mind and become nameable for the patient. The authors comment: "Enactment by contrast [to acting out] is related to primitive unconscious elements which find in the act their first expression" (Zanocco et al., 2006, p. 150).

Hart (2008) discusses the particular kind of countertransference enactment that Lebovici describes based on her work with a patient who moved into a state of hypoarousal (following overarousal), when reexperiencing extreme helplessness that she felt resulted, almost, in metabolic shutdown. Such a state of hypoarousal cuts the sufferer off from both internal and external stimuli in order to prevent cell death and damage that might otherwise result from a continuing state of overarousal. She argues that the effect on the therapist who is in the presence of such extreme manifestations may be a sense of having what feels like a lack of countertransference, which initially seems to diminish the possibility of meaningful reflection. She describes what seems to have been a flight into pseudo-thinking that she experienced as she worked with a severely traumatized child, a 3 1/2-year-old little boy, whom she calls Zack, who had been removed from his family because of neglect, violence, and suspected sexual abuse. The flight into thinking occurred in her at moments when he moved into severely dissociative states. Hart describes the state she was experiencing as a defended sort of thinking about her patient's difficulties. On these occasions it seems that what she experienced was an involuntary shift into left-brain cognitive activity, perhaps as an unconscious protective dissociative strategy that matched her patient's dissociative state, while avoiding a mirroring experience that would have led to the extreme and damaging right-brain manifestations that were being demonstrated in her patient.

What I find so moving about her account of the vicissitudes of Hart's (2008) countertransference experience is the shift she describes to a right-hemispheric body-, image-, and feeling-based empathic countertransference as the child became more able to be in touch with his bodily experience and also became able to cry. She describes her countertransference response on one occasion as consisting of sharp pain in her abdomen, which then emerged in "images of daggers" (Hart, 2008, p. 65). Linking with the left hemisphere occurs as she then begins to ponder the unthinkable—that is, she finds herself thinking of the sexual abuse that the child may have experienced. In thinking about this processing, she is reminded of Schore's (2003a) observation that projective identification is "a very rapid sequence of reciprocal affective transactions within the intersubjective field that is constructed by the patient and the therapist" (p. 73).

Closing Thoughts

A patient toward the end of her treatment chose to sit cross-legged on the couch during one session, looking at me pensively as she explored the transference patterns in her mind that had caused her such difficulty early in the therapy—patterns that had so easily made her feel as if I might be a monster, or that she might be something monstrous, that she would fall into the abyss, that I must hate her, be bored by her, be always wishing the session would end, just waiting for her to leave. She tentatively mused about how it might have felt to be me at some of those times and about how it distressed her now to think of how it might have affected me then. As she spoke I was reminded of the difficult countertransference feelings that I had experienced—feelings of anger, rage, uselessness, failure, even despair. With gentle warmth she reflected on how gradually but inexorably the deep affective engagement that had occurred between us had allowed those old patterns, based on fear and distrust and rage, to slowly change into a new way of experiencing as she began to know something of containment and security within the analytic dyad. The reader will meet Holly and will experience something of the changes in her inner world over the course of her therapy in the next chapter.

Part II
Tools for Change:
*Relational, Experience-Dependent Plasticity
in the Service of the Developing Self*

5

The Double Helix:
Affective Encounter and Interpretation

ATTACHMENT, AFFECT REGULATION, AND AWARENESS of early patterning have become increasingly accepted as the basics of good therapy because they underpin each individual's capacity for successful relating. My concept of therapy is something like a double helix, in which interactions involving left-brain and right-brain processes intertwine in order to make a whole. One aspect of therapy deals with the implicit, arising from the right hemisphere; it is predominantly affective, composed of the affective encounter between therapist and patient. The other deals with the explicit, arising from the left hemisphere; it is predominantly cognitive, manifest in interpretation. With Stern et al. (1998), Cambray and Carter (2004) note two similar strands of therapeutic action. One strand is "explicit through verbal, content-oriented interpretation of the transference, the other is implicit through nonverbal, process-oriented knowing in the context of the shared current relationship" (p.133). They conclude that the focus of therapy should be on "facilitating a coordinated integration of explicit and implicit relational memory and knowing as manifest in images, dreams, stories, and narratives, as well as the analytic relationship" (p. 144). Cozolino emphasizes that "the blending of the strengths of the right and left hemisphere allows for the maximum integration of our cognitive and emotional experience with our inner and outer worlds" (Cozolino, 2002: 115). No therapy is complete without both and I find that interpretations, particularly those that involve putting feelings into words, arise out of the experience of relationship as it unfolds and brings about increasing connectivity, making possible healthy and integrated functioning of both hemispheres of the brain. M. L. Miller (2008) argues that "with each successive advance in our theoretical understanding of emotion the analyst's emotional participation becomes more central to the analytic process, opening new avenues of therapeutic relatedness and intervention" (p. 4). There is now a growing consensus that left-brain interpretational work is simply not enough and that right-brain empathic relating is essential, especially for patients who have experienced early relational trauma. Haven (2009) points out that "people process their trauma from the bottom up—body to mind—not the top down" and concludes that "if trauma is situated in these subcortical areas, then to do effective therapy, therapists need to do things that change the way people regulate these core functions, which probably can not be done by words or language alone" (p. 212). The second half of this book explores some of these avenues. The American Psychological Association's Presidential Task Force on Evidence-Based Practice (2006, p. 277) asserts that clinical expertise is characterized by "interpersonal skill, which is manifested in forming a relationship, encoding and decoding verbal and nonverbal responses, creating realistic but positive expectations, and responding empathically to the patient's explicit and implicit concerns."

Integrating Cognitive and Affective Approaches

For those who have experienced early relational trauma, it seems that only this dual approach of empathy and interpretation will enable clients to address the point of pain while staying "in mind" and able to work, rather than retreating into defensive dissociative states of mind. Interpretation alone is simply not enough to redress damage to early implicit structures in the mind. Haven (2009) comments: "Trauma does not sit in the verbal understanding part of the brain but in the much deeper regions—the amygdala, hippocampus, hypothalamus, brain stem" (p. 211). Our task is not merely that of making the unconscious conscious but rather of restructuring the unconscious itself (Alvarez, as cited in Schore, 2007a). Lane (2008) points out that the adaptive value of primary emotional responses is the reason for their survival in the evolving organism that is the human being. Schore (2008b) argues that "emotional processes lie at the core of not only early developmental processes, but also in the re-evocation of these processes in the psychotherapeutic relationship" (p. 22). Stern (2008) emphasizes the unconscious aspects of the therapeutic process, explaining "Just as inevitably as the patient unconsciously affects the analyst, the analyst unconsciously affects the patient. From this point of view, the relationship is understood to take place between two unconsciously intertwined subjectivities" (pp. 404–405).

Whereas the explicit can be thought about in words by the therapist and client together, the implicit is most effectively addressed through the actual quality of the relationship that is established in therapy. I argue in favor of an approach that regards both affective encounter and interpretation as vital and complementary aspects of therapy. I have come to take what I think of as a "double helix" approach to therapy, one that pursues increasing neural integration of right- and left-hemispheric activity.

Jung consistently emphasized the dual aspects of the encounter between two beings. He regarded the meeting of minds at both conscious, explicit and unconscious, implicit levels as necessary for change and transformation. I have utilized Jung's (1946b) exploration of one of the images from the Rosarium Philosphorum, in order to better illustrate the levels at which this transformation occurs (see Fig. 5.1).

Jung understands the joining of the left hands as representing "the unconscious side . . . the affective nature of the relationship" (Jung, 1946b, par. 410). The left side of the body connects to the right hemisphere of the brain, and the right side of the body connects to the left hemisphere. The joining of the left hands in this image may be understood to signify right-hemispheric, implicit interactions and emotional responses, and the crossing of the flowers held in the right hands (which Jung understands as compensatory) to signify the exchange of ideas or cognitions arising in the left hemisphere. Both figures are standing in a way that permits gaze and gaze-away exchanges to take place between them, reminiscent of the earliest ways of relating between mother and infant. The way the gaze of each engages the other points to the importance of the "language of the eyes" for the understanding of the other (Baron-Cohen et al., 1997; Baron-Cohen, 2001; Hirao, Miyate, et al., 2008). For a considerable time analytic theory privileged left-hemisphere functions over those of the right. However, each has a part to play. As M. L. Miller (2008, p. 11) argues, "our brain is as much, if not more, an emotional organ as it is a cognitive one," and he notes that "cognitive schemas organize our declarative knowledge whereas emotional schemas organize and interpret our subjective and interpersonal worlds" (p. 8).

The Right Hemisphere and Cognition

Recent research has focused attention on the process by which the unconscious is made conscious, seemingly an essentially cognitive process. However, both fMRI scanning and electroencephalography (EEG) recordings have detected increased activity in the anterior superior temporal gyrus of the right hemisphere, where new insights involved what might be termed the "aha" factor. Researchers describe this as the activity that reflects the moment at which "the unconscious becomes conscious" and note that "this right anterior area is associated with making connections across distantly related information during comprehension" (Jung-Beeman et al., 2004, p. 506). They further observe: "It is striking that the insight effect observed in the RH [right hemisphere] in our experiments occurred when people solved verbal problems, which traditional views suggest should involve mostly LH [left hemisphere] processing with little or no contribution from the RH." They conclude that such insight solutions are associated with "early unconscious solution-related processing, followed by a sudden transition to full awareness of the solution" (p. 507).

Inadequate development of the left hemisphere is the result of early relational trauma and prevents adequate processing of information (Panksepp, 2008). For the mind–brain to function effectively the two hemispheres need to function in an integrated way. Both are linked through the corpus callosum, the midsection, which has been identified as the brain region most severely reduced through early traumatic experience (Teicher et al., 2006). It seems likely that such linking and integrating of the two hemispheres is best able to develop in a therapy that embraces the affective as well as the cognitive dimension. Beaucousin et al. (2006) stress that emotional verbal communication has a fundamental part to play in human relating and that emotional comprehension emerges from the processing of both linguistic and pragmatic information, thus being the product of the integrated functioning of both hemispheres.

Recent research has also highlighted the importance of the ventrolateral prefrontal cortex (VLPFC) in the integration of cognitive and emotional information from one's own internal states, both in normal subjects and in patients with a diagnosis of schizophrenia. The VLPFC, "in addition to cognitive information on external object identity through the ventral visual pathway . . . also receives motivational and emotional information from the OFC [orbitofrontal cortex] and subcortical areas such as the mid-brain and the amygdala" (Hirao, Miyuta, et al., 2008, p. 172).

Other researchers focus attention on the integrative role of the cerebellum, "a vastly complex structure . . . [with] almost as many neurons as the cerebral cortex" (Cozolino, 2006, p. 285). This complexity, in conjunction with its dense connectivity into surrounding areas, suggests that the cerebellum may play a significant role in "the modulation and timing for language and affective communication" (p. 286). Levin (2009) further highlights the importance of the functioning of the cerebellum in relation to the processing of emotion and the linking of implicit and explicit memory. I would speculate that the cerebellum ultimately can the integration of affect and cognition that is mediated by the cerebellum ultimately can lead to therapeutic change and development of mind.

It must be clearly acknowledged that from a therapeutic viewpoint, words have limitations. Words can be used defensively in the consulting room by either member of the dyad. A patient may use a stream of words or may report rather meaningless life narrative material in an attempt to shut out the analyst. Words are rarely neutral, and words spoken by the analyst may be experienced by the patient as attacks that harm the fabric of the self. Knox (2008) notes that at the wrong stage of psychic development, even the lightest interpretation can be experienced by a patient as "inadvertently taking away a whole world" (p. 31). She goes on to argue, both sensitively and cogently, that "interpretation is about words which, by the fact we need to use them, convey the separateness of one mind from another and so may be unbearable to someone who cannot yet be sure that he or she can be allowed to have a much more direct emotional impact on the analyst, that the analyst is not afraid of the patient's need for close attunement" (p. 35).

I am aware that much interaction in the twosome will be fast, automatic, and below the threshold of consciousness. Cozolino (2006) observes that "when it comes to the processing of facial expressions we have a wide span of attention, a low threshold for detection and obligatory and automatic processing" (p. 177). Such research makes clear that to "watch what we say" will not be sufficient on its own; equally vital will be to attend to "how we are." A shrug of the shoulders, on its own, or with a certain look or sound may indicate disdain; a shrug of the shoulders, again on its own, or with a slightly different look or sound accompanying it may rather indicate despair. A smile which does not reach the eyes may have the quality of a grimace—sometimes this will reveal itself as annoyance, at other times the therapist may be instantly aware of underlying fear. Watt identifies two routes for perception of the feelings of another person. One is very fast and he terms it the contagion route; it is essentially a right hemisphere, affective process occurring below levels of consciousness. The other is a slower process involving left hemisphere, cognitive processing; that is, thinking about what a sound, a look, a gesture might mean. Fear may be identified almost instantly. Thinking about why the patient might have become afraid is a slower but equally important process for the therapist. Quiet attentiveness from the therapist can help the patient to feel safe enough to reveal the material that has come to mind, which may well be very frightening, and short, open-ended questions can invite further exploration of the feeling and encourage the patient to attend to the affect.

Mundo (2006) points out that "when patients are asked to remember the significant moments inducing change during their treatment they usually remember affect-charged moments of interaction with the therapist" rather than the interpretations that were offered (Mundo, 2006, p. 684). Indeed Fonagy and Target (2008) point out that "as arousal increases, in part in response to interpretive work, traumatized patients cannot process talk about their minds" (p. 29). The Boston Change Process Study Group emphasize the importance of the implicit realm as the facilitator of therapeutic change, of the experience of "moments of meaning" within the dyad rather than moments of insight or intellectual understanding (Lyons-Ruth et al., 1998).

"Moments of meaning" are processed by the prefrontal cortex of the right hemisphere, the emotional executive of the brain, which is densely connected vertically into the limbic system, the brain stem, and into the body, just as the body, the brain stem and the limbic system are richly connected to the prefrontal cortex. Such connectivity enables the prefrontal cortex to process, organize, and inhibit, feelings, impulses and bodily emotions. It also has strong horizontal connections into the left hemisphere, via the corpus callosum, which enables more cognitive processing. Such connections are reciprocal. There are horizontal connections at the limbic level from right to left and vice versa. Cozolino (2002) notes "transcortical networks in both hemispheres feed highly processed sensory-motor information forward to the frontal cortex. Simultaneously, multiple hierarchical networks, which loop up and down through the cortex, limbic system and brainstem, provide the frontal cortex with visceral, behavioural and emotional information" (p. 132). Cozolino concludes that factual and affective informational development layered upon early experience requires "simultaneous re-regulation of networks on both vertical and horizontal planes" and observes that much of this is mediated "through interactions among regions of the prefrontal cortex, our primary executive system" (p. 30). Such reregulation can only be the product of a therapy that addresses movement between and within each hemisphere. As a result of their exploration of fMRI scans, Beaucousin et al. (2006) concluded that the accurate affective communication involves activity in both hemispheres in that semantic, affective prosody and mind-reading neural networks are activated (Beaucousin et al., 2006). Chused (2007) suggests that in such circumstances "the communication that takes shape back and forth between patient and analyst may have more mutative power than an explicit communication" and argues that "in some instances such implicit communications lose their power to alter a patient's inner world if they are made explicit" (p. 875).

Locking on to an emotional understanding of another via pattern completion (see Chapter 4) allows a quick response to present experience based on past experience. When past relational experience has been seriously flawed, familiar pain in relating is privileged over fear of the unknown. Javanbakht and Ragan (2008) point out that "such a neuropsychological template fit offers abeyance of the insecurity of the unknown in favor of . . . easily accessible pattern-completion" (p. 270). When early experience has been very difficult or present circumstances have given rise to very stressful relational experience, then such locking in of a past pattern may result in a very powerful negative transference that may destroy the unique opportunity that therapy offers to experience something other. Left-brain interpretational work will prove to be ineffective when confronted with such a negative affective engagement based on past early, right-brain experience. The solution lies in the relational approach: Lewis et al. (2000) point out that "people do not learn emotional modulation as they do geometry or the names of state capitals"; rather they learn it implicitly from "the presence of an adept external modulator" (as cited in Dales & Jerry, 2008, p. 305). The therapist must be sufficiently present to mitigate the too intense transference that would paralyze the patient and lead to a stalemate in the treatment.

Promoting Neural Integration as a Means to Achieve a Learned Secure Attachment

Images associated with early trauma may be called forth through the powerful affective engagement that may occur in therapy when the core work is understood as affective and relational in nature. Lichtenberg (2004) notes that "through words, images, gestures, metaphors and model scenes, analysts and analysands forge linkages between presymbolic, procedural, verbal, symbolic and imagistic symbolic encodings of experience" (p. 140). Such images, if characterized by novelty and creativity, are often metaphorical, and as such stimulate brain activity and facilitate change and development in the mind-brain-body being. Zabriskie (2004) comments "images carry our analysands beyond their here and now toward their could and would be. Images give form and shape to the mutual vibrations of the emotions, as they move back and forth along the highly charged connections between analyst and analysand" (p. 240). Such images are conveyed not only through the patient's story but also through the evolving symbolism in dream sequences and in paintings. Insight arising out of exploration of the symbolic as it presents in image and metaphor facilitates the development of a secure attachment, adequate affect-regulation, and a more coherent sense of self. Because some metaphorical material may represent an early state of emergence from the implicit, it may be difficult at first for patient or therapist to get hold of in a meaningful way. A measure of a deepening capacity for trust can be seen in the ways in which such images change over time, as the patient becomes more able to process early experience on both cognitive and affective levels. The patient's inner world becomes more benign as a result of intersubjective experience within the analytic dyad. Holly (whom we met in Chapter 1) worked in therapy with difficult experiences of relating to her mother. Holly's images, often taken from dream images, were remarkable in that they played a transforming role by functioning as the steppingstones by which she became able to put difficult feelings into words. Hartmann (2000) notes that as we move from focused waking thought to dreaming, "our mental processes become increasingly metaphoric" (p. 70). When a patient brings a dream, I often ask when during the night he or she thought it had occurred. Holly's reply was that it usually felt as if she had dreamt just after dropping off to sleep or just before waking. Holly described these dreams as "snippets." I have found that such dream snippets, despite their fleeting nature, are often highly significant precursors of change, particularly changes in the analytic attachment.

Throughout the course of therapy, Holly and I worked with cognitive and emotional schemas, the exploration of which offered an opportunity to reshape her understanding of her intrasychic and interpsychic worlds. Holly had experienced quite severe early relational trauma (Wilkinson, 2006a, pp. 149–150). Her mother had had a difficult early start herself and found it difficult, if not impossible, to mother her children. She had returned to work soon after the birth of each baby, leaving the children with a succession of carers. She would disappear from time to time totally unexpectedly. Holly has hardly any memories from her earliest childhood and few that include her mother. She felt that she always displeased her mother, who left her in no doubt about this, attacking her verbally and occasionally physically. She remembers her mother as an angry person and would often lie awake in bed at night listening to her parents quarreling, particularly her mother's raging. Holly was sent away to school and was desperately unhappy there. At school her elder sister seemed to take on her mother's mantle. To Holly it seemed that, together with her friends, her sister used seniority as an excuse to persecute Holly, bullying her at every opportunity. Holly failed dismally at school, left as soon as possible, married young, had children, and only much later, with the help of therapy, was able to embark on higher education and a career.

First Phase of Therapy: Acknowledging Terrifying Feelings. *Material arising from the implicit that indicates a disorganized attachment and that is dominated by subcortical, amygdala-driven states of fear and aggression.*

Holly came to see me for the first time in the middle years of life. She was in a state of seeming numbness and confusion, impelled by a recent overwhelming loss that had occurred in her life. Her underlying rage and fury were expressed in her first remark. She experienced the rocky mill-stone grit moor edge, which has towered high above the village in which I work from time immemorial, as threatening and fearsome. She commented: "Isn't it frightening to be here? Isn't it dangerous? It was frightening driving along beneath the edge." She continued, "I thought that the huge black rocks would come crashing onto my car. They don't look safe; it looks like they could crash down on us." Often when she became fearful of me, she would build a pile of pillows on the couch between her and me so that she could not see me and I could not see her. She experienced the rocky edge on her way to that first session, much as she had often experienced her mother and would come to experience me at times in the "rocky edge" of the transference.

Symbols express underlying emotional schemas. For Holly the black rocks and the pillows represented an opportunity for either a repetition of old patterns or a chance to form new patterns of connectivity in the mind, based on the new experience of relationship that the therapy would provide. I have been struck not only by verbal material brought by patients as they attempt to process trauma, but also by the visual images that they bring and the enactments that occur. All become of great significance as the patient slowly, painfully, and with great difficulty seeks to put words to the emotional schemas that the images represent. The countertransference experiences of the therapist may be acutely painful and difficult to bear at these times, but they are but a tiny amount of the pain felt by the vulnerable, hurt, and raging child aspects of the patient. Hart (2008) has described similar states of being as "a mirror neuron dance of the affective transference" (p. 275).

In my work with Holly I frequently asked myself a series of questions:

- How will I deal with Holly's fear, which she experiences as overwhelming?
- How will I approach her towering anger?
- How can her actions be translated into words?
- How can her underlying emotional schemas be transformed into cognitions that we may then think about together?
- What is the most appropriate way for me to be with her?
- How am I feeling?
- How does Holly make me feel?
- What am I not feeling?
- What is it appropriate to say?
- How can I open this moment up?

In the therapeutic encounter the matter of timing is everything, and therefore the empathic engagement of the therapist will be crucial: Too much or too soon and the trauma patient may feel unsafe, confused, intruded upon, and even penetrated against his or her will; too little or too late and the patient may feel unsafe and uncontained. For some time our work was dominated by Holly's experience of me as the hostile, persecuting, destructive mother-analyst, as I carried the projection of her internalized destructive and persecuting mother. As we worked together, she would suddenly change in a moment, it seemed; her face would show fear and then would become hard as she closed off completely from me. For Holly, sometimes just too strong a tone in my voice—the use of what has been termed as "primary not pastel colours" (Williams, 2004) in my way of speaking would remind her of her strident, overintrusive, and fearsome mother within. Almost a whole session would pass wherein Holly would struggle with her experience of me as the bad mother.

A turning point came when Holly went home after one such session and dreamt a dream with one terrifyingly vivid image that she felt compelled to paint. She brought the picture to her next session: It was of a fearsome black cat mauling a baby cat (Figure 5.2). It filled her with fear. Haltingly she was able to discuss her uncertainty about whether I was the bad black cat mother attacking her, or whether she was the bad black cat tearing me to shreds. So through this image we became able to talk about experiences of aggression long past being experienced in the relationships of today. Toward the end of the session we noticed a little cream cat curled up in the center of the picture. For me this seemed like a symbol of hope in that it was uncannily like a much-loved, happy little cat I had once had, that Holly had never seen or known about consciously (Wilkinson, 2006a). The meaningful image of the little cream cat may be understood as the product of her unconscious imagination (Decety & Chaminade, 2003; for an explanation of this concept, see Chapter 4). It was an indication of a softening in her primitive splitting mechanism that brought me hope that her anger would no longer be experienced only in projection. For Holly the image brought the possibility of putting her angry feelings into words as we looked at the image together; for the first time Holly became able to speak about her anger. This was the first of many pictures that Holly was to make at home and bring to therapy. Some, such as this one, she would bring immediately; others would arrive after several months had elapsed since their making. Lyotard (1993) reminds us that the primary motivation for the artist is a search for truth. Sometimes it may be a visual image that assists the patient in moving from a wordless state of rage and terror to a state that permits the unthinkable to enter the mind.

Second Phase of Therapy: From Image to Mind. *Fostering neural integration by verbal interpretation of images arising from the implicit and symbolizing cingulate-driven, dyadic attempts to connect*

One day some months later Holly came into the room saying "Some people dream vividly with long stories. I can never bring dreams, I only dream in snippets." I replied, "Perhaps if you had a book and kept a record of those snippets they might begin to make some sense for you." Here I was hoping that the act of writing might help to stimulate memory and lead to meaningful links that would assist the meaning-making process and ultimately enrich her personal narrative.

Dream: "Why was I trying to clean the outside?"

She thought for a moment or two and then said, "Well, last night I dreamt of a vase and that I was trying really hard to clean it. What meaning could there possibly be in that?" I replied more directively than I would ordinarily because I sensed the importance of making sense of the image for her. "Well, for starters what does the vase symbolize?" After a while I added "Is it something to do with it being a container?" "Mm, maybe," she replied. I continued, "Well, yesterday we were talking about the difficult relationship that you had with your mother and how she made you feel you were a no good, bad baby from the beginning. It's been so difficult to know whether you were a bad baby or whether it was actually your mother who was having difficulties." Holly asked anxiously, "I was trying to scrub the outside—why the outside?" "But isn't that what you are often trying to do, wanting to look good on the outside, trying to please the other person, just as you so longed to please your mother and for her to see you and to love you?"

There were some moments full of sadness, then our dialogue continued. I pondered aloud, pausing between my thoughts to give her time to follow the thread; "I wonder whether the container might be this relationship where you also want to have an experience of being seen as a nice, clean container. Because of what we were talking about last time we met, I do think it probably has to do with your mother." We sat in silence for a while then I added, "What about the vase? What was it like?" Holly replied, "Oh, I know it well—it was a glass vase, cut in a rather modern way. It was something my sister gave me." We talked more about the early dynamics of the family and what her sister had given her in terms of negative feelings about herself when her sister acted the bossy goody-goody at boarding school. Like her mother, Holly's sister always made her feel that she had got it wrong, that she was bad rather than good, that her outward way of being with others was inadequate, that she needed to "clean up her act." In her therapy we often worked at the edges of this sort of experience and I had to tread carefully at first so that I did not provoke massive projections that would have been too overwhelming for her to process. Gradually we began to be more able to relate implicit to explicit, to explore our current experience of relating in light of the patterning that she brought with her from the past. The next session Holly felt confident enough to bring another dream, which she still called "a snippet," but it was slightly fuller and involved her current attachment relationships.

Through her engagement in the therapeutic relationship Holly sought to process her experience of another in a different way to that portrayed in the dream. She had longed to be a loved and valued child. Perhaps she might not always be seen as "bad" or "dirty." She made many images that conveyed the plasticity of her mind and the uncertainty she experienced about me at this time.

Painting: "Is It Safe to Trust Her? How Does She Feel about Me?"
The painting in Figure 5.3 showed Holly sitting on the couch with two images of me sitting side by side in the room; in the more dominant image in the foreground I had a clock face, as my face and the time it showed was the time that our sessions ended. "Was I sitting there longing for her to leave?" Holly wondered. Sitting behind but yet leaning forward and so appearing to be in front of the clock-face analyst was a fainter picture of me with a real face listening attentively but also rather anxiously. That this figure was fainter seemed to indicate that it was an aspect of me that was still in the shadows of her other experience of me. The picture reflected the uncertainty of her experience but also indicated her hope, for there was not just one possibility of how another might be with her, but two. Was I similar to her mother? Did I see her as "no good"? Was I just waiting to get rid of her at the end of each session, just as her mother had packed her off to boarding school? Would she prove to be too much for me? Might she actually become able to experience and internalize someone who sat with her and listened to her attentively? As Holly looked at this picture she was able to explore what it said about her way of relating to me at that time. She felt that she was portrayed by the child sitting hunched up, withdrawn, and alone and also by the simple line drawing of a figure lying close to death; both were encased in a protective bubble (representing her dissociative defense in the face of possible intimacy). The cushions from the couch were piled up around her, adding further protection, and were also represented as the wall that she so often built between us. In those early months of therapy she would almost always accidentally dislodge one of the tassels from one particular cushion, a cushion in exactly the same blue material that covered my chair. She would then work really hard to repair it and to reattach it to the cushion, acting out in a vivid way her fear of the damage that might come from her attachment to me and her wish that there might be a possibility of an experience that was reparative. She thought the child in the bubble might be trying to repair the blue

cushion. The little cream cat, which had also come to stand for her, was shown as taking the risk of being outside the bubble, struggling in a frenzy of motor activity, arms and legs flailing, with two heads, one with a grimace of a smile, the other with mouth open, possibly in a silent scream. This reminded her of rushing off into a frenzy of physical activity when things became too much for her both at home and later at school.

Painting: "What Do I Feel about Therapy? How Do I Feel about Her?"
In the next painting (Figure 5.4) we are sitting together in an imaginary garden; I am sitting in a relaxed way and listening attentively to her. This time there are two images of Holly, not me. One Holly lies comfortably and listens attentively, half-turned toward me, but another, a darker figure, also recognizably her, lies alongside, turned away from me with her face toward the wall. Again her picture reflected her uncertainty. Could she trust me? Could she engage in a relationship? What about her hurt, angry self that really only wanted to turn away to avoid the risk of being hurt again? This picture was not brought until much later in the therapy. Significantly, these two pictures (in Figures 5.3 and 5.4) were brought to therapy together.

Holly looked again at this picture with me much later on in the therapy and began to explain that the fountain in the shape of an egg that sometimes played in my actual garden had been very important to her. She felt that it had come to symbolize "the breast" for her; if the water was flowing then there could be a hope of a feed. She would feel very sad if it was switched off. Holly had said nothing of this to me at the time. It was as if her internal struggle to risk relationship had been symbolized in the availability of the life-giving fountain but in the very concrete way, that characterizes the thinking of those who have experienced early relational trauma. For her at that time there was no certainty that another would be reliably there for her in a life-giving way and she found herself unable to risk putting such painful feelings into words. While the notion of meeting together in the garden was symbolic in the second picture, I was reminded of its power as a symbol when I read Martha Bragin's (2007) account of her work with a survivor of torture, with whom she actually met in an enclosed garden, which she felt conveyed safety, freedom, life, and nurturance—all of which were crucial to the ability of her patient to engage in the treatment.

Painting: "To Try to Relate Feels Dangerous"

Because the making of mind is an implicit, emergent, and relational process, traumatic complexes, or splinter psyches (Jung, 1934a: par. 203), form when the psyche is presented with inassimilable experience, resulting in undigested contents. Sometimes a vivid image such as Holly brought next may emerge that helps to move the patient from a wordless state of rage and terror and enables the beginning emergence of such split-off feeling-toned, archetypal experiences into mind (Figure 5.5).

In this complex metaphorical picture Holly was struggling again with her perception of our relationship. The most significant point for me about this image was that the bad black cat mother had begun to become more human in a somewhat Picasso-esque way. There is a mouth that is open and can speak, albeit a rather fierce mouth that might bite, much as her mother's remarks had been biting. The meat cleaver of her/her mother/her mother-analyst's anger is held behind her back. As I look closely at the picture with Holly, I note to myself with horror that the cleaver is about to fall on the little cream cat that has now taken on human form, albeit an emaciated one, bearing a crown of thorns. The theme of victim, abuser, and the need for a rescuer was to play out over many, many sessions in the transference and countertransference relationships.

Stern (2008) stresses that whatever content is discussed will also be expressed through the medium of the analyst's unconscious way of relating, which is evoked by a particular patient out of the dissociated content of his or her mind. It is clear that the analyst who remains unaware of this process is in danger of making interpretations that reinforce, rather than illuminate, the transference. Stern (2008) notes the probable outcomes: "The analyst of a masochistic patient makes sadistic interpretations of masochism; the analyst of the seductive patient who is nevertheless fearful of sexuality makes seductive interpretations of the patient's fear; the analyst of a narcissistically vulnerable patient interprets the narcissism in a way that wounds the patient's self-regard" (p. 403). Such ways of interpreting can trigger early unconscious memory and leave the patient feeling "as though a layer of my skin had been peeled off"—in these words of one patient describing an earlier assessment interview in another setting in which far too much had been said too soon, ultimately leaving the patient in a more defended state of mind. Another patient described an earlier attempt he had made to engage in therapy as feeling "as if the therapist had opened the top of my head surgically without anaesthetic, and was sitting behind me poking about with wires inside it." That patient persisted with the therapist for some time before deciding it was actually a sadistic process. It was years before the patient risked embarking on therapy again, this time choosing a therapist who always sat where the patient could keep an eye on her if he wished.

Final Phase of Therapy: Learned Secure Attachment. *Material indicating state of neural integration and more complex cortical development and capacity for self-regulated affect.*

Painting: "I Can Feel Safe"

The next picture that Holly brought was of another twosome, but a very different one (Figure 5.6). It was an image of an attachment from which a child might begin to look out at the world a little more confidently, the beginnings of a coherent sense of self within. Perhaps we may infer that the new relational experience in the therapy and the evolving symbolizations to which it gave rise had assisted the development of new neural pathways in the brain, enabling the beginnings of a change in attachment style for Holly. As we looked at this painting together, I noticed that it was painted on a paper that had a rather rough, raised surface. I wondered aloud why Holly might have chosen that paper. Holly replied, "Oh, it was the first piece of paper that I pulled out of my drawer." Almost instantly her mood changed from being companionably at ease to feeling criticized and a failure. She said, "Oh, I've spoiled it, it's no good . . . well, maybe I will do it again." In turn I quickly felt that I was an insensitive, no-good therapist-mother who had, with a few words, managed to spoil for my patient what had been a good experience of making something. As she left Holly murmured, "Oh, well, maybe I'll do it again." She arrived the next week and almost immediately said, '"You know that picture?" I simply said "Yes," remembering well my previous mistake and also knowing that she found it hard to believe that I might keep her in mind. She continued, "I decided I wouldn't do the picture again. It's on rough paper but I thought to myself that it was actually an appropriate choice because it's been a rough road." Once again I marveled at both the pertinence and the healing power of the symbolic.

Painting: A Learned Secure Attachment

It was with joy a year or so later that Holly painted another picture (Figure 5.7) that portrayed the new attachment she found as a result of the repeated experiences of rupture and repair in therapy, an attachment that I call "learned secure" (Wilkinson, 2006a, pp. 182–83). Holly spoke of this picture in relation to the last one. She said that, although in some ways she experienced the new one as quite primitive and the colors quite crude, she felt that that this one marked the completion of the process. She felt both mother and child had become more human. She had become able to experience and speak freely of these images from her internal world as symbolizing aspects of herself. She liked it that the child was able to reach out and touch the mother's face in a loving way, and she felt that her inner child might, at last, begin to feel more secure. She felt it was significant that the two aspects of the mother's face again become important as they reflected the different moods she was able to experience within herself: sometimes feeling smiling and joyful, sometimes feeling pensive and sad. She felt that it was important that her anger was still in the picture, in the form of the little black cat, but that it was now in manageable proportions. She said that "the little black cat" was how she thought of the picture, that it reminded her of a cat they'd had when she was a teenager that had been a really nice cat.

She remembered that it had been called Togo. Earlier in the same week that she brought this picture, she had said for the first time she could actually conceive that the therapy might be able to end at some time. On reflection I found I was not altogether surprised that the little cat who represented her ability to contain and use her anger constructively happened to remind her of a cat called "to go" . . . perhaps Togo signaled the arrival of self-regulation, which would permit the possibility of termination. Holly said she had wondered whether the heart in the picture might be a bit naive, but then she had felt it was the way people ordinarily spoke about love and affection. I found myself thinking about the baby's earliest experience of the warmth of the mother's body, the comfort of the rhythm of her heart beat and the warmth that had grown between us. She spoke last about the snowdrops that were blooming in the bottom left corner of the picture. It seemed that in the realm of the unconscious hope had flowered, that the bitter winter ruled over by the wicked ice queen no longer had her in its thrall.

Conclusion

Mancia (2005) suggests that "the defining element of the therapeutic action of current psychoanalysis appears to be that of transforming symbolically and putting into words the early implicit structures of the patient's mind" (93). Mancia makes clear that such experiences cannot be remembered in the ordinary way but can be accessed only when they are "re-experienced emotionally and enacted in the intersubjective relationship" (p. 93). Therapeutic experience acts as a "bridging function" that enables the patient to find his or her own way, as Holly did, to process the unconscious traumatic experiences of the past. It is deep emotional engagement that makes this process possible and enables the patient to heal.

The making, bringing, and discussing of these pictures, representative of the symbolic work that is the stuff of analysis, made crystal clear to me that, for Holly, it was the relational style of psychoanalysis, with its capacity to address early trauma deep in the implicit memory store of the developing right hemisphere, that was crucial to the successful process of change—that assisted in the integration of the mind–brain hemispheres that then permitted the self to emerge more fully through the process of individuation.

6

Metaphor and Metamorphosis

METAPHOR CAN TAKE MANY SHAPES OR FORMS and heralds change. Its emergence, in whatever form it takes, leads to a greater understanding of previously unprocessed feelings. It seems that such feelings may pressure the patient from within to find some way of expressing them, of putting them "out there," so to speak, so they can be felt, processed, and integrated more easily. In an early therapy session one patient, whom I have called Peter (Wilkinson, 2007a, p. 325), brought a vivid, visual metaphor that captured his early trauma. He had managed the distress that he was experiencing over the weekend break by spending his Saturday making an Advent calendar, and he brought it to his next appointment. It was a picture of a frozen land of ice, with a few small dark pine trees, the only hint of color in the landscape. In the center of the picture loomed a huge stag, dominant and aggressive. Almost hidden behind the stag was a tiny baby deer. Such a vivid, visual metaphor both arose out of and stimulated right-brain activity concerning feelings, lodged in the implicit, as we began to think and talk about the picture together.

The picture affected me deeply as I sought to be available to the feelings that the patient wished to communicate in this metaphorical way; I felt chilled, and deadness was provoked in me by the utter desolation of the gray and white wasteland of the patient's internal world that confronted me. As we began to talk together both of us were seeking to engage with the novel metaphor that the picture presented. I wondered out loud why the patient might have found himself choosing that image; very quickly the patient began to get in touch with sad and frightening feelings that he had not been able to explore with me before. He explained that as he looked at the picture with me he felt frightened that the little Bambi might not survive for long after losing its mother to the hunter. I immediately thought of the verbal connection with *bambino* or child, only to find my patient explaining that he had just that moment thought that for an Italian, *Bambi* must mean child. The fast unspoken processes of empathy enabled such connections in our minds, and neural integration was fostered as we were able to speak about these feeling-toned ideas together. The patient began to realize that he himself had felt quite young as he had sat making it, perhaps about 8 years old. He did not yet relate the scene he had portrayed so vividly to his own early trauma, but I began to realize that deep inside this patient there was a defensive, frozen self state and some crucial early loss.

In later sessions it became clearer that this frozen state had arisen through the very early loss of his mother and the difficult interactions that had dominated his experience of his father, who, overwhelmed by his own loss, could not allow himself to draw close to his son. It had been further compounded by the deep loneliness he often experienced when sent away at boarding school at 8 years old. Although he was told he was privileged to go to boarding school, he felt he must have done something wrong to be sent away when other children went to day school and got to live at home.

In the early session when he first brought the image, I sought to engage with my patient so that we might begin to explore what this image meant for him. In so doing I was beginning to understand my patient's personal use of metaphor, and I began to gain insight into the dynamics of his internal world. It took much longer before the patient began to risk the pain that attaching to another might bring. Right-brain activity was dominant in so many aspects of this early exchange. In this early stage of therapy the patient was relating to early feelings, early self states; such experience was enabled through engagement in an affective relation to another. One might say that feelings dominated the therapeutic picture at this stage, but in a wholesome creative way that contrasted with the threatening stag, enabling "the processing of the nonsalient meanings of the novel metaphor" (Mashal et al., 2007, p. 115), inviting a changed sense of self through a new safe affective experience with another.

Metaphors can emerge to capture and convey our earliest experiencing. Cozolino (2006) comments: "Abstract notions are tied to our bodies through metaphor, thus connecting our minds to the world through the experience of our bodies" (p. 73) and suggests that "our ubiquitous use of physical metaphors to describe our inner experience may also betray the sensory–motor core of both our subjective experience and abstract thought" (p. 190). Pally (2000) observes that "by containing within them sensory, imagistic, emotional and verbal elements, metaphors are believed to activate multiple brain centres simultaneously" (p. 132). Metaphor stimulates brain activity and facilitates change and development in the mind–brain–body being. Levin (1980) suggests that metaphor is a particularly effective medium for the therapist to use for transference interpretation because "metaphors cross modalities: they relate one sensation to another and the various hierarchical levels of experience to one another" (as cited in M. L. Miller, 2008, p. 11). Bucci (2001) notes that affective engagement with the therapist may call forth imagery that is as yet unrealized to a patient who is still working at a subsymbolic level. It seems that metaphor has a dual role to play in therapy for at these times the sensitive use of metaphor by the therapist, as well as a careful entering into and exploration of metaphor offered by the patient, will facilitate change.

Proto-Metaphor

How does our powerful response to metaphor arise? Perhaps it may emerge from a child's earliest experiences. Schore (2002) describes the mother's face as "the most potent visual stimulus in the child's world" (p. 18). Jacques was the first child of a couple in their 30s, whom I observed weekly from 6 weeks to 2 years of age (Wilkinson, 2006a). At different stages of development Jacques used a Venetian mask, a large vividly colored toy parrot, and a long-linked necklace, both to stand for his mother and to help him process difficult feelings in relation to her.

- At 2 months old I noted that Jacques tracked his mother with his eyes and that often when she left the room, he would look at a painted Venetian mask of a woman's face that hung above the sitting-room door, seemingly as a way of holding on to her image in some way, albeit displaying some distaste for it. His eyes would meet his mother's on her return, and he would lall and gurgle to her in delight as he "found" her again.
- Later, around the time that solid foods were being introduced, Jacques was given a large, brightly colored toy parrot. It hung on a perch just near the high chair in which he was fed. It seemed that for Jacques it was an exciting object that could also suddenly

become scary. On at least two occasions it seemed that the moment at which it became scary coincided with the moment that Jacques was offered a bright green soup, which he tasted, then made absolutely clear that he didn't like. I have wondered about the fact that the predominant color of the parrot was also bright green, and that Jacques's mother also often chose to wear green. Was one standing for the other? Was the color a link that made this association possible in Jacques' newly developing mind?

- At about 1 year old Jacques used to like to play with a long, silver chain that I wore often when I visited. One day his mother was called away unexpectedly and we were left alone together for almost an hour. His mother had rarely left him for that long. He played with the chain almost the whole time, so much so that I marveled at his concentration. He sucked the chain, held it up, looked at it inquiringly, and chewed on it again; he salivated copiously as he did so. When his mother finally returned, he took a long look at her, then threw the chain to the floor, no longer needing to substitute an object for Mother once his real mother had returned and was once more available. It seemed that my chain had become a link to Mother, on this occasion enabling him to allow another to stand in for Mother in her absence.

In using metaphor we are allowing one thing to stand for another, and in Jacques' way of managing here, I felt I was seeing the beginnings of the capacity for metaphor and symbolization. It seemed to me that each of these instances might indicate the beginnings of Jacques's ability to use one thing to stand for another, the ability to use a transitional object in the way Winnicott suggested (1975a), and the ability to think symbolically, to use what might be thought of as proto-metaphor. These instances seemed to represent a very early stage in the development of mind that becomes possible through interactive experience with another mind; interactive experience with his mother formed an integral part of Jacques' experience in these sequences. Fosshage (2008) emphasizes the infant's very early ability for nonverbal symbolic processing in all sensory modalities and understands this as a precursor to thinking, which he terms "imagistic thinking."

As we observed earlier with Naja (Chapter 2), research indicates that 2-month-old infants stimulate what, in the left hemisphere, will later become their language network by looking at their mother's face

(Tzourio-Mazoyer et al., 2002, p. 460). From my observation with Jacques it seems that this interactive process also fosters the capacity to symbolize, to use metaphor, in effect, to facilitate the early development of mind.

Neurological Substrates of Metaphor

Although basic language functions are associated with the left hemisphere, a plethora of research studies is beginning to show considerable involvement of the right hemisphere in the processing of metaphor especially when novelty, creativity, and imagery are involved (Faust & Mashal, 2007; Mashal et al., 2007; Mashal & Faust, 2008). Right-hemisphere specialization in the very early stages of processing emotionally charged words has been established (Ortigue et al., 2004; Atchley et al., 2007). Mitchell and Crowe (2005) outline a bihemispheric theory of the neural basis of language, noting that some language functions, including metaphor, are mediated by the right hemisphere rather than the left (Mitchell & Crowe, 2005, p. 963). While familiar, conventional metaphors (e.g., "food for thought") are processed as part of regular left-hemisphere language functioning, an fMRI study of the neural correlates underlying the processing of novel metaphoric expressions (e.g., revealed "stronger activity in right posterior superior temporal sulcus, right inferior frontal gyrus, and left middle frontal gyrus . . . suggesting a special role for the right hemisphere in processing novel metaphors" (Mashal, et al., 2007, p. 115).

The significance for the therapist is that, as Fosha (2003) reminds us, "emotional experience is not processed through language and logic; as the right hemisphere speaks a language of images, sensations and impressions . . . therapeutic discourse must be conducted in a language that the right hemisphere speaks" (p. 229). Of course a metaphor that is conventional for one may be novel for another. Discussing metaphors with an American friend proved enlightening; as we talked on the telephone I remarked that it was "raining stair rods," a familiar phrase in the North of England but one that I found had not crossed the ocean to California, whereas "raining cats and dogs" was a familiar metaphor to us both. This seeming digression makes clear that in choosing what metaphorical speech to use the therapist must listen carefully to the patient's language, for the metaphors that will be most likely to effect change in the patient are those that are developments of the patient's own use of novel

metaphor or those that are new to the patient and are therefore stimu-
lating. Loker (2007) also points out that

> a metaphor that is used in the waking state in verbal form can also
> be used in dreams in pictorial form, because the mode of cogni-
> tion and language of the unconscious, or of the right brain, which
> produces dream thoughts, is believed today to be concrete-
> analogic and is the source of both dream thoughts and waking
> metaphors. (p. 44)

Evolving Symbolizations

Evolving symbolizations (such as those contained in Holly's series of
dream pictures [see Chapter 5]) often emerging in the form of novel
metaphors, have long been established as indicators to the therapist and
the patient of progress in the healing process. The activation of the
implicit in this way requires connection at a deep emotional level. What
emerges may be healthy early experience, too early to be available to
explicit memory processes, but the result of healthy early dyadic experience. However when early experience has been traumatic, what emerges
from implicit memory will have a very different quality to it; being born
of deep uncertainty and insecurity, it will be defensive and dissociated. As
the therapy develops so symbolization evolves, with damaging early
experience beginning to be modulated more by deep emotional connection with another than by cognitive, linguistic processing. Inevitably, as
material from the implicit emerges, the left hemisphere has a role to play
in the process of putting the images into words, which then become
available to the processes of explicit memory storage and retrieval.
Cozolino (2002) suggests that language combined with emotional
attunement is "a central tool in the therapeutic process; it creates the
opportunity to blend words with feelings, a means of neural growth and
neural network integration" (p. 210). Nowhere is this experienced more
powerfully than in the realm of emergent metaphor, when a patient haltingly struggles to express the feelings that have emerged in a picture,
dream, or image.

M. L. Miller (2008) emphasizes the importance of Levin's understanding that emotional memories are encoded in "multiple hierarchically
ordered levels of experience, with the lowest level being various sensorimotor schemas that organize sensory and motor experience." Higher

levels become more complex with "sensorimotor qualities but are also amenable to symbolization," and the final layers are those that are "amenable to verbal symbolization" (p. 10). Defensive dissociative processes may mean that layers don't interact easily with one another and that movement through layers becomes blocked. Two patients who suffered severe relational trauma before they were 5 years old independently described how they had, as children, developed a way of being in which they retreated into hectic motor activity whenever circumstance triggered any possibility of recalling their traumatic early experience. One told how in later life she had become a sculptor and had realized that she had chosen this field, and enjoyed it, because it was such a slow motor process that she could actually feel its calming effect. She produced work that she was later to realize was deeply symbolic of her early trauma. At the time, the pieces were made without any conscious understanding or ability to make links, far less to verbalize her experience.

Case Example: Clare

The gradual development of the ability to move more easily from primitive levels of functioning can be seen in material drawn from the treatment of Clare, a successful businesswoman, whom we met in Chapter 1. I have written elsewhere about Clare's description of the similarities and differences in the initial transference to her therapist in her two experiences of therapy, a transference quality that emanated from her early relationship with her dominant, aggressive, and persecutory father (Wilkinson, 2007b). When we deal with the interactive regulation of implicit memory products, we are by definition dealing with material so early, or so traumatic, that it cannot easily be brought to mind, the unconscious emotional exchange within the analytic couple may be used as a means of knowing and understanding the otherwise unknowable and inexplicable.

Early Therapy: Amygdalar Terror Emerging in Metaphor

Clare's early therapy could easily become dominated by an experience of her male therapist as the archetype imbued, hostile, persecuting, destructive monster; all too frequently the therapist carried the projection of her internalized destructive and persecuting father, or rather the destructive, persecutory aspects of her own inner being that were so hard for her to contemplate. At these times Clare would feel herself freeze; it was hard for her to hold on to the reality of the gentle, enabling person that she knew this therapist to be at other times. She remembered her father as the terrifying person who would summon her to his study to berate her for her shortcomings. In retrospect, her own anger, which she would later describe as manifesting a desire to "hammer home" her point, was as yet totally inaccessible. Clare felt that both of us worked with her in a containing way but nevertheless her first therapist, a man, could easily be experienced as "a monster," a fearsome black beast, in a moment. At such times she would become so anxious that she imagined that she "saw" a tall, monstrous black-cloaked figure whom she felt would tear open her chest, almost like a surgeon pulling apart the two sides of a patient's ribcage, to remove her heart. Later she felt that this image was the beginning of her awareness of the overwhelming anxiety and bodily fear that she had experienced as a child in the presence of her father. In a way the process symbolized her terror of her father's attempts to open up her mind, her terror of him finding, yet again, that she was inadequate, that there was not enough knowledge inside her. But it also carried the knowledge that the therapist, the surgeon of the metaphor, was trying to help. Clare's metaphor captures something of the pain involved in opening up one's mind in this way and of the therapist trying to help with difficult early experience that is hidden inside and affecting all aspects of the patient's functioning—just as the surgeon seeks to repair the heart, buried deep inside the patient, yet influencing every aspect of living and being.

Second Stage of Therapy:
The Emergence of Shame-Related Metaphor

In the beginning of her work with me, Clare struggled with her experience of me as the condemning parent analyst. We found ourselves grappling over and over again with the effects of shame, the neural substrates of which are formed in the second year of life (Schore, 2003a, 2003b). Healthy early experiences of misattunement, permitted by the parents at a manageable level for the toddler, lead to an acceptance of difference, a growing awareness of the other, and enable the development of the capacity for socialization (Stern, 1985). However, when the rupture in attachment caused by shaming has been frequent, prolonged, and unmitigated by experiences of repair, the neuronal pathways for self-hate and fear of the other become strongly established and the other becomes a source of terror and dread rather than a source of supportive relationship.

After working together for a while, Clare gradually became able to trust me a little, and sometimes I seemed to become more human, more accessible as a real person. But nevertheless her internalized critical father was still waiting in the wings to be experienced through me as a severe critic, as the "one who often summoned her to the door of his study to berate her for her shortcomings, often adding as a veiled threat, 'And I don't even have to touch you to break you'" (Wilkinson, 2007b, p. 355). Badenoch (2008) observes that "shame-imprisoned people say that it feels intolerable to be visible, to be known, because of the hateful core they perceive within themselves" (p. 105). At this stage at the best of times it was difficult for Clare even to speak in sentences. She would begin, hear her father's condemning voice in her head, interrupt herself; begin again, only to stop and start on a new tack. I would wonder whether to finish the sentence for her, whether this would make her feel even more inadequate or whether my silent waiting would be damaging, seeming to her like a critical, condemning father. This pattern of interrupted speech happened again and again as the internal persecutor condemned each new attempt to express herself. Her particular form of wordlessness was the most striking feature of her state of being at these times, as she became dominated by right-brain functioning, by deeply held ways of being and behaving arising out of the traumatic quality of her earliest relational experience, lodged in implicit memory. At this stage it seemed that I might be experienced as a frighteningly sadistic figure at any time. Clare, it seemed, would slide away from me, much as she had tried to slide away from her father's summons to the door of his study. If there was anything that was too difficult to talk about, particularly if it involved a task at work in which she felt she might fail, she would begin to miss her sessions. If she did come, her body language and the sliding of her gaze away from me told me that she could barely bring herself into the room, for fear I would actually become the critical, controlling person that deep down she feared I might be. At these times the image of her father shouting at her as she stood fearfully at the study door became a metaphor for her fear of my anger, the anger of those that she found difficult at work, and most of all for her own rage, which lay buried deep within her. At such times as she sidled in, I would have almost a physical sensation of having grown very tall and that she had become someone much smaller than me. It took many experiences spread over time for her to trust that I might not want to attack her, that I might not see a failure but the very competent and pleasant woman she actually was.

One of her worst memories was of the remedial English exercises that her father forced her to do for what seemed like hours on end every evening. She always felt that her efforts fell short of her father's standards, and each time she would feel she had failed yet again and further displeased him. As one might expect, situations at work that involved creative writing were probably the most difficult for Clare, especially when appraisal, assessment, or examinations were involved. Clare had to struggle with herself not to slide away from the task, not to leave it undone rather than risk failure. When she undertook such work, she would begin the task only to cast what she had done on one side, begin again, cast it away again and begin again, over and over, writing and rewriting, haunted by the ghost of her father standing once again at his study door.

Clare brought vivid memories of endless sessions with her father commandeering the blackboard, easel, and chalk, which her aunt, who was a painter, had bought her when she had noticed Clare's artistic ability. Instead of providing a chance to explore her creativity as her aunt had hoped, the blackboard became associated with failure, with her inadequacy when faced with the long sums written on it for her to solve as her father attempted to improve her arithmetic. Years later she only had to touch chalk for her hands to break out in allergic eczema—a tendency that abated only after she had worked on the experience in therapy. Gradually she became more able to risk engagement with me through the shared exploration of these internal images, such as the monster, the surgeon and the angry father, which she haltingly became able to verbalize. As she did so the process helped her to understand her difficulties with both her external father as a child and her internal father, the stern critic, the one whose legacy meant that she also had to grapple with her own anger and her tendency to hammer home the point with others.

Third Stage of Therapy: A Sense of Safe Relationship

Why and how did Clare come to experience our relationship as safe? I think Clare would reply that it was the experience, over time and on many occasions, of a nonretaliatory other who sought to understand her apprehension rather than condemn her before she started. It seemed that through the medium of nondirective psychodynamic psychotherapy she was gradually able to encounter me, another person, separate but with whom she could engage at a deep affective level and with whom she was gradually able to experience a sense of safety rather than of threat. Gradually new neural pathways began to build that permitted more comfortable and comforting states of mind. I gradually found my eyes meeting not eyes that slid away but eyes that seemed to peep up at me, at first timid, and then, after a while, I became aware that I had lost the sense of a smaller person. Gradually I noticed hints of laughter and humor in eyes that dared to hold my gaze as an equal and in an adult way. The eyes have been shown to be the most direct route for recognition of mental states and emotions in others (Baron-Cohen et al., 1997, Baron-Cohen et al., 2001; Hirao, Miyata, et al., 2008). This is often particularly true for patients who have learned vigilance through repeated traumatic experience; the young child may learn early to read the mind of the abuser in his or her eyes. A child or indeed an adult patient with this sort of early experience may need to be able to look and look away, to gaze and be free to break the gaze. I have chosen here to write briefly about the eye contact that Clare made with me at this stage, about the eye talk that leads to "I" talk (Solomon, personal communication, 1999). I could equally well have written of changes in body language, changes in the content and emotional tone of the material the patient chose to bring.

Evolving symbolizations may emerge in a series of pictures or dream images, which I understand as emergent metaphor, one thing gradually being revealed as standing for another and carrying with it the capacity to enable change into a more mature state of being (metamorphosis). Such metaphors stimulate brain activity in a more thorough way; such processing, utilizing as it does brain plasticity, brings with it more possibility of change than any other form of human communication (Pally, 2000). Sometimes a series of images will emerge close together over a very short period of time. As such they seem to indicate a crucial point in the therapy, usually where a difficult emotion, previously held only in the body, is beginning to be able to be known as a recognizable feeling for the first time. Sometimes the series will be spread over time and will contain frightening images which as the therapy progresses metamorphose into something more human and accessible. In Clare's case what started as a frightening black monster changed to the father who regularly summoned her to his study and berated her as she stood at the door, to the therapist who seemed to argue with her and finally became "the one who I can discuss difficult things with and know that my point of view is heard."

Neural Substrates of the Metaphorical Aspects of the Dreaming Process

Emergent metaphor has long been one of the most powerful vehicles by which the self may achieve greater integration, and nowhere is this effect more marked than in work that emerges from the dreaming process. Grabner et al. (2007) note that the functioning of the right hemisphere in its more free-associative primary process (which we may associate with emergent metaphor) has much in common with the states of dreaming or reverie. Bar-Yam (1993) suggests that during sleep the mind–brain is active but is mainly isolated from sensory neurons and therefore from sensory input. He speculates that during sleep the mind further subdivides into isolated neuronal groups and that this makes possible the breaking up of experience from the waking period into pieces that become the building blocks for creative learning and enable adaptive response to future circumstance. The role of the zif-268 learning gene in rapid eye movement (REM) sleep is emphasized by Rossi (2004) who draws our attention to animal studies of REM sleep in which this gene is expressed after the animals have been allowed novel, enriching experience, and that as a result of this gene expression new neural pathways develop. In humans it seems that one result of such processing is that, through metaphor, the unconscious is conveyed to consciousness. Thus dreaming, arising from sleep that is a fundamentally dissociative state, may yet be said to revitalize the mind–brain in an associative and integrative manner.

Many researchers now adopt a stance that understands dissociation from a broader perspective, embracing not only the unusual dissociative phenomena at the extreme end of the spectrum that present in dissociative identity disorder (DID) or in complex cases of posttraumatic stress disorder (PTSD), but also understanding the sleep process as an essentially dissociative state of mind, and all dreams as dissociative phenomena. Such a view considers the dissociative strategy to be part of the normal functioning of the mind–brain as it screens out the nonessential in order to maintain optimum functioning. Our concern as therapists is often with the negative aspects of dissociation; in the dreaming process, a dissociative phenomenon, we are able to make creative use of our understanding as we work with the metaphorical aspects of remembered dreams.

As early as 1910 Prince suggested that dreams had more in common with dissociative phenomena than with repression. His views did not find favor in the Freudian community at the time and were refuted by Jones, in particular (as cited in Gabel, 1990). Jung, however, took a stance concerning dream content that was much more in keeping with current theory concerning dissociation. He understood dreams as the compensatory products of the unconscious that sought to help the dreamer to understand aspects of his or her own inner world of which he or she was not yet aware and which would be helpful. Jung (1946a) commented: "Dreams do not deceive, they do not lie, they do not distort or disguise, but naively announce what they are and what they mean. . . . They are invariably seeking to express something that the ego does not know and does not understand" (par. 189). He felt that dreams put the dreamer in touch with aspects of his or her inner world, which were currently unavailable to the conscious mind, through the metaphorical images that they contained. While Jung felt that initial dreams were "often amazingly lucid and clear-cut" (1934c, par. 313), he understood every dream to be essentially integrative in nature, bringing dissociated aspects of experience into conscious mind.

Hartmann (2000) has argued that a dream offers "the explanatory metaphor for the dominant emotion or concern of the dreamer" (pp. 69–70), and Mancia (2005) has suggested that the function of the dream is to create images that are "able to fill the void of nonrepresentation, representing symbolically experiences that were originally presymbolic" (p. 93). Dreams can be understood as metaphors that enrich the mind–brain, in an associative, integrative manner (Wilkinson, 2006a, 2006b).

At the early stages of life the affective experiences captured in these vivid visual and emotional "pictures" are products of right-brain activity, recorded in implicit memory. Mancia (2005) points to the very primitive origin of some dream material; awareness of implicit memory has extended the concept of the unconscious to include the place where "emotional and affective—sometimes traumatic—resymbolic and preverbal experiences of the primary mother-infant relations are stored" (p. 83). As such these will inevitably emerge in dreams. They will not have been encoded as part of an autobiographical narrative that is easily accessible because the hippocampus that tags time and place to memory would not yet have been online. Rather they will remain as part of amygdaloidal memory and will emerge when a stimulus, such as a similar feeling, tone, sight, or smell, rouses them from their long "sleep." As such they contribute to "the formation of an early unrepressed unconscious nucleus of the self" (Mancia, 2005, p. 85).

The exact nature of the biochemical and regional differences in dreaming from waking states preoccupies many researchers who reach very different conclusions. Hobson (1999) emphasized the role of the cholinergic system in the dreaming process and argued that dreaming activity begins in the brainstem, progresses through the limbic system, finally reaching the medial frontal cortex, while the executive portions of the frontal cortex (i.e., the dorsolateral cortex and the orbitoprefrontal cortex) remain less active. His earlier understanding of the dreaming process as essentially chaotic has been rejected by some prominent critics, who argue that he underestimated the degree of cortical control over the dreaming process (Jones, 2000; Domhoff, 2005), and indeed Hobson modified this view in his later work. Solms (1999) suggested that dreaming is generated by a different mechanism from the one that generates REM sleep itself. He understands the activation of the dopaminergic mechanism to be crucial to the generation of the actual dream in all sleep states. Braun (1999) argues that neither the cholinergic nor the dopaminergic hypothesis will prove to be the sole explanation of the dreaming process but that the pattern of activity may actually be driven by differential patterns of information transfer between cortex and thalamus.

Domhoff (2005) suggests that it is most helpful to consider the features that dreaming shares with both normal waking cognition and waking hallucinatory thinking and to blend that understanding with a thorough knowledge of dream content. He examined several large-scale studies of dream content, all of which failed to find bizarreness and intensity of emotion. He concludes that dreams have more in common with stories than with psychosis (Domhoff, 2005). This approach seems to resonate with the experience of many. Be that as it may, all seem to agree that the dream is in a unique way the expression of the internal, the intrapsychic world of the dreamer (Braun, 1999).

Inevitably expression of this inner world emerges in metaphorical images, which represent evolving symbolizations that may lead to metamorphosis as they are processed in therapy. Metaphors act as windows to the psyche, to the soul, to the self as we work with our patients in the relational encounter that is special to the consulting room.

Case Example: Jill's Dreams

Jill could not remember her father, who had died in a car accident soon after she was born. Jill was an only child and was very close to her mother when she was young. However, she learned early on that her mother was unpredictable: She might be nice or she might be cross and strike out. Much later, in her teens, she realized that her mother had had a drinking problem from early on, which was part of the reason for her frightening mood swings. When she was almost 4 years old Jill was excited to learn her

FIGURE 2.1

Naja shows us that face, voice, sense of self, and sense of the other are all intimately linked with early right-brain functioning—in this instance, providing
stimulus to the later developing language centers in the left hemisphere.

FIGURE 2.2
The Bunnikins plate.
Memory privileges emotional truth.

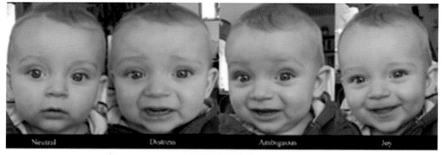

FIGURE 2.3

Example of a set of expressions shown to mothers. Lenzi, D., et al. (2008). Neural basis of maternal communication and emotional expression processing during infant preverbal stage. Cerebral Cortex, 19(5), 1124–1133. Reproduced with permission of Oxford University Press.

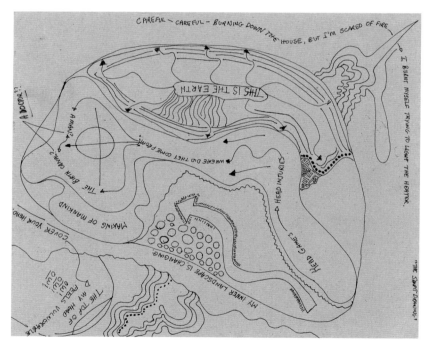

FIGURE 3.1

Steve's pen-and-ink drawing, the "Sandpit drawing," reveals the emergence of early trauma.

FIGURE 5.1
The king and queen from The Rosarium (Jung, 1946b, p. 213). Affective engagement enables change.

FIGURE 5.2
The bad black cat mother. This picture first appeared as plate 1 in Wilkinson, M. (2006). *Coming into mind: The mind–brain relationship: A Jungian clinical perspective*. London: Routledge. Reprinted with permission of Routledge.

FIGURE 5.3
The clockface analyst. Is it safe to trust her?

FIGURE 5.4
The analytic garden. How do I feel about her?

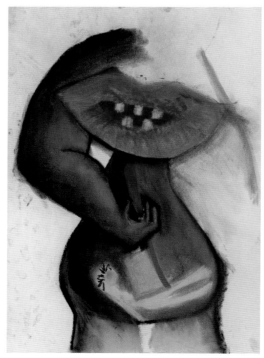

FIGURE 5.5
To try to relate feels dangerous.

FIGURE 5.6
A good enough attachment.

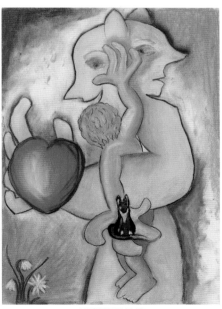

FIGURE 5.7
The little black cat learned
secure attachment.

FIGURE 7.1
Dream sandscape.

FIGURE 7.2
The years of my life.

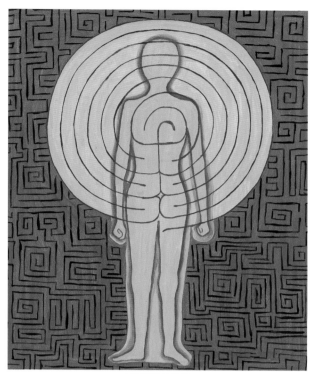

FIGURE 7.3
The labyrinth.

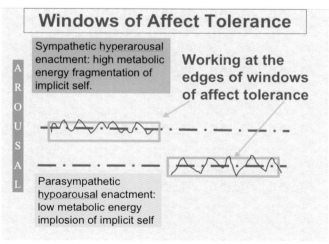

FIGURE 8.1
Psychobiology of high and low arousal enactments.
Reproduced from Schore (in press).

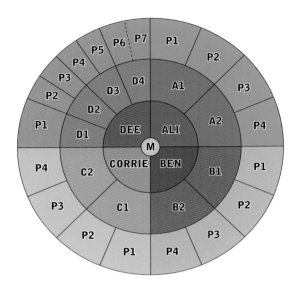

FIGURE 9.1
The complex dynamics of relationship in group supervision.

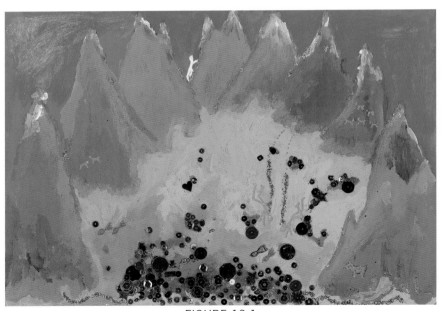

FIGURE 10.1
The riches of attachment.

mother was to marry and that she was to have a new daddy. Recently Jill, now middle-aged, had been wondering what, if anything, had happened between herself and her stepfather when she was a child and could not remember. She was aware of his unremitting hostility, and little else.

Jill arrived in the consulting room in a rather frightened state and recounted the following dream sequence:

> I was staying with Evelyn, an old friend in the country, or maybe in her London house. It felt like a main home. I was beginning to lay the table. It was an old, Georgian long table, slightly rounded at the ends. I shook out the rather pleasing new cloth that was of linen, a rather soft, loose, light weave. Its pattern was a large, slightly oblong check, in soft shades of pink, blue, and lavender. As I placed it on the table what I thought was a dry old lump of excrement was suddenly revealed. I became aware of a further lump on the floor quite near me. I noticed that a small, dark-haired Hispanic-looking man was standing at the far side of the table holding a soft broom. I thought he would clear up the mess, but he walked past me through an open doorway into another room. As he did so he stepped on the dry turd that was on the floor, denting rather than completely flattening it.
>
> Suddenly the scene changed; I had gone onto the terrace. I was at the corner, with my hand on the balustrade, just at the point where there was a narrow, slightly curved flight of steps down into the garden. I seemed to be about to stroke the silver-gray tabby cat that was on the balustrade. Instantly, I became aware of something stuck between the fingers of my left hand, partly caught by my ring. I thought it was a wasp; I was terrified that it would sting me. I looked more closely and became aware of short, rather stiff hair-like whiskers, and then I saw its hard black back. I thought it would stick itself into me. I was horrified; I could find no way to get rid of it. I woke in terror.

Jill's first comment as she began to explore the metaphorical language of her dream was that she had been wondering if anything had happened between her stepfather and herself when she was a child, in addition to the hostility and verbal abuse that she had suffered from throughout her childhood and had never forgotten. Jill went on to think about the checked tablecloth linking the dream to my consulting room, which had somewhat similar soft furnishings at that time, then she moved quickly back to what she felt had really frightened her in the dream. Later she realized that the table reminded her of the dining table belonging to a happy family that she had known well when she first left home, a family to which she had yearned to belong.

She went on to wonder whether there was a link between the two parts of the dream. She began by saying "I wondered about the dark Hispanic-looking man." Then her thoughts seemed to move on and she rather tentatively likened the black, hard-backed, bewhiskered beetle to her black-haired stepfather, who had put a ring on her mother's finger. I asked if he had had whiskers. With difficulty she articulated that the hair seemed to her to be more like genital hair. Jill became distressed at this moment and said that she remembered how as a young teenager she had walked into her parents' room and had seen her stepfather with all revealed. When she was calm again she went on to say that when she was about 11 for a period of time she had slept in her parents' room, probably to free a room for her aunt, who had come to stay after an operation. She wondered what she had been aware of then, what that time had been like for her. She returned repeatedly to her terror of the beetle. She thought it might be a reference to her stepfather, but it remained unclear exactly for what it stood. She noted that wasps penetrate with something in their bottom, not with a proboscis, as she had haltingly tried to describe as she explored her fear of the dream creature. Referring to the dream later in therapy she realized that *proboscis* was the sarcastic joking word used to describe her stepfather's large nose by her mother. She also wondered whether the little girl she had been had become confused between two different words beginning with *p*. Later she came to think of the soft female things in the dream, like the checked tablecloth, as not unlike one her mother had and the silver tabby cat rather like the tabby female cat of her childhood home. They seemed to her to be reminders of the lost happy times with her mother, which had quickly become out of reach as her stepfather's rule became the dominant force at home.

A few days after this dream, she came to a session and told of a frightening incident that had happened the previous evening:

> I was in the garden last thing at night. I was aware of a winged insect buzzing fiercely near the glass door, attracted to the light in the porch. I came into the sitting room. I suddenly saw/felt this

horrible gray, slug-like object fix onto my thigh; I was wearing trousers but I became absolutely terrified. I was too terrified to shake it off because then it would become loose in the room and could harm me or others. I shouted to the children to keep away. I was frightened it would hurt one of them as much as me. I took my coat and somehow managed to get it off and then stamped on the coat until I was sure I would have killed it. My feelings were panicked, frenzied, out of control rather than being in control of the situation.

Again the actual incident took on a metaphorical meaning for my patient as she returned again and again to the pain and distress of the little girl who could not emotionally withstand the hostility of her difficult stepfather. His fury had penetrated her and made her whole internal world feel unsafe and damaged. She was terrified of anger yet was often consumed with anger.

Jill tried to think what this incident might have symbolized, but the creature remained an unnamable, unidentifiable source of a terror that had fixed on her and might have penetrated her and damaged her. Over time, and through talking to her aunt, it became clear that her memories of her stepfather as verbally and physically abusive were accurate. The aunt had also feared for some while that he was also too intimate physically with his young stepdaughter. Her grandmother and aunt had spoken to her mother, who denied it vehemently, but it was about then that the stepfather's attitude toward his stepdaughter seemed to change from inappropriate intimacy to the unremitting hostility that my patient had always remembered. The early part of the analysis was concerned with sorting out her feelings about her now-dead stepfather, grieving for the kind stepfather he had never been, while also grieving for the real father whom she had never known. Most of the later therapy and transference centered on the much more complex feelings that this patient had for her volatile and rather tempestuous mother, who loved and hit in turn, who always claimed to love her daughter but who never really managed to convey this love to her or to protect her.

In this period of the therapy, the metaphorical aspects of both dreams and real life happenings were used by Jill to help her to process difficult emotions which had remained locked in her body. The gradual transformation of emotion into feeling that is its mental representation (Damasio

1994, 2003), which was facilitated by this processing, enabled Jill to begin to think about the unthinkable in relation to her early experience and to tolerate the inevitable uncertainty that accompanies this process.

Conclusion

These case histories illustrate the importance of metaphor in helping the therapist and patient explore the quality of leftover affect and trauma caught in body memory, while not foreclosing on the uncertainty and lack of clarity that there is for such patients in terms of their earlier experience. Just as the body never lies and can put us in touch with appropriate affect, emergent metaphor helps us to understand the emotional truth of our inner experience while still tolerating uncertainty. Most importantly, emergent metaphor heralds metamorphosis, the capacity for healthy change in the mind, enabling a more coherent sense of self.

7

The Neuroscience of Narrative: Experience and Meaning-Making

NARRATIVE NEUROSCIENCE IS A RELATIVELY NEW AREA of exploration, but a significant one. Just as metaphor lights up more centers of brain activity than any other form of human communication, so too does story; story gives shape to emotional experience and often relies on metaphor to develop aspects of the narrative. *The Concise Oxford English Dictionary* (Sykes, 1976) offers a definition of narrative as that of "story told in first person." Therapy is so concerned with the personal story of the client that the neuroscience underpinning the development of story is an exciting area of development for the therapist to explore: "What fundamentally constitutes our consciousness is the understanding of self and world in story" (Young & Saver, 2001, p. 73). Currently the study of the neuroscience behind narrative draws principally upon imaging studies of volunteers responding to various kinds of narrative material as well as on studies of patients' brain lesions. However, what is yet to be fully explored is just how narrative develops in the consulting room and how personal story may emerge in a way that enables minds to change.

Ferro (2005) suggests that therapy can be understood as bringing about transformations by grasping the emotions underlying patients' narrations "in such a way that they feel it is understood and shared, thus progressively activating their narrative competence" (p. 100). The right hemisphere is, in this respect, the master of the left: The affective experience, meaning-making process, and emergent sense of self that are the hallmarks of coherent narrative as it develops in the consulting room, all arise in the right hemisphere and draw upon the linguistic capabilities of the left to produce the story. Let me elaborate: The right hemisphere processes visual, tactile, auditory, and olfactory experience and is the original source of much of our experiencing in the broadest sense of the term.

Given its central role in affective experiencing, the right hemisphere enables much of the affective engagement and communication that occurs within the therapy session. Only then are the analytic and linguistic processes of the left hemisphere able to begin to formulate personal story in the more fully developed form that we more usually describe as narrative. A striking aspect of the research on narrative for the therapist is the degree of hemispheric integration that is required for story production and the stimulus toward such integration that secure relating, which includes coconstruction of story within the therapeutic dyad, offers.

Coherent narrative is characterized by a causal event structure, a lack of superfluous or tangential information, and a depiction of events in an imagined world that parallels the world of real experience (Mar, 2004). In contrast, patients' initial trauma narratives may have confusing and distracting elements, a disjointed rather than coherent quality, and be intruded upon by flashbacks. Early story, generated out of the relation to the mother, lays down the patterns of being in the world that give rise to ways of being and behaving in it in relation to others. Such patterns of being and behaving manifest themselves afresh in the therapy room, but may become modified through the development of a secure attachment. "We need to tell someone else a story that describes our experience because the process of creating the story also creates the memory structure that will contain the gist of the story for the rest of our lives" (Schank & Morson, 1990, p. 115).

Our Earliest Stories

From the very earliest days of life, inner experience is organized out of interactive experience with the primary caregiver. Schore (2008a) notes that "it is a fallacy that all language is in the left hemisphere, for the right hemisphere is dominant not only for prosody but also for processing of emotional words, the detection of one's first name, social discourse, metaphor and the organization of information at the pragmatic-communicative level." Mother and baby, in their earliest, right-hemisphere-based affective exchanges, engage in proto-conversation that leads to what I call proto-narrative, which arises "from our emotional nature through a musical-prosodic bridge" (Panksepp, 2008, p. 49). Ultimately this proto-narrative develops into one's personal story and makes possible a sense of self. Bollas (1987) observes that "a generative respect toward every representation in thought of the origins of the true self, and of the countless speeches mother and infant make through their curious dialect, enables us to face that knowledge we possess but cannot think" (p. 282).

From how early can experience be available to us as we engage in this process? To begin to examine this question I would like to explore some of the earliest memories that have been recounted to me, the difference in their quality, and the significance they may hold for understanding the individual's earliest life. Such memories illustrate the integrity of the individual mind–brain–body because they tend to center on bodily and sensory experience. One patient told me a very early memory of being left outside in the stroller, cold, white flakes falling from the sky onto her face and hands, and her dislike of this. She remembers her anger and sense of helplessness as she experienced it beginning to snow and still being left outside. This patient's mother suffered from an enduring post-natal depression, and one can assume that the patient may well have been left unattended for long periods of time, the advent of the snow gone unnoticed by her mother. Another patient recounts her earliest memory of being in her stroller in the garden near the hedge. She remembers her surprise when the green hedge with its white flowers gradually started to move and to turn upside down. She does not recall any fear. Her mother later told her of her own anxiety and horror at coming into the garden and finding her baby hanging upside down in the stroller—the old-fashioned, high-backed stroller had turned right over. The patient would have been about 15 months old and perhaps rather too active to have been left in the stroller unsupervised in this way. This same mother forgot her baby on more than one occasion; another time she left her outside a shop and arrived home (half an hour away) before she missed her, another time she went off to work, forgetting her. On that occasion the child's crying alerted neighbors to her plight. The same child fell into a lake at 3 years old and into the fire that burned in the living-room grate not long after. This mother's ambivalent care for her child affected my patient deeply; gradually it formed a part of her internal world with which she had to struggle for the rest of her life, as she sought to become an adequate caregiver for her own self.

In contrast, another woman describes a fleeting but very happy memory of preparing for a photograph on her second birthday: "We were going for my second birthday photo; I have a sense of my parents' overwhelming pleasure as they got me ready in my special dress . . . there was a cake." Another remembered, in a very tactile way, her dress that was a present for her third birthday:

> I have a lovely pale blue silk dress made for me by my grand-
> mother. I remember the slippery feel of the silk. I loved to trace
> with my fingertips the outlines of the embroidered farmyard
> animals that go around the hem. I remember what the goose looks
> like. I think there was a duck with little ducklings, following in a
> line behind her. I don't remember what else.

These happy memory fragments may have been preserved through, and
will certainly have been affected by, the later encounters with the photo
and the dress.

Two female patients dealing with the arrival of their first sibling
recount—and, in so doing, seem to explore—memories that carry the
first inklings of experience in the world of the feminine. Again the
sensory qualities of the memories are dominant. The good smells associated with Mother, for one, and Grandmother, for the other, remain into
the present.

The first commented:

> I remember my maternal grandmother coming to stay and
> plaiting my hair when my mother was in the hospital and my
> sister was born. I remember on my mother's dressing table a
> bottle with the perfume of Devon violets with 'made in London'
> written on it. London was clearly a wonderful place. [In later life
> this woman was to travel halfway across the world to make
> London her home.]

The second recalled:

> I remember going to spend the day at my grandmother's house
> because my mother had gone to the hospital. My grandmother's
> dressing table was so pretty and there was the wonderful smell of
> her spilled powder, the 'untidy mess' (my mother's words about it)
> on top which, as a child, seemed to me to be a veritable treasure
> trove of perfume, lipsticks, brooches, and bracelets. I can still
> smell her powder. I can smell it now.

It is interesting to note that the narratives highlight smells, colors,
and emotions associated with the experience being recounted: products

from early implicit memory are from the right hemisphere where emotion and visual, tactile, and olfactory experiences are processed. (The process of memory making is discussed more fully in Chapter 2).

Neurological Substrates of Narrative Communication

Recent advances in cognitive neuroscience suggest that the creation of narrative communication is mediated by a regionally distributed neural network. Mitchell and Crow (2005) highlight the importance of right-hemisphere functions for successful social communication. Beeman et al. (2000) emphasize the cooperation between the hemispheres for story comprehension and development; they attribute to the right hemisphere initial predictive inferences concerning the development of story and to subsequent activity in the left hemisphere the coherent inferences that follow. Components of these regionally distributed networks include the amygdala–hippocampal system, responsible for initial encoding of episodic and autobiographical memories, the left peri-Sylvian region where language is formulated, and the frontal cortices and their subcortical connections, where individual experiences are organized into real and imagined narratives (Young & Saver, 2001, p. 75). Young and Saver (2001) cite Bruner's (1991) assertion that narrative is the instrument of mind that constructs our version of reality and gives meaning to our experience of life. However, they suggest that this explanation is only partial because Bruner "fails to address the neurobiologic underpinning of the centrality of narrative in human cognition" (p. 75). They argue that it begs the question of how the brain determines that such experience should be organized with narrative as the core structure that gives meaning. Here Bruner and Young and Saver seem to get caught once again into the old Cartesian split, Bruner emphasizing mind and Young and Saver stressing brain. It is not a question of either brain or mind as the sole source but rather a series of interactive processes between not only mind and brain but also body.

My view is that mind responds to the changes that occur in the brain as a result of mind–brain–body interactions with another mind–brain–body experience; brain is modified again in response to mind, and so on. Intrasubjective experience arises from earliest intersubjective experience and is, in turn, modified by further intersubjective experience and reflected in the narrative that emerges. Schacter and Addis (2007a,

2007b) emphasize the constructive adaptive nature of memory processes. The brain is able to learn from experience and to modify future expectation in the light of what was learned.

Networks within the brain connect in a multiplicity of ways, permitting the most complex patterns of information processing. Examination of functional imaging in volunteers and clinical reports of the changes in individuals who have suffered focal brain injuries provide "a convergent view of how the brain narratively organizes experience" (Young & Saver, 2001, p. 75). The development of narrative is a dynamic, variable, and vulnerable process; experience processed in the right hemisphere becomes the determinant of the narrative that is developed into its final form in the left. Addis et al.'s (2007) research using fMRI scans draws attention to the activation of the right hippocampal region that takes place when an individual constructs a narrative concerning the future that is novel and of a personal nature. They note that the right frontopolar cortex is also uniquely recruited in prospective thinking, which is characterized by intentionality, and the right ventrolateral prefrontal cortex in planning.

Research using fMRI scanning has demonstrated that both an intact left hippocampus and left amygdala are required for optimal encoding of emotional material in retrievable form (Richardson et al., 2004, p. 283). Further research highlights the complex specialization that takes place within the hippocampal region and that provides evidence of a specific role for the anterior hippocampal region in the successful associative encoding of memory that inevitably underpins the development of a personal narrative (Chua et al., 2007). These complex neural activity patterns and interactions provide the elements by which imagining and meaning-making occur. Episodic memory is thought to be extremely well adapted, drawing on past experiences to facilitate the imagining of what may happen to us in the future. Other researchers emphasize the meaning-making function of episode memory "to help us make sense of the past and the present" (Schacter & Addis, 2007a, p. 778). Much of the forward-looking, imaginative, relational exchange between therapist and patient depends on these aspects of the mind–brain relationship.

Mar (2004) notes that cross-temporal and cross-modal processing are necessary for effective encoding, retrieval, and expression in words, with the right-hemisphere networks enabling global coherence. The corpus callosum, the major highway between the two hemispheres, forms from right to left at about 20 months old, enabling interaction and integration of such inter-hemispheric activity. Mar reviews the available evidence and concludes by summarizing the five main regions that appear to be the neurological substrates of narrative. He stresses that it will most likely be the pattern of interaction among these, yet to be explored, that will prove most enlightening concerning the central role that narrative plays in the human being's interior world and interaction with others. He suggests the following associations between functions of mind and brain structures:

- Comprehension, selection and theory of mind—medial prefrontal cortex bilaterally
- Narrative understanding and expression—lateral prefrontal cortex in the right hemisphere
- Story comprehension and production via the attribution of mental states and mental inferencing—temporoparietal region bilaterally
- Many aspects of story production, but possibly especially theory of mind and propositions—anterior temporal region bilaterally, including the temporal poles
- The imagery and episodic memory processes associated with story-making that are affective in nature—posterior cingulate cortex

Basic "memory packets" or storage forms are created without our conscious awareness; "one such packet organizes scenes and since we remember in scenes, these . . . allow us to travel from scene to scene" (Schank summarized by Ekstrom, 2004, p. 669). Another more complex group of memory packets deals with themes: These enable the processing and bringing together of scenes along with the integration of more abstract information. Such stories are encoded in neural patterns that the brain matches against new experience. The right hemisphere, dominant for novelty, particularly notices new deviations from the expected (remembered) pattern and creates new refinements of the pattern based on the new experience that has been noted. Such knowing consists not only of cognitions and emotions, but also that which is bodily and for the most part unconscious. Young and Saver explain that "To be without stories means in Schank's telling to be without memories, which means something like being without a self" (as cited in Young & Saver, 2001, p. 74). Not surprisingly Mar (2004) reiterates that "both lines of evidence, imaging and patient, indicate the importance of the right hemisphere areas in sharp contrast to the traditional portrayal of left lateralized language processes" (p. 1,429). As Schore (2001) stated so cogently: "The center of psychic life shifts from Freud's ego, which he located in the 'speech area on the left hand side' (Freud, 1923) and the posterior areas of the verbal left hemisphere, to the highest levels of the right hemisphere, the locus of the bodily based *self* system" (p. 77, emphasis in original).

Emergent Narrative

Affinity for narrative emerges at a very young age (Mar, 2004). It seems that the earliest narrative emerges initially out of the proto-conversation that occurs between mother and child and then develops as does the relationship between mother and child. The mother's face is "the most potent visual stimulus in the child's world" (Schore, 2002, p. 18). Ferro (2005) cites Bion's view that every mind, at birth, needs another mind in order to develop and suggests that proto-emotions and proto-sense impressions are transformed into visual pictograms that carry the emotional qualities of primitive feelings. Such elements then "undergo further operations in order to attain the status of thought and narrative image" (p. 2). Thus Ferro describes the processes whereby "a narrative fabric is woven" (p. 2). Mar (2004) also notes the contribution of the processing of affective experience in the story-making process.

In good-enough circumstances, patients will have experienced warm exchanges with the mother, such as empathic looking, touching, and being held. Out of these emerge proto-conversation and the exchanges that lay down the neural patterns for later developing speech and social exchange. In less fortunate circumstances the baby may experience indifference, anxiety, ambivalence, terror, or hate, in which case very different neural patterns are laid down in the baby's developing brain. In such exchanges the baby mirrors "the rhythmic structures of the mother's dysregulated states [in the] stress-sensitive corticolimbic regions of the infant's brain that are in a critical stage of growth" (Schore, 2003a, p. 251).

Traumatic experience can be an overwhelming single event but also may be composed of "a synergetic accumulation of repeated traumatic micro-experiences" (Ferro, 2005, p. 104). The therapist's ability to engage in what I might describe as a containing or holding way will (1) contribute to the patient's ability to draw on painful experience in the reconstruction of his or her story, (2) allow for the experience of implicit relational knowing (Lyons-Ruth et al., 1998), and (3) provide the best opportunity to test the old patterns of expectation against the reality of experience today.

In the same group, mentioned earlier in the chapter, who offered early memories, there were several accounts of a first memory, from around the age of two to three years, that contained scary moments wherein the central experience of the memory was a sense of separateness and loneliness.

> Woman: "Our new house was being built . . . a neighbor fetched me and took me to her house. She was minding me. We were in the garden; her son and I were in the stroller together. They were talking and thought I didn't understand. I knew they were saying that they shouldn't have to mind me. I felt that I wasn't wanted there. . . . I could see our house across the garden. I felt I wasn't wanted there either. I didn't belong anywhere."

> Woman: "I was in bed, and it was shadowy dark. I had been put to bed as it was my bedtime. Across the hall there was the warm yellow glow of light from the room where my parents and their friends were. I felt alone."

> Man: "My parents were in their bedroom. I was alone in my room. I thought 'What is going on? Why am I not in the room with them?' (*After pausing and seeming to explore the memory for a few minutes*) I used to press my face into the pillow . . . I could see pictures . . . each time I wondered 'What will I see?'"

The first of these extracts may contain within in it a sense of loss for the first house leading to a sense of loss of the first container, mother. The last memory recounted hints at primal scene material. Each child has a sense of separateness, a sense of what it is to be a separate self.

Such stories can be recalled freely, as these were, or they may be hidden, only to emerge over time in the context of the therapeutic relationship. But why might they be hidden? It may be that they are formed from very early experience or it may be that they arise from experience so traumatic that it is inassimilable to the conscious mind. It seems that early autobiographical memory may arise in the right hemisphere and be transferred to the left, where it reaches its fullest development. The capacity of the high right hemisphere (i.e., the orbitofrontal cortex and the anterior cingulate) to regulate the right amygdala and to enable the transfer of information across the corpus callosum from right to left becomes very significantly diminished in patients with severe early relational trauma. When the different elements of an unbearable experience get dissociated or split off from one another, there can be no proper memory of the event. It will not be processed by the hippocampus, which tags time and place to memories, and so it cannot be stored as explicit or narrative memory. It cannot be recalled in the ordinary way because it has not been stored in the ordinary way. Instead it is encoded implicitly in the emotional brain and the body to remind and warn if similar danger should threaten again. In a sense the person may have lost a substantial part of who he or she is, of what constitutes that person's unique self. The memory of such trauma may be stored implicitly in the patient for many years until mind and psyche are strong enough to integrate the unbearable experience. Sometimes the trauma is made manifest via narrative material or a dream narrative that seems to point to the earlier traumatic experience.

Porges (1997) describes three levels of neurological response with which a child may react when afraid. The optimal response is a social one mediated by the ventral vagal system and available to the child with good-enough early experience; such experience enables a turning toward others for help at such moments. Children with poor early experience may turn away from others when they become afraid relying on the sympathetic nervous system and its alternatives of fight or flight. As early as 1980 Fraiberg's research showed that when a baby's distress reaches intolerable limits, a cutoff mechanism comes into play analogous to that associated with intolerable physical pain. Schore (2002) makes clear how when both flight and fight fail, the parasympathetic nervous system comes into play, allowing a shutdown, frozen state to ensue—the way of escape when there is no escape.

Many who sustain trauma over time lose memory of it. If the trauma occurs prior to when the child is about 3 years old, the hippocampus will not be fully online and capacity to remember is not yet available. Terr's paper (1996) "True Memories of Childhood Trauma: Flaws, Absences, and Returns" seeks to grapple with the problem that confronts both patient and therapist as each struggles with what is not remembered, half remembered, remembered only in patches, retained only in body memory yet portrayed in the transference and experienced by the therapist in the countertransference. For patients whose trauma memory is held in the body, the body becomes "a kind of stage upon which the unfelt psychic pain can be dramatized" (Sidoli, 2000, p. 97). It seems to me that this is particularly difficult for the therapist to think about because it is an indicator of the slow drip, drip of suffering that may have occurred in a vulnerable child's early life.

As a child, Harriet used narrative defensively and for survival purposes as a place of escape. She was able to immerse herself in story and in so doing evaded something of the harsh reality of her childhood. However, she was also able unconsciously to begin to process something of the traumatic experience of her early years. Harriet became a child who was always "lost in a book." Some stories that remained with her were the ones that had secretly terrified her, reflecting as they did the frightening aspects of her internal world; others were more nurturing and carried the hope that enabled her spirit to survive. She explained that *Snow White* was terrifying because the Witch [mother] gave the girl poisoned fruit. *Alice in Wonderland* terrified her because Alice fell into a world she couldn't understand, where she almost drowned in a pool of her own tears. *Bambi* was horrifying as the hunter killed the mother and left Bambi alone with the father. *The Wizard of Oz* was the most frightening of all because there the girl encountered a man without a heart. There were more gentle nurturing themes but significantly in these books someone other than the parents cared for the children (Wilkinson, 2006a, pp. 49–50).

In the consulting room I sometimes felt that she still used narrative defensively, just as she had in childhood; she would tell of events at work or with friends, bombarding me with words, allowing me no chance to communicate with her, avoiding eye contact and keeping difficult feelings at bay.

Trauma and Narrative in Therapy with Adults

Creation of a coherent narrative has been suggested to be of fundamental importance in working with patients who have experienced trauma (Covington, 1995; Beebe & Lachmann, 2002; Cambray & Carter, 2004). It is the adequate regulation of emotional arousal that allows the creation of such narrative. "A traumatized patient with an abuse history including an intrusive, critical and abandoning mother may experience . . . through voice, intonation and expression [of the analyst], acceptance and connectedness" (Cambray & Carter, 2004, p. 132). The regulation of emotional arousal that can occur through such interactions permits the creation of a new narrative.

There are divergent views in cognitive neuroscience as to the exact nature and extent of the limbic system within the brain and the centrality of its role in the regulation of emotion, the way in which trauma-induced memory loss occurs, and what sort of remembering is possible. Traumatic experience and the associated endorphins that are released, along with raised cortisol levels, may interfere with the efficient functioning of the hippocampus and therefore with effective explicit memory consolidation. Amygdalar activity, however, is stimulated by experience that is traumatic, leading to enhanced emotional, implicit memory storage. Negative arousal seems to cause a narrowing of the attention so that negative, visually arousing encounters appear to be remembered more strongly and with more awareness of the central emotional elements (i.e., gist) as well as the visual detail of the event, than nonemotional ones. There is a consistent memory tradeoff: Central emotional events are retained over peripheral or background nonemotional elements of visual memory that occurs (Kensinger et al., 2007). Across a number of these studies emotion has been shown to enhance gist memory but impair memory of detail; thus emotional memory becomes dominant in the recall of past distressing events. The fluctuating degree of connectivity between the amygdala and the hippocampus, between the implicit and explicit memory systems, in the contextual processing of fear means that if the degree of emotional arousal is moderate, then explicit, declarative memory formation is strengthened, but when arousal is strong and highly stressful, then explicit memory formation may become impaired. However, the implicit becomes highly charged and operates adaptively. In experiences of extreme distress, feeling, sensation, behavior, image, and meaning may become dissociated from one another (Levine, 1997). The earlier in life and the more sustained the traumatic experience, the more likely this dissociation.

The adaptive constructive aspects of memory (and therefore of work with personal story) are being extensively explored (Addis et al., 2007; Kensinger et al., 2007; Schacter & Addis, 2007a, 2007b). Inevitably, the coconstruction of narrative becomes an integral part of therapy for patients who have experienced early severe relational trauma, but it must be undertaken with an understanding that the nature of such recall is primarily emotional rather than an accurate snapshot picture of the trauma. The high right hemisphere holds the key to emotion regulation and indeed much of the learning that will take place occurs through the emotional regulatory qualities of the transference experience in the therapy. Bohleber (2007) discusses what he terms "the battle for memory in psychoanalysis." He understands, on the one hand, that "trauma is a brute fact that cannot be integrated into a context of meaning at the time it is experienced because it tears the fabric of the psyche" (p. 335), but nevertheless he feels that a search for the truth concerning trauma is necessary in order to recognize adequately what has been suffered. He deplores earlier psychoanalytic attitudes that privileged psychic reality and devalued external reality. He argues that today's emphasis on the relational also tends to discount the value of reconstruction. He also fears that an emphasis on narrative may mean that "the real world goes unmentioned" (p. 377). In raising these issues Bohleber draws our attention to the complexities of working with narrative, with past and present, inner and outer realities.

I would argue that an emphasis on coconstructing narrative may play a vital part in assisting the patient not only in coming to terms with the reality of his or her internal world, but also in the process of mourning what was and what might have been, which then enables a greater capacity to live life as it is now in the real world. This mourning process, essential to work with those who have experienced early relational trauma, can be undertaken only if there is respect for the fact that "real traumatic events . . . happen to children and that these real events exert a strong developmental influence" on the way children experience the world and relate to others in the future (Eagle, 2000, p. 126). Indeed, Bohleber (2007) himself argues that it is necessary to appreciate fully the causative traumatic reality in order to distinguish between fantasy and reality and to avoid retraumatizing the patient; in this he seems to be reacting to the earlier overemphasis on fantasy rather than developing a cogent argument against the development of a coherent narrative as an important aspect of psychotherapy. Ferro (2005) draws attention to the complexity of the therapeutic task, suggesting that "the psycho-analyst's entire 'art' lies in knowing on which angle to focus . . . the locations of the infantile history, those of the internal world and the transgenerational field, and those of the present relationship in the present field" (p. 47). Bohleber (2007) warns that the appalling aspects of trauma may arouse defensive repudiation, not only in the patient, but also in the therapist, and give rise to the danger that the traumatic aspects of the patient's story will not be given sufficient space in the therapy.

Narrative, Meaning, and a Sense of Self

There has been a plethora of publications, books, and plays of what one might term "survivor narratives," some of which have become popular bestsellers. Why should this be so? The search for meaning, for making sense out of suffering, of giving shape to emotional experience, is perhaps such a fundamental need in us all that the public responds warmly to those who attempt to process and make something out of their experience in this way. Positron emission tomography (PET) scanning has been used to show that access to effective deductive logic depends on a right ventromedial prefrontal area devoted to emotion and feeling, demonstrating that emotion and feeling have a part to play in effective thinking (Houdé et al., 2001). Young and Saver (2001) stress the need to "create a notion of the self that is understandable." I have sought to recreate something of the experience of working with patients with early loss through the vehicle of a case study of someone whom I call Rachel. In this composite I emphasize the effect of the death of a father on childhood experience and beyond.

Case Example: Rachel

Rachel's father died suddenly when she was only 6 years old. She felt that their mother had been unable to recognize or cope with her children's need to mourn or to understand the difficulties that they were experiencing. The mother was overwhelmed by her own difficulties and by trying to provide for her young family. Rachel blamed herself for what had happened to her father. She felt that if she had been a good girl, her daddy would not have died. Her brother, in his raging, became the epitome of the difficult teenager, whereas Rachel became the good girl who sought to do well at school and to try to reconcile the warring members of her family. She became a doctor but, after a while, found that she was often exhausting herself by offering extensive help to dying patients; suddenly in her early 30s she lost part of her field of vision in one eye. After investigation her consultant concluded that it was a stress-related illness, and she came to see me. The physical symptom pointed to the trauma and in a sense represented an attempt to process it; up to that point the symptom had acted as a protective barrier that helped to keep the traumatic attachment loss "out of mind."

Her transference, not surprisingly, was characterized by an instant awareness if I felt under par, accompanied by quite an intense need to protect me. Underlying this response was a much more difficult-to-access rage that I might become ill and leave her. Unconsciously she always feared that if she loved, she might lose the loved one again. Gradually over time in therapy we became able to piece something of her story together. She talked a little to her mother about her father's death after she had been in therapy for some time. Her mother told her that she had "fixed on a remark" of her mother's which she had heard as "the ambulance did not come on time" (her mother had actually said "the ambulance did not come *in* time"). Rachel had just kept asking whether, if Daddy was dead, that meant that he would not be coming home in an ambulance. Probably she was actually trying to ask, in a rather indirect way that mirrored her mother's way of dealing with the distress of her children, "Will Daddy ever come home again?" It was a question that her mother, struggling with her own shock and grief, could not bear to hear, much less to answer. Rachel thought she and her older brother had been sent away immediately after the death. In fact, when she talked to her mother and brother, she found out that that had not been the case. She came to understand that she had felt shut out, "sent away" in a symbolic sense. The children had not been allowed to go to the funeral; Rachel's brother remembered that they had stood at the school railings and watched the hearse and their relatives arrive because the school was next door to the church. Rachel had no memory of this.

It was only very late in therapy that she gained some inkling of a memory of this small fragment of very emotionally charged experience, which still felt quite dissociated and which she experienced as her brother's memory rather than her own. Her "memory" of the events around the death and the funeral shows clearly how emotional gist is privileged over background detail. The emotional gist of her memory was accurate but the detail was flawed or absent.

After working on the emotional aspects of her early story, she became more able to see how her medical practice had become a constant and draining enactment of her early trauma. As she came to this realization, the pattern began to change and she no longer felt compelled to act out her early loss. Rachel had always enjoyed food and eaten well and continued to do so during the therapy, but at stressful times in her life, particularly those that involved a close personal relationship with a man, she had a real struggle to keep at a healthy weight; seemingly the weight just dropped away from her, a reaction to stress that she had experienced all her life. Partly it seemed to represent her unconscious fear that she herself might just fade away, but it was also partly a feeling that if she had been bad and that made Daddy die, then she herself should not thrive. "Her sight gradually returned to normal over the first two years of therapy and she became able to conceive a child, something that had eluded her for many years. It seemed that working through her grief and guilt had made it safe enough for her to conceive of being a parent" (Wilkinson, 2007a, p. 327).

Young and Saver (2001) stress the primary role of narrative in organizing meaning and a sense of self, concluding that "the potent adaptive value of narrative accounts for its primacy in organizing human understanding (as opposed to pictorial, musical, kinesthetic, syllogistic, or multiple other forms)" (p. 78). In this they perhaps ignore patients such as Holly and Sophie, who accessed their ability to think about their experience by means of vivid visual images rather than narrative, or those whose access tends to be through music—indeed, all of them would find words a much more difficult medium to use as an initial way of experiencing and thinking about meaning. Each of these patients also experienced significant early relational trauma that disturbed their primary attachment to their mother and early proto-conversations with her. In therapy each not only has used the initial therapy sessions but also has explored her inner world at home using her own medium, bringing artwork or experience of music back into the session as a way of communicating about and exploring early trauma. Gradually in the therapeutic relationship it has become more possible to access words and to build narrative for both early and current relational experience. Bucci (2001) describes conscious processing as "the tip of the psychic iceberg" (p. 45). She stresses the use of multiple modalities of unconscious mental processing and emphasizes the human being's capacity for verbal and nonverbal modes of symbolization. Citing examples from art, music, and dance, she argues that information may exist "in a form that could not be fully captured in words" (p. 48). Persinger and Makarec (1992) suggest that intensely meaningful moments of experience may be the result of accessing nonverbal representations that are the right-hemispheric equivalents of a sense of self; they argue that this probably occurs as a result of enhanced firing in the left hippocampal–amygdalar complex. Early processing, especially of negative emotion, may well be captured only in implicit, amygdalar memory and may emerge most easily in vivid visual or prosodic forms of expression, linked to the earliest forms of experiencing and processing of emotion. Ferro (2005) suggests that one function of the analyst may be to "facilitate the creation of affective-climatic coordinates so as to activate the patient's 'imaginopoietic capacity.'" He stresses that whereas narrations create images, they are in turn derived from them (p. 101).

Case Example: Sophie

When she entered therapy, Sophie was in her late thirties. She gradually began to use painting as a way to develop a coherent narrative of her life; such stories have the power to change our understanding of our personal world, both past and present.

Early Stage of Therapy: *Encountering the Burden of Sophie's Depression*

Sophie came to therapy in a state of depression. She had been off work for some weeks and had reached the point where she felt unable even to get up and prepare breakfast for her children before they went off to school. Early in the therapy she brought a picture that she came to call "dream sandscape"; she felt that it reflected the intolerable burden of trudging through the years of her life. In the picture are a series of images of herself, each trudging after the other much like prisoners in a chain gang (Figure 7.1). She could feel no hope at all at this time; even when she determinedly painted two images of herself as breaking out of the line and dancing, the feeling of the movement portrayed was heavy and despairing.

Second Stage of Therapy: *The Emergence of a Coconstructed Narrative and a Coherent Sense of Self*

Much later she came with another picture which she titled "The years of my life" (Figure 7.2). This time the overall effect of the picture was that of a stained-glass window, full of light. She used several sessions in therapy to discuss the significance of each of the tiny paintings that occupied one pane of the window and which represented 1 year of her life. We found we were reviewing the narrative that had gradually become her story as we had worked together in therapy. There were early years of appalling pain and sadness, latency pictures that showed her engaged in those interests that have always brought her consolation, particularly her love of the natural world, and later panes pictured her engagement with therapy. There were empty panes for the years that stretched before her; they were full of light, blazing her new-found hope.

These pictures provide a useful portal into understanding just how much Sophie's inner world had modified and just how much any patient's mind and perception of earlier experience can change as narrative is worked with in the context of an enabling relationship. Images, painted seemingly randomly by her at the time, gradually began to reveal the emergence of a changed sense of self that developed in response to therapy. She moved from feeling trapped in a sarcophagus whose walls were made of her painful early experience, to a dawning awareness of the difficulty that there had been in the mother–child relationship and the way in which this had been internalized. Once this work had been accomplished, she gradually became able to portray a softening of the walls, leading to a gradual emergence, an awakening of her true self to the possibilities of what life might hold for her (Wilkinson, 2006a, plates 4–9). I have included a new one here because it symbolizes the emergence of a coherent sense of self (Figure 7.3). It shows her centered position in a labyrinth, a symbol that had great meaning for her as representing her life journey.

Conclusion

Emotional security fosters the coconstruction of an individual's self-narrative. This is what one might expect, given that the earliest encounter with narrative is often experienced safe on Mother's lap, or listened to last thing at night while the child looks sleepily into a loved parent's face. The secure therapeutic relationship, with its reliable affective tone over time, enables the affect regulation that makes possible the development of a coherent narrative. This in turn allows "the old present"—the trauma that may have recurrently seemed to be "now" to the patient—to be placed firmly as "then," in turn encouraging the development of neural circuits that enable more effective affective regulation. It is the plasticity of the brain that permits such therapeutic gains throughout life. Within the context of an affective engagement with another mind, the part that narrative has to play in changing minds should not be underestimated. In Cozolino's (2006) words, "The simultaneous activation of narratives and emotional experiences builds neural connection and coherence between easily dissociable networks of affect and cognition" (p. 306). In so doing, narrative construction fosters both hemispheric integration and neural integration at all levels.

8

Dissociation and Regression Revisited

A CENTRAL CONCERN OF THIS BOOK HAS BEEN with what Schore (2007b) termed "the current paradigm shift from not only cognition to affect but also from repression to dissociation" (p. 753). Young (1988) suggests that dissociation is an "active inhibitory process that *normally* screens internal and external stimuli from the field of consciousness" (p. 35, emphasis added). We dissociate all the time as we allow our mind to concentrate on one particular experience and effortlessly filter out what might otherwise be distracting stimuli. As I write this, I have suddenly become aware of the washing machine at work in the next room, the wind rustling the leaves of the trees outside the window, the interaction of wind with the sunlight making subtle changes in the light reflected on my keyboard. As I concentrated on the task in hand, I had completely eliminated all these stimuli until this moment.

The dissociative response resulting from traumatic experience is also purposive. The *Diagnostic and Statistical Manual of Mental Disorders— Fourth Edition* (DSM-IV) identifies dissociation as disrupting the usually integrated functions of consciousness, memory, identity, or perception of the environment (American Psychiatric Association, 1994). The *International Classification of Diseases—Tenth Edition* (ICD-10) (World Health Organization, 1992) makes reference to partial or complete loss of the normal integration between memories of the past, awareness of identity and immediate sensations, and control of body movements. I understand the dissociative response to be an adaptive defensive structure developed to protect the nascent or traumatized self. Bromberg (2008) describes traumatic affect as not merely "anxiety with its volume turned up," but rather "affective flooding intense enough to disrupt thought because it is *inherently chaotic*" (p. 416, emphasis in original). He

suggests that "defensive dissociation shows its signature through discon-
necting the mind from its capacity to perceive that which feels too much
for selfhood to bear" (p. 416).

Overview of Dissociation and Regressive States

Teicher et al. (2006) regard the "consistently reported hippocampal
volume reduction, particularly on the left side" in research populations
who have experienced early relational trauma as a significant factor in the
development of the dissociative defense, noting the consistent reporting
of such diminished hippocampal volume in studies of adults who have
experienced early sexual abuse whereas those of sexually abused children
do not show such marked changes (p. 193). Earlier animal research
(Andersen & Teicher, 2004) investigated delayed effects of early stress on
hippocampal development in rats. The results of the more recent study
(Teicher et al., 2006) suggested that early maternal separation produces
a regionally specific delayed effect on the structure of the hippocampus
by attenuating rates of synaptic development. The researchers concluded
that "early life stress may affect a brain region in a way that is not immediately apparent on a gross morphological level, but may become
apparent with continued maturation" (p. 194).

Mundo (2006) notes that the excessive stimulation of the amygdala,
such as that associated with traumatic experience, "would interfere with
the correct functioning of the hippocampus, thus affecting the possibility
of proper symbolic representation and conscious awareness of the experiences." He observes that several studies have shown that "under
stressful conditions the amygdala is hyperactive while the hippocampus
may show reduced activity" (p. 684). Thus dissociation may become
increasingly significant in individual lives as those who have been traumatized begin to struggle with the demands that face a young adult and
which are manifest again in later life as the ageing mind struggles with
the difficult emotional and bodily experience associated with the latter
phase of life.

Jung (1934b) appreciated the significance of the dissociative defense
arising from early trauma; he described disturbances caused by affects as
phenomena of dissociation. He appreciated the possible time lag before
the tendency to dissociate is fully recognized, observing that "the real
emotional significance of that experience remains hidden all along from

the patient, so that not reaching consciousness, the emotion never wears itself out, it is never used up" (Jung, 1912, par. 224). It is often such experience that brings a new patient into therapy, and part of the work may well be to deal with the pressures from within that are perhaps leading to the possibility, first of painful awareness of emotional suffering, and then of the development of a more integrated experience of the self. Jung warned that dissociated content, which he described as a traumatic complex, may suddenly return to consciousness: "It forces itself tyrannically upon the conscious mind. The explosion of affect is a complete invasion of the individual. It pounces upon him like an enemy or a wild animal" (Jung, 1928, par. 267). It is for patients with just such extreme experience as described by Jung that the new research provides insight for therapists to enable a different, more benign experience of dissociated states of mind. Issues of empathy arousal and affect regulation become crucial to successful therapy and are discussed later in the chapter.

Regression has been a much debated part of analytic tradition and technique. But to what and where do patients regress? Where are they in their minds at such a time? Is the process helpful or unhelpful in regard to the psychodynamic process of changing minds? How do we avoid the dangers of drowning in a regressive fusion with a patient, on the one hand, or being destroyed by the unbridled forces of primitive rage, on the other? How do dissociation and the dissociative defense relate to regression? Should we allow regressive states of mind? If so, how may such experience in the consulting room help the dissociative patient? The goal of therapy for dissociative clients is to promote integration within the personality. This integrative process inevitably involves overcoming dissociative defenses in order to explore dissociative states of mind so that maturation, full integration, and affect regulation can take place.

Dissociation is a defense that is employed as a means of surviving and adapting to the effects of traumatic experience, and for some it is the means that makes it possible to adapt to life in a hostile environment that involves repeated traumatic experiences that are inescapable. As such, dissociation inevitably involves regression to primitive states of mind. It is to these dissociative states of mind to which a patient, overwhelmed once more by psychic pain, may regress and that the therapist will of necessity seek to engage. The words of Emily Dickinson (c. 1862) both evoke the unbearable mental pain associated with terror and point to the dissociative defense that alleviates distress but at a price.

There is a pain—so utter—
It swallows substance up—
Then covers the Abyss with Trance—
So Memory can step
Around—across-upon it—
As one within a Swoon—
Goes safely—where an open eye—
Would drop Him—Bone by Bone

What are the hidden hazards of treating this client group? Both therapist and supervisor at one remove may experience secondary traumatization from repeated exposure to a patient's experience of abuse through the overarousal of the patient's highly sensitive limbic system. Such patients bring complex issues, not the least of which is the need to work through earlier abusive ways of relating as part of their exploration of the past patterns lodged in implicit memory. Supervision offers the opportunity to reflect and helps to diminish the very real possibility of the therapist and patient becoming locked into unhelpful and prolonged reenactments of earlier abusive experience. Guidelines for the treatment of this group of patients note that "much of the material can be violent and shame inducing for the psychotherapist" and recommend that "psychotherapists need professional support to acknowledge the impact of the patients' material on themselves" (McQueen et al., 2008, p. 86).

The romantic, amusing, and deeply moving film *Eternal Sunshine of the Spotless Mind* (2004) highlights some of the hopes and fears of traumatized patients as they seek to deal with past experience. In the film Dr. Mierzwiak's clinic offers "The Lacuna Procedure," which guarantees permanent erasure of particular distressing memories from which the patient would like to be freed. The central character, a young man called Joel, is horrified to discover that his girlfriend has had her memory of their intense, turbulent, and painful relationship erased by this technique. He seeks the same course of treatment but then rejects it as he realizes he still loves her, and together they then move on to struggle with early memories of his that it feels important to work through rather than forget.

("The stuff of science fiction" you may be now be muttering, but as I write I discover *Nature's* section on neuroscience carries an article entitled "Beyond Extinction: Erasing Human Fear Responses and Preventing the Return of Fear" [Kindt et al., 2009]. The researchers found that oral administration of the *b*-adrenergic receptor antagonist propranolol before memory reactivation erased the behavioral expression of the fear memory 24 hours later and prevented the return of fear. The researchers concluded that disrupting the reconsolidation of fear memory in this way opens up new hope for patients with hitherto recalcitrant emotional disorders. This research has been greeted by some as a psychopharmacological breakthrough for patients for whom conventional treatments have failed to bring relief, but others see such a treatment as potentially damaging and emphasize the importance of preserving the integrity of memory. They value the warning aspect of traumatic memory, which is much like the early warning system provided by the pain response.)

Symbolically, we can understand *Eternal Sunshine of the Spotless Mind* as highlighting several of the dilemmas that face the therapeutic dyad: how to deal with dissociated trauma experience, how to process distressing memory, how to modify the trauma response, how to manage levels of arousal, how to develop new patterning, how much to help the patient let go of and what to retain in a manageable form. Every patient who has experienced early trauma has to deal, one way or another, with the patterning that such difficult experience provides. To work through a portion of the trauma in a safe relationship may help to remove something of the "here-and-now" quality of such memory that leads so easily to states of overarousal and dysregulation, and which will then permit something more of a "there-and-then" quality to emerge, which frees the patient to live life more in the present. The empathic relationship is the therapeutic measure that facilitates such change and development.

Dissociation Up Close

Pierre Janet (1889) first used the term *dissociation* to refer to the uncoupling of the mental processes, the splitting apart of psychological functions that normally go together. Dissociative patients may complain of absences, amnesia for patches of recent time or for trauma experience, depersonalization, and derealization. Such patients may be either easily aroused and overcome by flashbacks to traumatic experience or "dampened down" or "switched off." In such states of mind (i.e., hyperarousal or hypoarousal), the past is not yet truly the past because it has not been possible for such unbearable experience to be processed in the normal way. It has not passed into explicit memory via the hippocampal memory system of the left hemisphere, which would have tagged time and place to it, enabling the sufferer to gain some distance from it. Such unbearable experience, in which psychic contents get dissociated or split off, inevitably cannot be properly remembered. Rather it remains as part of the individual's "implicit knowledge" that is associated with the amygdaloidal memory store of the early developing right hemisphere. In early relational trauma occurring before the age of 3 years, dissociation may reflect an earlier stage of mind structuring wherein the cognitive flexibility to be provided by the later developing left hemisphere was not yet fully developed. Indeed Teicher et al. (2006) argue that it is the impairment of the development of the hippocampus as a result of early relational trauma that may generate such dissociative states of mind (p. 193). Once again our concern is with processing that occurs in the right brain rather than the left. When early attachment experiences are traumatic in nature, they become, as Schore (2002) comments, "burned into the developing limbic and autonomic systems of the early maturing right brain, and become part of implicit memory, and lead to enduring structural changes that produce inefficient stress coping mechanisms" (p. 1).

In revisiting aspects of early trauma in the consulting room later in life, the right hemisphere may inhibit the activity of the left when a patient enters a state of high arousal. Decreased activation of Broca's area may inhibit the patient's ability to articulate what is felt as overwhelming at that moment. The deeply dissociative defense mechanisms that may emerge as a result may mean that traumatic experience becomes available only in flashbacks; such dissociative manifestations have been described as primary by Dutch researchers Nijenhuis and van der Hart (1999). When different aspects of experience become dissociated from one another (e.g., affect from meaning), presenting as memory fragments that may be visual, verbal, a smell, a sensation, or a feeling unattached to narrative, they are classified by Nijenhuis and van der Hart (1999) as secondary. Tertiary dissociation is their term to describe dissociation in individuals who manifest several dissociated identities. Patients whose traumatic experience has led to any of these dissociative defenses have found some aspect of their experience unbearable; a dissociative response enables intolerable pain to be kept at bay, out of mind.

Trauma patients may come for help because some aspect of the amnesiac defense is failing, and as their trauma is beginning to emerge into mind, it feels too much to manage alone. For some, manifestations may emerge as scary bodily experience or overwhelming emotion.

Case Example: Jennifer

A patient whom I call Jennifer lived in a war zone in early childhood, a place where it was dangerous for people of her race to be seen on the streets. As a child she was sent out in the fog to fetch supplies because a child in the fog just might go unnoticed, whereas in broad daylight she might have been stopped. Jennifer and her immediate family escaped and came to England when she was 7 years old. She has virtually no memory of any experiences before they arrived here. Jennifer arrived asking for therapy because she'd had a terrible panic attack on the street. She told of being taken to hospital in an ambulance, whose siren had sounded weirdly terrifying as it echoed in the fog. Only gradually, in the safe context of the emotionally engaged relationship provided in therapy, did she haltingly become able to make the links to her terrifying early experience. In the safety of the therapeutic relationship, in a series of rather regressed experiences, dissociated states of mind were felt by Jennifer and gradually the unthinkable became able to be thought, the unbearable to be felt, just a little at a time. Jennifer began to explore her terror of being caught, which had had to be buried at the time, and had remained buried until the tendrils of the fog reached into her hidden memory store. In time we both came to understand how the panic that had been so long denied had overwhelmed her and had become a full-blown panic attack, when the trigger of the fog stimulated the old neuronal pathway.

Working with Dissociative Processes

When faced with overwhelming trauma, the dissociative defense—by which feeling, sensation, behavior, image, and meaning became split off from one another—acts as a protective maneuver that preserves the integrity of each area (Levine, 1997). Such experience may not have been processed by the hippocampus, which, as noted several times, tags time and place to memories, and so it cannot be stored as explicit or narrative memory. Rather it will be encoded in the emotional brain and in the body, experienced only in implicit ways. For such patients the body becomes "a container and signifier, as a kind of stage upon which the unfelt psychic pain can be dramatized and eventually relieved" (Sidoli, 2000, p. 97).

Establishing Emotional Connections

If an adult is troubled by early relational trauma, it is "because as a child he or she extracted patterns from early attachment relationships and these patterns form attractors in the limbic brain" (Dales & Jerry, 2008, p. 285; the pull toward pattern completion in these circumstances is discussed more fully in Chapter 4.) Lewis et al. emphasize that "when a limbic connection has established a neural pattern, it takes a limbic [i.e., a new, powerfully engaged emotional] connection to revise it" (as cited in Dales & Jerry, 2008, p. 285). The affect regulation that occurs through a relationally based psychotherapy, supported by supervision that encourages such meaningful affective engagement, is the key to treatment in these circumstances.

Regulating Levels of Arousal

In the consulting room such patients can be easily triggered into states of hyperarousal that affect both psyche and soma and that blot out the ability to think. Such states may escalate very fast, eliciting fight, flight, or freeze responses when even a minor element of current experience, such as a feeling, a noise, a color, a shape, a touch, or a smell, elicits a dissociated fragment of previous trauma. Cozolino (2006) points out that words are problematic at such times of terror because decreased activation in Broca's area occurs in such states and the patient literally finds it difficult to speak. Afterward patients cannot always recall what happened because the encoding for conscious memory may also be affected in states of extreme arousal. This means that both patient and therapist struggle with the task of constructing coherent narrative. In states of overarousal the secretion of endogenous opioids may come to the rescue, calming the amygdala, which has a high proportion of opioid receptors, and thereby calming the patient (Cozolino, 2006).

However, frequent experiencing of extreme states of arousal in therapy may lead to overdependence on the release of opioids as a way of self-calming. The therapist must find ways to help the patient return to a more regulated state of arousal without this sort of extreme escalation occurring. Should the therapist fail to achieve this then the patient may move to the further state of hypoarousal, wherein disengagement (the escape when there is no escape) and the rag-doll-like state of collapse may ensue, accompanied by the release of endogenous opioids. An understanding of the intensity of projections that may emanate from these patients at such times and be received by the therapist is central to adequate understanding and supervision of what one might term the inner workings of the therapeutic alliance in these circumstances. The way in which the therapist may also get pulled into an enactment is particularly relevant here. Stewart (2002) comments: "The supervisor can provide a cathartic holding experience, a space to think, or in Schore's (1996) terminology the opportunity to co-regulate or recover to a more mature mode of functioning" (p. 76).

Processing Affect

A young child or even an adult may communicate with noises. Here the therapist may wish to resist the temptation to respond merely in noises but perhaps will follow the rhythm and lilt of the patient in speaking phrases such as "What is it that you want to tell me?" or "I know" or "I see." With a child, identifying the state as hypoarousal or hyperarousal and therefore responding appropriately may come through an exploration of the way in which the room and the objects in the child's box are used. Are they attacked, squashed, pushed, pulled? Are they collapsed onto or not touched at all? What do the sounds evoke in the therapist? What is the therapist's bodily countertransference?

Dissociative episodes in the consulting room and dissociative states of mind can be unnerving to the onlooker and can become counterproductive for the individual once the trauma is past. Bromberg (2003) warns that unintegrated affect from psychic trauma

> threatens to disorganize the internal template on which one's experience of self-coherence, self-cohesiveness, and self-continuity depends . . .
>
> The unprocessed "not-me" experience(s) held by a dissociated self state, or by several dissociated self states in the case of patients with DID, as an affective memory without an autobiographical memory of its origin 'haunts' the self. (Bromberg, 2003, p. 689)

At the time of the original trauma(s), when meaning was unbearable and experience unthinkable, the dissociative defense may have been a mind-saving one. Because of the way the "unformulated" (Stern, 2008, p. 402) traumatic experience is remembered in the body rather than held in mind, many clients struggle to engage with such psychic pain. As we have seen, experiencing these states arises from the realm of the implicit and as yet there will be no encoding in explicit memory for such trauma. Stern (2008) explains that such experience is "highly charged with affect. Sometimes, in fact, that experience is virtually nothing *but* affect, affect that can feel completely inchoate to the patient" (p. 402). Research has already shown clearly that the experience of emotional pain "lights up" the anterior cingulate cortex just as actual physical pain does (Eisenberger et al., 2003). By contrast the recall of trauma in the context of the holding, containing therapeutic relationship can do much to modulate the intolerable nature of previously unbearable memories and thereby to modulate the associated affect, in turn modulating the quality of the remembered experience. When such states of mind are addressed in a relational and affect-regulatory manner, a greater integration may gradually take place that enables an explicit memory, at least of the experience in the consulting room, to be held in mind.

Regression in Psychoanalytic Literature and Its Relation to Affect Regulation

Regression work, used as part of the therapeutic technique, was initially associated with Breuer's work with his patient Anna O and developed by Freud after Breuer renounced it in reaction to his patient's extreme hysterical response (Breuer & Freud, 1895). Its use as a psychoanalytic technique became a contentious issue for two reasons: The first relates to Freud's renunciation of his early use of hypnosis to achieve altered states of mind, which for him were an integral part of working with regression, and the second relates to the profession's understandable renunciation of Ferenczi's (1988) later unboundaried exploration of regression in the service of therapy, which may best be explored in his clinical diary.

Despite these difficulties, I would like to highlight certain aspects of this early work that still have relevance for us as clinicians today. First is the understanding of regression as involving altered states of mind that are primitive in nature; second is Ferenczi's understanding that what was provoked by the use of too abstinent a technique on the part of the therapist was not a therapeutic improvement but rather "a replay, a reenactment of original traumatic experiences that the patient as a child had undergone at the hands of adults resulting in an under—or over-stimulation of the child" (Stewart, 1992, p. 104). Third, I would draw attention to the current concern that interpretation used alone and in the context of an abstinent approach may actually be antitherapeutic for some patients at certain stages of treatment.

Lastly Stewart (1992) also notes Ferenczi's interest in exploring the degree of tension that a patient could tolerate and his assertion that to work at the edge of what was bearable could bring about therapeutic results. If we look at the work of Ogden, Minton, et al. (2006) and of Schore concerning the appropriate level of arousal, we find that this latter assertion of Ferenczi has a curiously modern ring to it. Schore explains the neurobiology of working with such states of mind by means of the following diagram (see Figure 8.1). He notes that the "self-destabilization of the emotional right brain in clinical enactments can take one of two forms: high arousal explosive fragmentation versus low arousal implosion of the implicit self" and argues for work to be done at "the edges of the windows of affect tolerance."

Affect regulation while working at the edge of what may be tolerated is desirable in most therapy once the relationship is secure enough to work with traumatic experience. Such work requires caution to avoid states of hyperarousal; when the clinician strays into methods of working that stimulate overarousal, frequent states of hyperarousal and the emergence of flashbacks may overwhelm the patient's capacity to think and reflect on the emotional state and aggravate the kindling process. The cautious therapist will watch carefully for signs of psychological kindling, that is, the changed pattern of neuronal responses in the brain, subsequent to emotional trauma, whereby they fire in response to internal stimuli rather than external stimuli. This changed pattern of neuronal response was first identified by animal researchers (Goddard et al., 1969) and has since been explored more fully by researchers, particularly in relation to posttraumatic stress disorder (Charney et al., 1993; Post et al., 1995) and posttraumatic illness (Miller, 1997; Scaer, 2001). Scaer notes that psychological kindling is most likely to affect the amygdala, leading to high levels of arousal and resulting in flashbacks and states of terror and dread. The goal is to avoid the development of the kindled state in the patient, with its inevitable misplaced release of powerful chemicals into the brain, chemicals designed to enable adequate response to life-threatening emergencies (Scaer, 2001). The kindled state, once aroused, may linger for some considerable time with detrimental effects to the patient's state of mind and general well-being. Cortisol levels may be raised, resulting in damage to the hippocampus and the thalamus.

Various ways of being in the room with the patient may help counteract such states of overarousal. For example, there is a need for caution in the use of lengthy silences with these patients; "silence is an ambiguous stimulus that activates systems of implicit memory" (Cozolino, 2002, p. 99). Such systems may be so persecutory that they lead patients to depths of affective despair. The therapist's aim is not reassurance or avoidance of the trauma, but rather to address the point of pain while enabling the patient to stay "in mind" and engaged in the therapeutic process (Wilkinson, 2006a). To this end the therapist should avoid sustained states of both overarousal and underarousal in the patient in order to work effectively (Ogden, Minton, et al., 2006).

Affect regulation, therefore, must be central to any therapy. A lowering of tone and slowing of speech help to counteract overarousal, triggered in the patient by the sudden flow of adrenaline. It may be possible to help the patient modify his or her experience by use of a simple phrase such as "It was then, not now." Cozolino (2002) suggests that this kind of verbalization is effective because it stimulates Broca's area and encourages the functioning of right and left hemispheres in a more integrated way. This overview endorses Ferenczi's understanding that interpretation solely in the context of abstinence is unhelpful for certain patients and introduces the relational perspective that implicitly underpins Ferenczi's thought about technique with regressed patients. Both Balint and Winnicott, who went on to develop theory and practice concerning regression, understood that the altered states of mind involved in regressive experiences in the consulting room covered a wide spectrum of arousal, from the numbing, switched-off mood of states that we would now recognize as dissociative to the more highly aroused dissociative states of mind often linked with flashbacks and kindled states of mind when traumatic experience is reawakened.

Regression in the Light of an Attachment Perspective: Balint

Balint (1968), the first to revive Ferenczi's work, proposed two types of pathological character structures that might be encountered in this group of patients, which he categorized in terms of their relation to the object. He described "ocnophilia" as a state in which there is a desire to cling to the object, and "philobatism" as a state in which the spaces between objects are preferred to the object. Here he describes, on the one hand, an anxious, clinging attachment style and, on the other, an avoidant attachment style. This aspect of his theory resonates with Bowlby's (1958) groundbreaking work on attachment and, indeed, Balint (1968) himself makes this link explicitly, as well as links to studies in ethology.

In his exploration of the therapeutic aspects of regression, Balint, in a clear-sighted way, did not restrict his perspective to merely the positive aspects of regression (a method that had led Ferenczi into substantial difficulty and the use of regression as a therapeutic technique into disrepute), but urged caution concerning what he termed "malignant regression," which he categorized as "regression aimed at gratification" (1968, p. 144). Balint understood the difficulties encountered in the regressive state of mind to be connected with the earliest relation to the mother and the experience of the inevitable frustration of what he termed "primary object love." He understood a benign regression as "a regression for recognition" and suggested that the analyst "must accept and carry the patient for a while, must prove more or less indestructible, must not insist on maintaining harsh boundaries, but must allow the development of a kind of mix-up between the patient and himself" (1968, p. 145).

Balint placed at least some of the responsibility for the type of regression that ensued in a session firmly in the psyche of the therapist. He argued that once a malignant type of regression is established, "the analyst will find it very difficult to resist its power, to extricate the patient and himself from it" (Balint, 1968, p. 140). Stewart (1992) notes that "The more the analyst's technique was suggestive of omniscience and omnipotence, the greater is the danger of malignant regression" (p. 123). Chu (1998) also warns that "passivity and withholding on the part of the therapist allow traumatic transferences to flourish" (p. 122). Chu continues: "Such transferences have their origins in a past reality and can rapidly become functionally psychotic" (p. 122).

A staged approach to the work within a session is important for patients with trauma histories (see Chapter 1) and may go some way in avoiding the development of a malignant regressive experience. For such patients the last part of the session devoted to recovery is essential to maintain so that they may leave in a safe state of being.

Winnicott

Winnicott (1965) also understood the need for regression, emphasized its value, and described two types that he felt occurred in the consulting room. The first he described as a thorough-going regression that some patients needed to achieve what he described as "unit status" with the therapist (Winnicott, p. 44). He understood the wound to these patients to be a primary one, just as in healthy early development "the infant becomes a person, an individual in his own right." This occurs in the earliest relation to the primary caretaker, which means that "the personal structure is not yet securely founded" (Winnicott, 1975b, p. 279).

Winnicott's and Schore's work both seamlessly integrate an understanding of the mother–baby couple as the source of the secure attachment and the unit status and also as the stimulus for, and definer of, the quality of the newly developing baby mind–brain and the baby's ability to self-regulate. Deep-seated early relational trauma requires sustained treatment in depth to effect change, thereby requiring a dependent experience over time for these patients.

The building blocks that establish attachment in the beginning of life are activated again in the very special kind of regression that may develop in the consulting room. The voice of the therapist may come to be extremely important to the patient as he or she begins to regress, and seeks to form, perhaps for the first time, a deep affective attachment that will give the confidence to move forward into a fuller experience of life. The inferior colliculus which stores the imprint of the mother's voice is the part of the brain which also becomes active when affective encounters occur throughout life. Panksepp and Bernatzky (2002) describe sound as "a special form of touch . . . built upon the prosodic mechanisms of the right hemisphere . . . [that] allows us affective emotional communication through vocal intonations" (p.136), and emphasize that sound is "an excellent way to help to synchronize and regulate emotions" (p. 140).

Winnicott felt that a thorough-going regression with a view to establishing a reliable attachment was of particular help to those patients whose attachment had been what would now be characterized as insecure, avoidant, or disorganized. Such patients, Winnicott felt, had developed what he termed a "false self" as a protective barrier against unbearable impingement and as a means of coping with the need to interact with the external environment. In Winnicott's exploration of what he described as the strain put on mental functioning that is organized in defense of a tantalizing environment—that is, an environment in which the mother does not manage to respond to the baby's needs in a "good enough" way—he noted that, in some patients, a method of managing emerges in which mental functioning becomes a thing in itself and acts as a substitute mother within the psyche but inevitably proves to be no replacement for real mothering.

Such a defense is reminiscent of Kalsched's (1996) identification of a powerful protector/persecutor figure, a split-off aspect of the self that develops in response to trauma (the protective aspect) but then comes to dominate the psyche (the persecutor aspect), reflecting the patient's internal attempt to regulate arousal and to manage the debilitating effects of lingering traumatic states of mind. Winnicott (1975c) warns that such false caretakers within the psyche will always prove inadequate, and breakdown may threaten or occur. He uses the term "freezing" to describe the effect on the developing psyche–soma of the failure of the early environment to provide adequate nurturing (Winnicott, 1975b, p. 281). We know that part of an initial response to a trauma experience is the freeze response and that after the threat is past, the healthy reaction is relaxation. What Winnicott suggests parallels our knowledge of the effects of an unresolved traumatic experience: that is, the sufferer may become fixed in the freeze response with detrimental effects on mind, body, and emotions (Levine, 1997; Scaer, 2001). Winnicott understood a regression that takes place within supportive psychotherapy, inevitably involving altered states of mind, to be a major therapeutic tool for such patients.

Winnicott (1975d) also understood that patients might move into altered states of mind in a less thorough-going but equally helpful way. In therapy with these patients he suggests that at the moment a patient becomes withdrawn, in an altered state of mind, if the analyst can manage to "hold" the patient metaphorically, then "what would otherwise have become a withdrawal state becomes a regression" (Winnicott, 1975d, p. 261). A quality of healthy dependency then characterizes the therapeutic relationship and enables the deep affective engagement that may bring about change in the patient's mind. Winnicott (1975d) concludes: "Danger does not lie in the regression but in the analyst's unreadiness to meet the regression and the dependence which belongs to it" (p. 261). Today, as we consider the value of such a relational stance, the added knowledge is available to us that affectively focused treatment alters the frontal lobes of the brain, which in the right hemisphere is the emotional executive of the brain, in a way that is detectable by functional imaging studies (Solms & Turnbull, 2002, p. 288).

Regression and Aggression

One of the reasons that Ferenczi brought working with regression as a therapeutic tool into disrepute was his failure to acknowledge the levels of aggression that can be uncovered through the engagement of primitive states of mind. Writing about traumatic experience in general, Grossman (1991) suggested that pain and painful affects stimulate, and are the sources of, aggression, and that fantasy formation may be damaged by trauma, leading to an ability to transform the traumatic experience through mental activity. Fonagy (1991) comments on the child's psychic response to parental abuse: "The parent's abuse undermines the child's theory of mind, so that it is no longer safe for the child . . . to think about wishing, if this implies the contemplation of the all too real wishes of the parent to harm the child" (p. 649). Inderbitzin and Levy (1998) note that "Destructive and self-destructive behaviors are prominent if not central, whether the source of trauma is a primary caretaker or external circumstances (illness, surgery, etc.) requiring help from an important adult" (p. 44). They argue that trauma gives rise to "intense frustration and ensuing aggression" and that the opportunities for aggression provided by "reexperiencing trauma" should not be underestimated (p. 40). We begin to have intimations of the quality and complexity of the transference–countertransference relationship with these patients.

Bragin (2003), in her discussions of the effect of terror on symbol formation, emphasizes the problems that occur when the natural destructive internal fantasy that is an inevitable part of the process of the development of mind seems suddenly to come into its own in external reality and points out that the "exposure to extreme violence may inhibit the ability to mentalize in order to protect against the knowledge of internal destructive capacity" that becomes too painful to bear (pp. 60–61). It seems that similar processes affect the nascent mind confronted with prolonged abuse at the hands of the primary caregiver.

Bragin also suggests that those who are afflicted by "survivor guilt" may regress to the state of early infantile omnipotence that acts as a defense against terrifying helplessness by seeing "themselves as the cause of the violence not its victim" (p. 64). In another paper she argues cogently for the need to enable the patient's awareness of the therapist's capacity for knowing terrible things very early on in therapy if the patient is to engage successfully in the incredibly painful task of undergoing treatment for the effects of extreme violence. In particular, she emphasizes that omnipotent guilt can be understood as "a defense against something far worse—being helpless and alone in the face of murderous rage within and the torturer without," adding "one is not then the helpless victim of someone else's nightmare but the author of one's own" (Bragin, 2007, p. 231). Knox (2001) developed a similar idea in relation to the patient who has experienced early relational trauma when she considered the effects of a child's dawning awareness of parental cruelty: "For any child to feel this is unbearable and . . . it might feel preferable in that situation for the child to construct a belief or fantasy that (s)he has done something to cause the parent to behave in this sadistic way; such an imaginative belief would allow the child to retain some sense of cause and effect" (p. 626).

Bragin (2007) argues that in the face of such internal pressures, regression to the earliest states of infantile omnipotence becomes inevitable, and the victim is "thrown back to an experience of early aggressive fantasy" (p. 231). She suggests that torture promotes regression to the preverbal defensive stage of the earliest months of life and intimates that identification with the aggressor may well be the ultimate outcome of abusive experience. Schore also concludes that the "spatiotemporal imprinting of terror, rage and dissociation is a primary mechanism for the intergenerational transmission of violence" (Schore, 2003a, p. 287).

Eigen (2001) delineated vividly the etiology of rage arising out of early relational trauma and argued for a similar effect to that described by Bragin and Schore:

> The individual was born into a frightened and frightening world, a world in which being frightened plays a significant role. . . . Personality [is] congealed or collapsed around or into the fright. . . . It spreads through body, the way it feels to be a person, through character. . . . Once personality is set in the mould of terror, it is difficult to move on. . . . Rage is fed by terror. (pp. 24–25)

It is essential for the therapist to help the patient understand that these terrible states of mind are not unthinkable but in fact knowable and that, as such, they can be acknowledged and worked with, especially in therapy. Bragin (2007) elucidates the central dilemma that such states of mind pose for the clinician: "how to convey the capacity to know terrible things without being destroyed by the survivor, while at the same time not conveying that one is dangerous oneself" (p. 229). It is only by acknowledging the aggressive fantasy that lies buried in us all that the patient can be helped to move on and to engage in the "struggle to reshape what relationship can mean" (Orbach, 1998, p. 70). Indeed Fonagy (1991) had already made clear that "the ability to represent the idea of an affect is crucial in the achievement of control over overwhelming affect" (p. 641). But how can this control be achieved in relation to aggression? For the answer I believe we have to return again to the earliest relationship, that between the baby and the primary caregiver, and allow the implicit relational knowing that occurs in that earliest dyad to inform our way of working in the consulting room. Regression, therefore, has a crucial part to play in treatment. One may summarize the process that Winnicott (1975b) conceived as:

- Providing containment in a way that gives the patient a sense of security
- Allowing regression to dependence
- Enabling a discovery of the self through the unfreezing of the early environmental failure
- Enabling an ability to feel and express anger
- Enabling a steady return to independence
- Validating a new quality of liveliness

The path of the therapy does not necessarily feel like a steady upward climb; more often than not, the struggle is more of a forward and backward motion, a struggle between progression and regression. Maybe a spiral staircase is a better metaphor, as both therapist and patient often seem to find themselves back at the same place again, but perhaps on a higher level of the spiral. In work that involves an encounter with younger self states that contain more regressed or frozen parts of the self, dependency is an integral part of the patient's experience. A patient described her need of her analyst over a short break in therapy as a need for her kangaroo mother. She knew that they were separate but still longed to be able to be kept close in a kangaroo pouch, much as neonates on a premature baby ward are "kangarooed" or snuggled by the parent close to his or her body inside a large sweater. At this stage the analyst's implicit acceptance of the patient's dependency at a nonverbal level is crucial. Of course, the acceptance could be put into words and no doubt later will be, but at this stage a much more fundamental sort of nonretaliatory holding is what is required. Chused (2007) emphasizes the analyst's capacity to allow him- or herself to be used symbolically in the role of "idealized care-provider," that is, to "accept the role of the all-important other has a significant impact on patients" (p. 878). Such dependency can be very difficult for the analyst to bear, and this difficulty gives rise to the danger that a premature attempt at separation will be initiated, with disastrous consequences, just as Stern (1985) noted that a misattuned mother can ask too much separation of her child too early. Later, the way in which analyst and patient are able to engage in the tasks normally associated with the second year of life will be crucial for the patient, who has needed to regress to earlier states of being. The inner child must also learn about a less than perfect fit to be able to manage in the world. Stern (1985) has described in depth the way in which well-attuned mothers gradually enable their children to accept this reality.

Chused (2007) notes that when a child patient is in the pretend mode which is a feature of imaginative play in the therapy room, "the defensive hyper vigilance and guardedness felt to be necessary in the 'real world' relax and the child is much more available for meaningful interaction" (p. 877). It is just so with the child part of the adult patient, and the wide range of therapeutic techniques that has developed attests to this. Perhaps what is most important about the playful, imaginative aspects of therapy—whether with child or with adult, and whether using toys, words, images, dreams, or imaginative interactions between patient and therapist—is what Chused describes as an exchange between patient and analyst, "where meaning is not fixed, [and through which] the implicit communication of availability, containment, accompaniment, and toler-ance allows for both the emergence of unconscious fears and conflicts and their eventual transformation" (p. 877). Chodorow (2006) observes that "the imagination creates symbolic images and stories that express the mood or emotion in a way that may be more bearable, [reminding us that] this completely natural process occurs in the symbolic play of chil-dren" (p. 223). The capacity for imaginative play helps patient and ther-apist together find a way through the defensive stance that hypervigilance would demand of the adult parts of the patient in response to regressive states of mind.

The Neuroscience of Changing Self States

Dissociation, such as these regressed patients may experience, involves the maintenance of effective defensive systems in protection of the self, on the one hand, alongside a separate system geared to managing the ordinary events of a daily life, on the other. Van der Hart et al. (2006) identify the "apparently normal personality" as an aspect of the patient's psyche that is "fixated in trying to go on with normal life . . . while avoiding traumatic memories" (p. 5). The apparently normal personality may be equated with Winnicott's adaptive, coping, or false self with which the patient manages the ordinary demands of living. In this sense Winnicott's term "false self" extends far beyond his original meaning.

The apparently normal self state is false in that it fails to recognize the experience of the traumatized self as its own; it is not able to identify with it and remains unable to feel its pain.

Van der Hart et al. (2006) understand the "emotional personality" to be stuck in the traumatic experience that persistently fails to become a narrative memory of the trauma. They note that the domain in which the emotional personality lives may be characterized by vehement emotion that is overwhelming and nonadaptive. In the hyperaroused states that occur in a regressed patient, the emotional personality is in the ascendance. In such states patients may unconsciously seek retraumatization in the consulting room in order to experience an endorphin "high" to which they have become accustomed from early and repetitive experiences of trauma. "Children abused by their caregiver will experience increased levels of endorphins as part of the traumatization and freeze response" (Scaer, 2001a, p. 88). Patients who had this type of early experience may continually seek to reexperience trauma in what may be thought of as an addictive state of mind. Such a pattern may also occur when a patient attaches to a therapist who unconsciously works in an abusive way, or is experienced as doing so in the transference. In each situation the patient unconsciously seeks the endorphinergic effects, with ensuing opiate-like reward, of the abusive situation. Reexperiencing or reenactment of this kind in the consulting room will become addictive rather than therapeutic. Thus the therapist must consider carefully the appropriateness of any reexperiencing or reenactment in the consulting room.

When dissociation has become the way to manage the trauma initially, it persists as a way of coping with stresses in life generally, and in the consulting room, in particular. Traumatized patients may find themselves escaping from reality by old familiar routes: When the going gets tough, they may enter states in which they believe "I was not abused"; in other states they may feel weak, helpless, and easily become a victim, whereas at yet other times they may find themselves unduly aggressive in an unconscious identification with the abuser. "Exposure to subsequent stress tends to reactivate not only traumatic memories, but also trauma-based schemes about self and others" (van der Kolk et al., 1996, p. 432).

Memories of the earliest trauma relating to the primary caregiver are held only in emotional and bodily memory. As such, when they are reexperienced there is a strong emotional and bodily quality to the "memoring," as one patient chose to describe the experience. When she used this term there was always a vivid here-and-now quality to the memory fragments that emerged, which would give rise to an experience of what I term "the old present."

Using EEG, Schiffer et al. (1995) observed activity indicative of left-hemisphere processing when patients were engaged with neutral memories, but a marked switch to activity indicative of right-hemisphere processing when they were engaged with trauma memories. Two small studies have explored the discrete regional cerebral blood flow (RCBF) patterns that are identifiable when patients listen to their emotionally neutral versus trauma focused scripts. The first study by Rauch et al. sought to explore the neurobiology of intense fear in eight patients with a diagnosis of PTSD. Cozolino (2002) reports this research and emphasizes their findings that, when listening to trauma scripts, the RCBF was greater in right-sided structures associated with intense emotion, "including the amygdala, orbitofrontal cortex, insular, anterior and medial frontal lobe, and the anterior cingulate cortex" (as cited in Cozolino, 2002, p. 273). Reinders et al. (2003), in a study of 11 female patients with DTD, used PET scanning to explore the possibility of one human brain being able to initiate two autobiographical selves. The results demonstrated that "these patients have state-dependent access to autobiographical affective memories and thus different autobiographical selves." Furthermore:

> The Traumatic Personality State (TPS) of the patient was identified as being able to store a traumatic memory and able to acknowledge that its reactivation affected them emotionally while the Neutral Personality State (NPS) reported to be emotionally unresponsive to that memory and had no awareness of having been exposed to that event. (Reinders, cited in Wilkinson, 2006a, pp. 169–70)

Areas that play a role in regulating emotional and behavioral reaction to pain were activated when the TPS listened to the trauma script but not when the NPS heard the same script. The existence of different RCBF patterns for different senses of self was observed in the medial prefrontal cortex (MPFC) and the posterior associative cortices. The right MPFC, thought to play a crucial role in the representation of the self-concept, was significantly deactivated when the NPS listened to the trauma script (Reinders et al., as cited in Wilkinson, 2006a, p. 170). Although the results of small-scale studies should be approached with caution, at the least they indicate possible lines of research that may profitably be pursued in larger studies or complementary studies.

Conclusion

Teicher's research into the aftereffects of trauma has shown that the effective functioning of the corpus callosum, which is the major highway between the two hemispheres, can be reduced through trauma (Teicher, 2000; Teicher et al., 2006). As therapist and patient affectively engage with one another and together develop words for the patient's experience, particularly for his or her previously inaccessible affects, greater interhemispheric connectivity is fostered in the mind–brain of the patient, helping to mitigate the earlier effects of trauma.

While researchers pursue the nature of dissociative states of mind and the way in which unintegrated affect may be integrated and unnecessary fear and negative affect modulated, what is clear is that therapy that addresses these issues will involve the circuitry of both hemispheres. Hugely important will be the therapist's capacity to foster an understanding that omnipotent fantasy is both an illusion and, as Bragin (2007) emphasizes, "the rage it is defending against" (p. 231). How can this level of therapeutic understanding be realized in the consulting room? Krowski (1997) comments: "It is only when a containing maternal object has been internalized [in therapy] that rage and hatred . . . can be faced" (p. 171). I conclude that it is the internalizing of the containing maternal object that is at the heart of a regressive process in treatment that emerges as truly therapeutic.

9

Mirroring, Resonance, and Empathy in the Supervisory Process

THE NEUROBIOLOGICAL PERSPECTIVE, AS YET UNEXPLORED, may have much to offer in terms of understanding the supervisory process. Supervision offers an important means by which practitioners may explore the clinical process and the changing nature of the therapeutic alliance as it develops with any given patient. It also provides an added protection for a vulnerable patient population. It seems essential to me that a practice that is valued so highly by our profession should look to exploring its grounding in the neurobiology of emotion. I have chosen to return to the processing of mirroring and empathy (see chapter 3) but with a particular emphasis on the relevance of these aspects of the neurobiology of emotion in relation to the countertransference aspects of the supervisory process. Watt (2005) describes empathy as "one of our most critical social abilities, and essential to the mitigation of suffering" (p. 187). He suggests that this extension of mammalian nurturing behavior that humans are capable of allows for an "increasing appreciation of the internal spaces of others," and of the "development of a theory of mind and perspective taking" (p.189). He identifies

- "native empathy," which he designates genotypic
- phenotypic empathy, developed through good early attachment experience
- empathy evoked by the specifics of the sufferer, noting that "we are far more empathically mobilized by the suffering of a small helpless creature with a rounded face and big eyes than by the suffering of a dominant, aggressive and powerful alpha male" (p. 198)

- empathy which is made possible by the current affective state of the empathizer, noting that "affect-regulation must be relatively intact in the empathizer, as must self-other differentiation" (p. 201)
- the automatic "primitive emotional contagion" aspects of empathy whereby unconscious, continuous automatic processing means that the individual instantly resonates to the emotion of the other (p. 202)
- the more complex cognitive aspects of empathy that give rise to emotion identification and theory of mind

Watt concludes that the brain's "early (short time-scale) receptive functioning prioritizes contagion responses while later responses may prioritize more cognitive processing" (p. 204). The success of the supervisory process will depend on the level of capacity for each aspect of empathy in the individual supervisor and also in the supervisee. Such an understanding of empathy implies that both therapeutic and supervisory skills cannot actually be taught but perhaps can be finetuned.

Schore and Schore (2008) note that "a neuropsychoanalytic right-brain perspective of the treatment process [and, I would suggest, of supervision] allows for a deeper understanding of the critical factors that operate at implicit levels of the therapeutic alliance, beneath the exchanges of language and explicit cognitions" (p. 18).

But how do implicit knowings impact on the therapeutic alliance and the supervisory process?

The Neuroscience of Mirroring, Resonance, and Empathy

Let us first explore the neural processes underpinning the mirroring that occurs in supervision. Gallese (2007) asserts that during our social exchanges, we "seldom engage in explicit interpretative acts"; rather, he describes our understanding of the other as "immediate, automatic and almost reflex-like" (p. 659). He argues that, although we are capable of thinking explicitly about another's mind in a complex and sophisticated manner, we actually have "a much more direct access to the inner world of others" (p. 659). Lyons-Ruth (1998) notes that "implicit knowings governing intimate interactions are not language-based and are not routinely translated into semantic form" (p. 285). The dominance of the implicit level in interactions must inevitably affect the supervisory process, which has sometimes been seen as dependent on verbal communications concerning the analytic hour. In supervision as in therapy, the right-hemisphere to right-hemisphere resonance that arises from the nonverbal aspects of communication, such as tone of voice, gesture, and posture, as well as the fast-acting communications that often occur below levels of conscious awareness will underpin the work. Words give rise to left-hemisphere to left-hemisphere resonance and enable the ability to think about the session and to develop of a coherent narrative concerning the patient (see Chapter 7). Detailed consideration of the process of developing such a narrative is as important for the therapist as for the patient. Empathy has both a cognitive component that can be communicated in words and an affective component—and both influence the development of a shared understanding.

What is the nature of this more direct access that we have to the other and how does it affect the process of supervision? Watt (2005), in a discussion of the meaning of empathy, suggests that all attempts to describe it "outline a common ground of a *positively balanced supportive response to the distress of another creature*" but adds that to define this core process is critical for neuroscience (p. 187, emphasis in original). Research has confirmed that empathy allows the sharing of experiences across individuals (Carr et al., 2003) by means of a mirroring process. Carr et al. (2003) make clear that we understand what others feel by a mechanism of action representation that enables empathy and our emotional responses. Exploring responses to a range of emotional facial expressions, these researchers demonstrated a fundamental role for the insula because of its capacity to relay action representation information to the limbic areas that process emotional content. Their data also show lateralized activation of the amygdala during imitation of facial, emotional expression. They conclude that the empathic resonance that is brought about by imitation does not require explicit representational content such as would involve the left amygdala. Rather empathy is grounded in a form of mirroring that occurs via an experiential mechanism involving activation of the amygdala in the right hemisphere. It may be that we should understand the left hemisphere's cognitive capacity as giving rise to cognitive empathy, whereas the right orbitofrontal cortex orchestrates a response that speedily involves the right hemisphere at every level. We might think of this as the fast route to affective empathy. Watt (2005) poses what appears to be a crucial question and ponders the implications of an answer in the affirmative:

> *Does a "categorical" and "preconscious"* [precognitive?] *recognition of the prototype states of separation distress, anger, fear, play, etc., emerge from the same basal forebrain, diencephalic and paralimbic regions necessary for the core affective states?* If so, then cortical receptive processing and recognition of emotion (organized largely in the right hemisphere) may be a cortical–cognitive "extension" of a more primitive receptive processing possibly invisibly embedded in the distributed subcortical emotion architectures. (p. 204, emphasis in original)

Schore (1994, 2003a, 2003b) suggests that the nonverbal transfer-ence–countertransference interactions take place at preconscious–unconscious levels and represent right-hemisphere to right-hemisphere communications of fast-acting, automatic regulated and dysregulated emotional states between patient and therapist. Such communications appear to develop out of the "embodied simulations" (Gallese, 2007) that arise from the earliest experience of right-hemispheric bodily, facial, and gestural communication between mother and child, out of which the capacity to relate and the development of communicative language grad-ually emerge. It seems that supervision exemplifies this process in a partic-ular way: Observation of another such as that which takes place in the consulting room, and again in supervision, is initially an implicit, auto-matic process, occurring at levels below conscious awareness, which may then gradually emerge into awareness and become possible to discuss.

Harrison et al. (2006) used fMRI scanning to explore the existence of emotion-specific autonomic signaling in affective communication. Their study provides the first evidence to support a role for the autonomic nervous system in perception–action models of empathy, as exemplified in the emotion of sadness. Their research has shown that "observed pupil size . . . influences the perceived intensity and valence of expressions of sadness" and that the "interaction between pupil size and (facial, muscular) expression induces contagious corresponding pupil responses in the viewer." Their findings provide "evidence that perception–action mechanisms extend to non-volitional operations of the autonomic nervous system" (p. 5). Using their fMRI results, they were able to demonstrate that these effects were "associated with neural activity changes in regions that process salient social cues, including the amyg-dala and superior temporal sulcus" (p. 274). They conclude that *"effective communication of emotional feelings engages visceral autonomic reactions underlying feeling states"* (p. 726, emphasis added).

Decety and Chaminade (2003) emphasize that "perception of emotion activates the neural mechanisms responsible for the generation of emotions" (pp. 583–584). They conclude that an understanding of another (in this case, supervisee and patient, and supervisor and supervisee) takes place as one represents the mental activities and processes of the other by generating in one's own mind (and body) "unconscious processes that might almost be described as *unconscious imagination*, that is, *a generating of neural experiencing at an unconscious level of similar activities and processes in oneself*" (p. 582, emphasis added).

From this material let us outline certain key aspects of functioning that the effective supervisor is able to utilize:

- The ability to receive communications concerning underlying feeling states, via what might well be described as the "gut reaction," which may be one aspect of an empathic response to distress in the patient.
- The ability to capture fleeting emotions in others
- A capacity for unconscious imagination, that is, an experiencing at an unconscious level in oneself the feelings experienced by the other.

Empathic understanding through unconscious imagination, such as is manifest in countertransference phenomena, is therefore key not only to the successful therapeutic process but also to its supervision. Cozolino (2006) defines such resonance behaviors as automatic responses triggered by mirror systems that are reflexive, implicit, and obligatory. Cozolino stresses the part played by both the insula cortex and the anterior cingulate in activating empathy both in our bodies and our minds. He cites the work of Phan et al. (2002), who found that both became activated during emotional recall as well as during tasks involving imagery. Cozolino (2006) explains: "In its role as an integration cortex the insula bridges and coordinates limbic and cortical processing as well as somatic and visceral experience" (p. 208). He argues that mirror and resonance circuits are required to "combine with visual–spatial, cognitive and abstract networks" to fully enable an empathic understanding of the other (p. 203). This process also describes adequate functioning within the supervisory process. As we have seen, Watt (2005) emphasizes not only perception, conscious imitation, and theory of mind but also the need to appreciate the centrality of affective activation within the empathizer. He advocates a complex and affectively sophisticated theory of mind that also includes primitive resonance induction mechanisms. Thus Watt offers a cognitive and affective foundation for empathy. If these dual bases for empathy are indeed the case, they would explain very clearly the extensive unconscious processes that are at work in supervision alongside the higher cortical, conscious processing that also takes place.

Some supervisors favor an approach to a supervisory session that is similar to Bion's approach to an analytic hour—that is, to be without memory or desire, to be in a seemingly restful state out of which a creative engagement with the material presented occurs. Although such a notion can only be speculative, it might be that in this unique resting state, the default network—that is, the system in the brain which appears to be active when the brain is seemingly at rest (see Chapter 4) is activated along with its connections to the hippocampus, which allow the creative connections between past and present to emerge and to be thought about in the supervision. Certainly the supervisory process requires the supervisor to think, to process and integrate both right- and left-brain functioning, including the affective and cognitive components of empathy, both of which must be engaged if therapy or supervision is to be effective.

A Psychoanalytic Perspective

A psychoanalytic perspective on the neuroscience understanding of empathy has been presented in a cutting-edge paper by Zanocco et al. (2006), "Sensory Empathy and Enactment." Here sensory empathy is defined as "that process which is based precisely on the ability to assimilate, through imitative identification, what another person is feeling" (Zanocco et al., 2006, p. 148). The paper explores the interaction in the analytic dyad and also sheds light on the unconscious aspects of the supervisory process. The paper opens by stressing the unconscious— what might be termed the "bottom up"—nature of sensory empathy which the authors link to Freud's concept of primary process. Zanocco et al. describe the analyst's dawning awareness of unspoken communications from the patient as "empathic intuition" (p. 148). No doubt a similar process occurs between supervisor and supervisee and underpins successful supervision.

Zanocco et al. (2006) value Gallese's (2007) work on mirror neurons and the understanding of observation of another as predominantly an implicit, automatic process that is grasped by another person by means of a mirror mechanism analogous to the reading of actions. It is just such an understanding that enables an empathic response. They see in this functioning confirmation of "the concept of intersubjectivity at the most primitive levels of communication" (Zanocco et al., 2006, p. 153).

Empathy achieved through the mirroring process is, by its very nature, not always comfortable. Let us imagine that a supervisee arrives, saying that she feels very low, her self-esteem is low, she is uncertain of her ability as a therapist. Almost as she speaks I might find myself uneasily drawn to thoughts about my own inadequacies. As I bring my mind back to the room, I find that my supervisee is describing an extremely difficult encounter with a new and rather disturbed patient, currently referred with problems of anger and depression. As she tells of the course of the session, it becomes clear that she has dealt sensitively with her patient's pain and unacknowledged anger. My supervisee reports feelings of low self-esteem that had attacked her in this very difficult session as she experienced her patient's very low, rather deadened, state of mind. Toward the end of the session her patient had been able to say a little about the severe trauma and neglect that had characterized his childhood.

As I continue silently pondering my experience at the beginning of the session, my supervisee gradually begins to recognize that her own acute experience of low self-esteem actually relates to her patient's inner world, which was so painful for him to acknowledge. A supervisor engaged in this process may be more or less active in regard to both intervention and disclosure of his or her own inner experience, according to the individual supervisee's needs. What the supervisor has experienced is the empathic mirroring of the supervisee's uncomfortable feelings as she, in turn, mirrored her patient's (until then) unacknowledged inner trauma and distress. Working at the edge of either extreme avoidance or unbearable encounters with pain requires great skill on the part of the therapist, and the enabling and supportive role of a skilled supervisor should not be underestimated. Such work requires supervision of timing concerning the stage in therapy at which it is safe to explore the client's inner world in this way as well as the timing within an individual session that will leave sufficient space to do such work but also for the client to recover before it is time to leave.

Meares (2005) points out that both therapist and patient are influenced by subliminal signals that potentiate change in the patient's state without, or in addition to, the use of words. The supervisor may need to differentiate between a thoughtful, empathic approach in a supervisee that enables understanding of the other and a supervisee's false assumption that his or her resonance experiences exactly match the inner world of the other, inevitably resulting in unhelpful consequences. In these situations identification or fusion may be being mistaken for empathy. Here it seems to me to be clear that what is required from the supervisor, as much as from the therapist, is a relational approach consisting of empathic responses that are also informed by clear thinking. The supervisor needs to help the therapist to be empathic while remaining separate enough to be able to think. Schaverien (2003) uses a metaphor to illustrate this point:

> Analysis is a drama that takes place between two people, the patient and the analyst (or in group work the group and the analyst). As if from the privileged position of the audience, the supervisor witnesses the drama, *sometimes moved by what is observed.* There is an attempt to help one of the actors de-role and to join the supervisor/spectator in observing the action from a critical distance. In order to do this the actor/analyst *makes a psychological split* that permits her *simultaneously* to stand beside the supervisor, as *a spectator* of this drama, *and to play a part in it.* (p. 170, emphasis added)

Although the notion of observing the action from a critical distance while sometimes being moved by what is observed perhaps privileges cognitive empathy over affective empathy, this description nevertheless does appreciate the value of both. What I would add is that great drama pulls audience members in so that they feel the action on the stage *as if within themselves.* The concept of a drama that involves the audience as much as the actors and in which emotional experiencing is key does allow for the more primitive automatic affective empathic response that is at the heart of countertransference experience in supervision. Effective supervision inevitably requires an empathic response of both kinds from the supervisor to both therapist and patient. Schaverien's (2003) analysis of the "psychological split" acknowledges the affective empathic response of the therapist as he or she plays a part in the drama, and the cognitive empathic response as he or she is the spectator. Schore and Schore (2008) suggest that it is the affective that conveys the personality of the therapist (and we may infer, the supervisor's as well) more so than conscious communications. The supervisor will experience the nature and quality of the work being presented through his or her countertransference at least as much, if not more, as through the words that are spoken.

Empathic experience in the supervisory session may give rise to moments of unease in the supervisor's countertransference. How do we deal such moments? Ultimately, of course, we hope that the supervisee will be able to explore the unconscious emotion (e.g., fear, anxiety, anger, or shame), that underlies the difficulty and gives rise to the affective empathic response of unease in the supervisor. Sometimes a pause, a moment before we respond, may be sufficient for this to happen. Sometimes it may be desirable to wonder out loud. What do I mean? I will demonstrate briefly.

Case Example of Supervision

A supervisee might describe a patient who, in several sessions, had suddenly become frightened, saying in a very young voice on each occasion, "Don't let Mummy come in here. Please, don't let Mummy come in here." Such encounters allow "clinicians to use their emotional reactions to better understand their patient's world" (Fonagy & Target, 1998, p. 110). Each time the supervisee might have replied, "It's all right, there's just us here." However, there are several responses one might make to this plea. My concern here would be to begin to help the supervisee figure out how to help the patient recognize and feel the fear that seems to be dissociated and to explore it without allowing the patient to become unbearably frightened. This therapeutic exploration of fear becomes possible because the feelings are experienced, contained, and voiced by the therapist. As a supervisor, I might feel a great pressure to remain detached and silent in an unconscious identification with the dissociated part of the patient. Alternatively, I might let the reassurance pass out of an unconscious identification with that part of both patient and supervisee that wanted reassurance. Or I might wonder out loud: "I wonder what would have happened if you had said something like 'We'll do what has to be done.'" Together we might come to the conclusion that such a statement might be experienced as quite persecutory, and the therapist might be in danger of being perceived as all-powerful and abusive. We might together reflect on the importance of timing and tone of voice as well as what might be said. Panksepp and Bernatzky (2002) and Andrade (2005) stress the importance of tone, lilt, and rhythm of the therapist's voice, which, they say, mirrors or modifies a patient's earliest experience of the mother's voice (held forever so close to those centers of the brain–mind that give rise to a sense of self). If the therapist were to wonder out loud, then the tone of voice would be crucial for this patient who is clearly both fragile and hypervigilant.

My supervisee and I might continue to muse together that whatever was said and how it was said would need to "hold" the patient and impart a sense of safety while still exploring how very frightening the original situation was, and how frightening the undoing of it is. The supervisee might say, "I guess I could have said, 'It sounds as if it was very frightening if Mummy came into the room.' " I might comment, "Well, yes, that sounds as if it might help to begin to allow the dissociated contents into mind." Countertransferentially, I may find it difficult to make such a comment and to encourage this development in the supervisee's work because of the patient's dissociative defense against pain. If I was able to realize this, I might add, "Sometimes it may be helpful to say something like 'That was then, not now" toward the end of the session, once some of the difficult work has been done." In this situation the then and now need to be clearly differentiated to enable the patient to leave with a feeling of being contained securely in the present, ready to deal with life as it is now rather than still drowning in past experience.

Supervision of a Supervision Group

Using my applications of neuroscience to clinical work, Bhurruth (2007) makes the following acute and relevant observations concerning therapy conducted in a group:

> Through the process of resonance, neural pathways in the listener are activated through hearing of experiences from another, as if they had the experience themselves. This does raise questions about group composition. It would seem that a group member with a history of trauma would respond well to exposure to how other non traumatised group members make sense of the here and now interpersonal experience and the expression of modulated associated affects, thereby integrating left and right brain functioning. However there is an implication that a group composition of a number of traumatised group members may kindle in

each other a fear response through the process of neural resonance that cannot easily be quenched without psychological casu-
alty. (p. 421)

Here Bhurruth underlines the importance of my extension of the
concept of resonance to analytic work with patient groups. The role of
the supervisor in exploring these issues with the conductor of the group
will be key.

Much supervision takes place within a small group setting. In these
circumstances Schaverien's (2003) metaphor needs to be developed to
include a number of plays, some with deeply disturbing content wherein
primitive states of mind predominate, with a group of spectators who
together listen to one member's account of excerpts from a particular play
in an emotionally engaged way, each bringing his or her own unconscious
empathic response into the dynamic of the group, each allowing an
unconscious psychological split within that will permit, through the
process of unconscious imagination, the generation of the mental ideas
and feelings of another to be born inside his or her mind. Complex neural
activity patterns and interactions provide the elements by which meaning
is made. The right hemisphere plays a significant role in the processing of
the forward-looking, imaginative relational exchanges. The key focus will
be the spectators' inner bodily and emotional imaginings, their cognitive
response to their inner experience, and their attempts to help the supervisee who is presenting his or her work with both aspects of experiencing
through the process of de-roling and making the psychological split that
Schaverien describes as simultaneously standing beside the supervisor as a
spectator of the drama as well as playing a part in it.

Over 1 year in one such group of say, four members may well bring with
them material from 10 supervisees, who may have presented, as together,
work with 20 patients. The processes of reflection, mirroring, and empathic
intuition within such a supervisory work group are immensely complex
because of the numbers of people whose conscious and unconscious
processes hover in the room, particularly in the form of transferences and
countertransferences. If this were to be represented visually, it might be as
an ever-changing kaleidoscope, made up of the colors and their mixes that
appear in Figure 9.1.

Such a group will be concerned with conscious and unconscious
communications and transferential and countertransferential experiences

at every level. The group will experience the interplay of both personal and cultural complexes. Most supervisees may be working with individuals for supervision, but one may see his or her supervisees in a group. Most of the therapists may do individual work, but one may have seen a couple. While one may have been working in a setting where the work is strictly time-limited and short-term, others may be engaged in longer work. Moreover, those therapists supervised in a workplace group will also have to contend with organizational complexes. The members of any such group will bring various levels of experience and competence to the process. The empathic capacity of the supervisor enables these conscious and unconscious aspects of relating to be held safely and in such a way that they can be discussed.

I want to offer a possible illustration of work within such a group. I have chosen to present an imaginary extract from supervision of a supervision group because, although complex, the processes of neuronal mirroring, resonance, and empathy are writ large when another layer of experiencing of the patient's material is added to the original supervisory process. One might say that the original encounter with the patient is sometimes literally reenacted, first of all in the experience of the supervisor, whom I will call Dee, and her supervisee as they work together, and then again in the experience within the group as the work is discussed. When the group is finally able to recognize just what is happening, it provides a powerful learning experience; it also provides an opportunity for the detoxifying of toxic contents. Driver (2002) comments: "Unconscious identifications by supervisees with the client's material and the subsequent reflection process and parallel process can open up the client's unconscious issues and aspects of the transference" (p. 95).

Case Example of Supervisory Group

In this imaginary account, the experiences of a patient whose dissociative defense system means that she is often in quite numbed and "switched-off" states of mind are mirrored in the experiences that occur in a supervisory group. Generally the therapist experiences the dissociative quality of the patient as a struggle to consciously keep the material and the patient in mind, and in supervision to present the material with clarity. For the supervisor there may also be a difficulty in following the material and in making the links that are so shunned by the patient. A nurse practitioner whom I call Eleanor was supervised by Dee, who in her turn received supervision in a group supervision. Eleanor began a psychodynamic psychotherapy training fairly recently. Dee had been practicing as a psychoanalytic psychotherapist for several years but had only recently taken on supervision. I explore here only the initial sessions of the supervisory group's encounter with Dee's work.

Dee came to her first presentation with thoroughly prepared notes and copies for each member of the group. Dee described how she quickly had found herself confused as she sought to supervise this young health professional who had been allocated an adolescent as one of her training cases. As Eleanor described some of the early sessions in her work with Kay, the patient, it became clear that on the first occasion Kay's mother had remained in the room, had done a lot of speaking for her daughter, and had described the reason for the therapy as "school refusal," that is, staying out of school because Kay was being bullied by other girls. As the group began to explore the material brought by Dee, we realized that Eleanor was faced with a 15-year-old patient who was struggling with the vicissitudes of florid adolescence. Kay, the patient, sometimes seemed to be fragmenting as she struggled in the grip of a recurring Oedipal experience in the context of current, extremely difficult, primitive, and rather dissociated states of mind. It became more and more apparent that she had never negotiated earlier developmental stages successfully. It seemed that Kay oscillated between overarousal and rather manic teenage acting-out with her friends and underaroused, switched-off, dissociated states of mind in therapy. This state of low arousal was mirrored very powerfully in the experience of the group.

Kay had come to therapy ostensibly because bullying at school had led to attendance problems; some of the hazy, indeed foggy, states of mind that the group experienced all so pervasively at the beginning of this supervision gradually lifted as we became more aware of the complexity of the relationships within the family. The father had left the family 2 years earlier; this behavior replayed an earlier occasion when he had left the family for some months when Kay was about 18 months old. This time after he left, he joined a fundamentalist sect and lived in a cult community with a new partner. For long periods of time Kay heard nothing from her father; she longed for even just a card on her birthday, but there was nothing. The sect did not observe birthdays, she later discovered. Even if she tried to visit him, she was not always allowed to see him. The sect had very particular requirements as to the clothing to be worn by women and also concerning the subjugation of women. Kay felt that she must conform when there, but in so doing she felt completely lost; her sense of self, tenuous at best, would vanish almost completely. Kay felt that she had lost her father, indeed that he had been taken away by another woman and another passion, the passion that he felt for "the cause." She found it difficult to be sure that she could hold onto her mother and swung from clingy to rejecting modes of attachment with her sister, her boyfriend, and others who mattered to her, including her therapist. It seemed that she must often feel as if she herself, as well as her life, was fragmenting and falling apart.

Affective empathy can feel uncomfortable in different ways; the particular feeling tone or bodily experience carried in the countertransference will relate closely to the unconscious affect that patients are not yet able to experience for themselves. The key to the work in the supervisory group lay in developing the capacity of the group to engage with and to think about their affective empathic experiencing of Kay's primitive dissociated states of traumatized mind. Probably it was what she was experiencing as an adolescent that first Eleanor, then Dee, and the group also went on to experience through the empathic mirroring process. It is likely that this experiencing actually arose out of much earlier states of overwhelming distress resulting in defensive hypoarousal that Kay must have experienced as a toddler when her daddy left. It seems she had experienced her own loss and her mother's uncontainable distress as overwhelming and had resorted to a defensive protective state of hypoarousal. In effect, her early experience of loss of her father was replicated as she entered adolescence. At a time, when as a girl, she would so need him to be there for her, he was once again absent. In reaction she was now reexperiencing an implosion of the implicit self.

The whole area of memory—what should be explored, what should be preserved and in what form, what may be thrown away or forgotten, what hazards might either remembering or forgetting hold for the patient—is a complex issue with no simple answer; rather, many questions arise that both supervisor and supervisee will need to explore together. Working with such traumatic memory brings its own complexities and hazards for therapist and supervisor as well as high degrees of pain and uncertainty for patients.

As Dee presented her supervisory material for the first time, I almost instantaneously began to feel fragmented and unable to think. As I listened to and read the description of this work, it felt as if my mind was dissolving, indeed was being wiped out. Dee spoke of her own confusion and the difficulty she had experienced as she sought to engage with

Eleanor. She found it difficult to get hold of the quality of relating between Eleanor and her patient. As Dee spoke rather hesitantly and quietly about the difficult feelings of inadequacy that she was experiencing in the work, so I too felt hesitant, confused, and inadequate as the seminar leader, as I struggled just to be clear who was who in the material that I was experiencing. I was aware of a certain numbness somehow pervading my being in quite a physical way that I had not experienced before. Others in the group began to ask clarifying questions that indicated that they were also experiencing similar difficulties.

The next time Dee came to present, she had organized her notes for the group in a different way to try to aid clarity. Yet once again the group immediately began to struggle with who was who, in what I can only describe as a fragmented sort of way. I became more aware of the under-aroused, somewhat dissociated quality of the mood that prevailed in the group. Dee once again described her own confusion and uncertainty, commenting hesitantly that she felt particularly fragmented and unable to think as she struggled to help her supervisee with the work. She felt that Eleanor seemed to maintain a rather distant, matter-of-fact attitude and at one point seemed to medicalize her patient's material. In the group we were able to explore, through the subdued affect we were experiencing, our unconscious imaginative experience of Kay's hypoaroused defensive state of being, which had become mirrored in our combined experience within the group. Adequate exploration of our feeling states enabled us gradually to work also from a cognitive empathic stance. Through the combined experience of affective and cognitive empathy, Dee gradually became able to realize how helpless, overwhelmed, and fragmented Eleanor felt. Slowly she understood that the rather distant and matter-of-fact attitude maintained by Eleanor was an old dissociative defense against emotional pain adopted by the supervisee in her years as a nurse.

Particularly significant for us as a group were the reenactments that we experienced over the initial weeks as we struggled to comprehend what was happening. An understanding of the intensity of projections that may emanate from these patients at these times and that are received by the therapist is central to adequate supervision of what one might term the inner workings of the therapeutic alliance in these circumstances. The way in which the supervision group may also get pulled into an enactment is particularly relevant here. All of these dynamics need support, exploration, and clarification within supervision. Stewart (2002) notes that "the supervisor can provide a cathartic holding experience, a space to think, or in Schore's terminology the opportunity to co-regulate or recover to a more mature mode of functioning" (p. 76).

At this time we struggled with states of underarousal that sought to deaden the group. Each member later described feeling confused, disso-ciated, unable to distinguish who was who in the presentation, and unable to hold on to the thread. We found it hard to know who was who in the narrative, whether Dee was referring to herself, her supervisee, even the patient or the patient's mother. There was no feeling of a central character with a central, lively core. The fragmented and fragmenting inner world of this adolescent got inside each one of us. Her confusion, dulled state of mind, depressed feel, and "switched-offness" often filled the room and the individual experience of each of us. As a group we grad-ually became able to explore the experiences of fragmentation and dead-ening switched-offness that overcame us in relation to the material; a similar fragmentation to that experienced by Kay, the patient, and in turn by Eleanor, as she sought to work with her patient, was also occurring in our experience of the material. We became aware of this as we each struggled with our own inability to think and make links in the material that was being presented to us.

For several weeks Eleanor struggled to establish the frame with this acting-out adolescent. The initial struggle had centered around whether Kay would come at all (which matched Eleanor's own anxieties around her ability to hold onto her patient), which—as Eleanor gradually became aware—mirrored Kay's own, much greater, anxieties about being able to hold onto and be contained by the therapy. There was also a struggle over just who would come to a session. If Kay did come, would her mother come with her, or her sister, or her boyfriend, or a friend? Eleanor struggled with just how she would manage to establish a twosome, as a third seemed ever-present. At first it was just as simple and as difficult as establishing that the session was just for the two of them. This acting-out we gradually understood represented Kay's experience of her family, at this particular stage in her development, which was domi-nated by her reexperiencing of Oedipal conflicts. Who was Dad? Did she have a birthday, an existence, an identity? If she tried to see her dad, who would he be with? Would she get to see him? What sort of adjustments would she have to make in order to retain even the most tenuous of rela-tionships with him?

The overall experience for the therapist and those involved in the supervisory process of this particular patient was of a consistent affective empathic experience of very primitive, defensively underaroused states of mind. Such an understanding of what occurs in the supervisory process gives a sound foundation for our understanding of transference and countertransference as emanating from the realm of the implicit and arising from the very earliest experiences of life. I understand the therapist's, and in turn the supervisor's, dawning awareness of unspoken communications from the patient as "empathic intuition" (Zanocco et al., 2006, p. 148).

Such awareness concerns primitive elements of experience that have not yet come into mind and become nameable for the patient. In my illustration the empathic power of these affects can be seen reaching out through the therapist to the supervisor and into the experience of the supervisory group as the group members encounter these primitive elements in the experience of the supervisor and in their experience as the material is being presented. Often awareness of these elements came through the bodily experiences of the group members, through tone of voice and conscious and unconscious modes of interchange, as they discussed the material that was being presented. Mathew (1998) comments that the body may be understood as the instrument of physical processes, an instrument that can hear, see, touch, and smell the world around us and that can tune into the psyche and search into its darkness for meaning.

It becomes clear from these imaginary extracts that the group found it difficult to get hold of even the simplest dynamics of Kay's relationships, and that this experience reflected Kay's limited capacity for mentalization. Zanocco et al. (2006) describe such experience, in turn, as "a part of the ego [that] has retained a primitive way of functioning" (p. 150). It was just such functioning that Kay was bringing to her session, that was then being experienced by the individual members of the group and the group as a whole as a struggle for any sort of coherent understanding that could be felt and then thought about.

Hidden Hazards of the Supervisory Relationship

Material that arises in the work, especially in work concerned with early relational trauma, may be sufficient to unsettle the internal world of either member of the supervisory dyad, especially if either is unduly stressed by trauma in his or her current circumstances. For example, a supervisor or supervisee whose early attachment style happened to be avoidant, and who is suddenly overtaken by severe emotional distress arising from a close personal relationship, may be thrown back from the acquired stance of learned security into the earlier mode of being and will seek to ignore and avoid the needy baby part of the patient that actually needs to be held and contained through the supervisory process.

An important boundary for the supervisor to be able to hold internally is the most fundamental one: It is the supervisee's patient, and the supervisee is the one who is doing the work. To stay in a "hands-off," enabling way of being may become most difficult when one begins to feel anxiety, envy, or anger. These feelings may be felt because the supervisor's own psyche is the problem, and unconscious emotion needs to be processed. Knight (2003) raises the issue of the supervisor's unconscious transferences to the supervisee and cites Stimmel's view that parallel processes in supervision provide opportunity for the enactment of, and resistance to, the awareness of such transferences (as cited in Knight, 2003). On the other hand, it may be a case of the supervisor's countertransference giving clues, for example, about the anxiety of either patient or supervisee.

There are several related boundary dangers to which the unwary would-be supervisor may succumb. Issues concerning boundaries will always form an integral part of supervision of work with patients whose boundaries have not been respected, and in the case of earliest relational trauma may not have been established adequately. The first is what I tend to think of as red-pen supervision. A colleague once described an experience in which he had felt that his supervisor was like a teacher who underlined every mistake and told him exactly what should have been said or not said. The supervisee eventually felt able to say, "Well, no doubt that is what would have happened if X was in therapy with you, and indeed she might do better, but she is actually in therapy with me." The supervisor looked startled, something shifted, and haltingly they found their way to a more fruitful experience. Of course, not every supervisee is able to be so clear about the boundary issue, and not all such situations will have the good outcome that occurred in this example.

Another danger takes the form of what Fiscalini has termed "analysis by ventriloquism" (as cited in Astor, 2003, p. 52). Astor suggests that in these instances the supervisor may be privileging the patient's unconscious over the supervisee's understanding, a hazard that arises out of the automatic mirroring and resonance processes that occur in the supervisory dyad's shared experience. This may well be the case or it may be that the supervisee, under the stress of such supervision, is functioning out of an adaptive false self, rather than working creatively from within. Such a way of being in the supervisee will have been learned in the earliest relationship to a parent who is predominantly self-aware and who is unable to fully allow the child the chance to find him- or herself. This dynamic may be more likely to emerge in supervision if the supervisor temporarily loses sight of the real person actually in the room with him or her. This response, of course, inevitably mirrors the abusive experience of the trauma patient who has not be seen and valued as a person but rather abused and shamed.

A further difficulty is highlighted by Mander (2002), who explores the concept of cloning, arguing that the supervisor must take care to avoid the danger of cloning that may occur "particularly when working with an impressionable, perhaps idealising supervisee" (p. 43). She comments:

> There is a fine line between influence and control and it is easily crossed, when the *furor didacticus* possesses the supervisor, perhaps in response to something in the clinical material which exerts a particular fascination and invites expansive analysing in the context of theory. . . . Equally difficult is the curbing of expectations, whether positive or negative, which, as with parents and children, can do much harm when the recipient is in a dependent relationship and then resorts to pleasing. (p. 43)

The Ethical Attitude in Supervision

Using supervision appropriately has long been seen as one aspect of adopting an ethical attitude concerning clinical work. Solomon (2007) has explored at length the origins of the ethical attitude from a developmental and attachment perspective. She understands the ethical function as a relational function involving the assessment of subjective and intersubjective states involved in self–other relationships. I am reminded of De Laurentis' (1966) view that individual subjectivity consists of the "patterns by which experiential and emotional contexts, feelings, images and memories are organized to form one's self-image, one's sense of self and others" (p. 5). The arrival at such a capacity, as Solomon (2007) understands the ethical function to be, involves a developmental achievement that is fostered by the initial empathic response of the mother to her baby and then develops through the quality of relationships that comprises the world of the healthy toddler.

The Neurobiological Substrates of the Ethical Attitude

Panksepp (1998) affirms that emotions are learned states which develop out of our earliest experience of relationship. Narvaez (2008) concludes that "the emotional circuitry established early in life relates to the brain's architecture for morality and later ethical expression" (p. 97). She posits three distinctive moral systems which are based on three brain areas. The first and most primitive is security, which she relates to primitive survival strategies arising from activity in the oldest brain structures described as the reptilian brain. Engagement is the second, which she understands as arising from the limbic or emotional or intuitive brain, and which enables the intuitive aspects of empathy, rooted in "the mammalian systems that drive us towards intimacy, such as *play, panic* and *care*" (p. 100, emphasis in the original).

Schore (1994) points out that, around 18 months, the parasympathetic nervous system begins to provide the decrease in arousal and excitement that makes socialization possible and that enables the development of "the neural substrate of shame." He argues that this is achieved through "socialization stress-induced, experience-dependent, structural transformation (rewiring) of the orbitofrontal cortex" and suggests that this enables the development of the "braking mechanism of shame" (p. 343). It may be argued that just as experience in the second year of life leads the child from a dyadic way of relating into triadic experiences, so the empathic third who is the supervisor helps to counterbalance the intensity of the experience within the therapeutic dyad and enables the development of greater insight and understanding. A capacity for separation and autonomy lays the groundwork for a capacity to behave ethically in relation to another. Many of the ethical problems that arise in therapy develop when some part of a person is not able to function in the "separate but aware of the other" way of being that characterizes the development of full agency.

The regulatory aspects of the parasympathetic nervous system arise from the regulation brought about through our earliest attachments. Narvaez (2008) notes that this occurs "in part via the regulation of the cardiac vagal tone, upon which emotional, behavioral and motor regulation are dependent" and explains that "the parasympathetic nervous system regulates cardio output through vagal tone under environmental stress" and that "responsive parenting with co-regulated communication patters leads to good vagal tone whereas nonresponsive parenting leads to poor vagal tone" (p.102). She adds that good early experience also leads to the development of healthy neuroendocrine functioning which inhibits defensive behaviors and enables "positive social interactions and the development of social bonds" (p. 102).

The last aspect of the ethical attitude that Narvaez proposes is that of imagination. She understands the capacity for this as arising from the neomammalian brain, stressing the importance of the frontal lobes, especially the prefrontal cortex. By imagination she means the capacity for free choice in ambiguous situations, the capacity for original and creative thought in relation to moral dilemmas, the capacity for fairness-related behaviors which she attributes to the dorsal lateral prefrontal cortex. She notes that damage to the prefrontal cortex "leads to poor impulse control, dysregulation of emotion and an inability to foresee consequences" (p.104). Although much of our ethical response is unconscious and intuitive, the prefrontal cortex, with its capacity for reasoned judgment may override the instinctual and the intuitive but may also listen to the needs for security and engagement as well. In supervising a therapist who is working with profoundly dysregulated patients such qualities are vital in the supervisor if he or she is to hold and contain the anxieties that may arise in the therapist in relation to the patient and in relation to those who may have responsibility for assessing his or her work, especially when the supervisee is working towards qualification with a training institution. The supervisory encounter itself is often appropriately opened to others—for example, in response to training institutions' or employers' requirements for reporting for the purposes of assessment and appraisal, or in the case of a supervision group, for assessment of the individual group members. Left-brain-dominated assessment and appraisal seems to increase in a world that moves inexorably toward the performative society. Ball (2001) warns that "performativity is a technology, a culture and a mode of regulation . . . that employs judgements, comparisons and displays as means of control, attrition and change" (p. 210). He argues that seeming transparency may actually lead to resistance and opacity and that continuous exposure to assessment can become a recipe for ontological insecurity. He highlights ethical dangers that lie in wait and cautions that "there is a real possibility that authentic social relations are replaced by judgemental relations" and "concern for patient need and professional judgement [are replaced] with commercial decision-making" (pp. 214, 223).

An ethical attitude toward our supervisee constitutes a form of boundary holding and enables the provision of a safe and reliable container that will facilitate, in turn, the supervisee's provision of just such a safe container for the patient. Martin (2002) discusses the question of theft in supervision; "Possibly the most insidious form of supervisory theft is the theft of the safe container" (p. 122), which often occurs when supervision is taken less seriously than therapy. He gives examples of failure to keep proper boundaries with regard to time, telephone-call answering, and many other infringements of normal analytic practice. In another paper he comments:

> If supervisors are tempted to offer "strawberries and cream" symbolically or literally (coffee and biscuits and the chance to gossip), or alternatively, "sour cream" (changes of room, time, a different fee structure, the establishment of a relationship that is more than a working alliance) then . . . they may be warning signals that ethical boundaries are in danger of being breached. (Martin, 2003, p. 150)

An ethical stance is sought for all aspects of therapy. After all, we guarantee to provide regular sessions that begin and end on time, to provide continuity of time, space, and environment. We seek to provide a room that is not overstimulating, that is containing and protected from intrusion. Within the analytic frame we respect confidentiality and aim to work in a way that facilitates trust. We seek to behave in an absolutely predictable way around management of breaks, holidays, and fees. The supervisee may learn a great deal about the patient's transference to him or her at any given moment in the therapy from any and all of these. In short, we regard boundaries as having an essential part to play in the therapy itself and as one of the ways in which the ethical qualities of the analytic relationship can be maintained.

Temperley (1984) notes the difference in her experience of working at the Tavistock Institute in London, where a colleague would have hesitated to knock on a door with an engaged sign even if it were to announce that the building was on fire, with her experience of working in a general practice surgery, where the receptionist walked in to access notes that were in the room, who couldn't understand why the two, who were "only talking" while the patient was fully dressed, should not be interrupted. From this experience of a senior colleague, we can easily imagine how difficult it can be for the inexperienced counselor or therapist to maintain the analytic frame. For example, a patient being seen in a voluntary center confronted the therapist on every aspect of the frame, from who answered the door onward. This supervisee struggled but was able to hold this very borderline patient in therapy with the containment provided by regular supervision. She was particularly fortunate in that she was able to increase the number of sessions for the patient and, through the greater frequency of meetings, the patient gradually became able to gain and hold down a job and to make use of the therapy in a way that enhanced her quality of life.

Conclusion

It is clear that supervision requires multitasking of extreme complexity, yet when done well it is often characterized by a simple sense of being at ease in a holding relationship while being deeply engaged in a meaningful task together. Schore and Schore's (2008) words concerning clinical effectiveness in therapy are equally apposite concerning supervision:

> Clinical efficacy is more than explicit left hemispheric technical skill in interpretation. Rather, increasing levels of clinical effectiveness . . . involves more complex learning of a number of nonconscious functions of the therapist's right brain . . . the ability to receive and express nonverbal affective communications; clinical sensitivity; use of subjectivity/intersubjectivity; empathy; and affect regulation. (p. 16)

10

Conclusion:
The Way Forward

I CLOSE AS I BEGAN, by musing again with Ian McEwan's (2006) character of Henry Perowne:

> A man who attempts to ease the miseries of failing minds . . . is bound to respect the material world, its limits, and what it can sustain—consciousness no less . . . the mind is what the brain, mere matter, performs. If that's worthy of awe, it also deserves curiosity; the actual, not the magical, should be the challenge. (from *Saturday* by Ian McEwan, published by Jonathan Cape. Reprinted by permission of The Random House Group Ltd., p. 67)

Those of us who engage with minds that have become unduly stressed also need great curiosity if we are to assist others who seek to explore their intra- and interpsychic subjectivity. It is a curiosity that is now presented with a plethora of sources of satisfaction as research into attachment, trauma, and the neurobiology of emotion burgeons.

As I was writing this final chapter, thinking about the many sources of information and how they might integrate with any one of the traditional schools of psychodynamic therapy, I dreamt the following dream.

I was visiting a country house that belongs to very close friends of mine, Sally and Alan. It is a very old and beautiful thatched cottage that has been carefully restored and modernized in a way that is in keeping with its original features. As one goes in the front door the large kitchen is off to the right down a few steps. On the left is the dining room, so often a hub of conversation and discussion of ideas. As my dream opened,

I was in the kitchen with a large group of seemingly rather distinguished guests. All were busy preparing their favourite soup, using tried and trusted recipes. Then Alan entered the kitchen carrying a very large pan with some new ingredients in it, which he set on the kitchen range. He carefully began to mix and blend quantities of the other soups into this, tasting as he went along to ensure that he had just the right mix to produce just the right flavor. When all was ready, we trooped out of the kitchen up a beautiful traditional dark oak staircase to the dining room, which in my dream had moved to the left at the top of the stairs. Some of the guests were still clutching the spoon they had been using to taste their favorite old soup.

The scene changed and I was sitting in the middle of one side of a long oak dining table. All the guests were sitting around the table, Alan was just across from me, and the old inglenook fireplace was just behind him. I thought the room had a rather Jacobean feel to it. Some people had chosen to bring the soup of their own old original recipe in the spoons they had brought with them from the kitchen, wanting at that moment only to conserve the soup with the old, familiar, much loved taste. Naturally with this already in their spoons, they found it difficult to taste the new flavor. A tall distinguished man, who reminded me of a very well respected American psychoanalyst who has blended the old established psychoanalytic teaching with the new insights from affective neuroscience, asked for a clean spoon. Alan brought fresh silver soup spoons, and several people took one and more readily began to appreciate the new flavor that had been mixed, blending the best of the old with the new ingredients that Alan had added.

As I woke and thought about the dream, I realized almost instantly that Alan, a much valued friend and the master chef of my dream who blended the old with the new with such care, stood for Allan Schore, who has made such an outstanding contribution to the consideration of how minds are changed in therapy by blending together for us the best of affective neuroscience, attachment theory, infant research, evolutionary psychology, and ethology—just as, in my dream, the new is blended with the old to produce something of outstanding worth, both in renovation of the house itself and in the delicious soup that has been concocted.

We very much need a theory and practice where the best of the old is conserved yet where the new can be integrated and used, just as in my dream. We need to go into the creative kitchen on the right—that is, to discover the riches of the right hemisphere that can then be taken and tasted, thought about, in the upstairs dining room that is the information-processing center of the left cerebral cortex. As in my dream it is in a sense a Jacobean atmosphere we wish to prevail, if by Jacobean one understands an atmosphere of enlightenment, of grounding ideas in the best experimental science of the day. The dream also warns that those who cling only to the old familiar soup, the old familiar ideas, may miss the new flavor that is made possible by the use of new ingredients, supped from a new spoon, ingredients that have now become available to us.

Psychodynamic psychotherapy stands at the interface of what might be termed the cognitive–affective divide. Traditionally this school of therapy has emphasized words, interpretations, and the changing of cognitions; currently we have come to a greater appreciation of the affective, relational aspects of our work and the way in which they relate to the early right-brained experience of the child in relation to the primary caregiver. Like so much in life, it is not a case of *either/or* but *both–and*. It is the capacity for integration and interconnectivity, both within and without, that gives rise to a mature mind. Regarding research, Panksepp (2003) warns against what he terms "cognitive imperialism" and argues that "if affective organic processes, ancient adaptive solutions that they are in brain evolution, are to a substantial degree distinct from those that mediate cognitive deliberation . . . then we must develop special strategies to understand them in neural terms" (p. 6). In effect, Panksepp rejects approaches that merely apply cognitive "information-only strategies" to research concerning affect, concluding that "emotions are not simply informationally encapsulated brain processes as some cognitively-oriented investigators seem to believe." He adds, "to succeed in this journey we must cultivate deep neuro-evolutionary points of view" (p. 12).

Not only does current thinking make clear that psychotherapy stands at the crossroads between the affective and the cognitive, it also directs our attention to the mind–body continuum, especially where trauma is concerned, in stark contrast to earlier practice, which seems to have envisaged a chasm between mind and body, in keeping with the old Cartesian dualism that dominated thought and practice. Sinason (2006) argues that in the past "to cope with the privileged access to the mind of the client a split has been made that excludes the body" (p. 51). Recent large-scale studies of the effects of adverse childhood experiences on later health in the United States and the United Kingdom (Felitti et al., 1998), involving more than 17,000 patients, identified a significantly increased risk of developing serious organic diseases, including cancer, heart disease, asthma, diabetes, and chronic obstructive pulmonary disease. Kendall-Tackett and Klest (2009) point out that trauma gives rise to health problems along five possible pathways: (1) physiological—affecting the catecholamine system, the hypothalamus–pituitary–adrenal (HPA) axis, and the regulation of cortisol and the immune system; (2) behavioral—high-risk behaviors may ensue; (3) social—affecting the capacity for successful relating; (4) emotional—leading to depression, anxiety, and PTSD; and (5) cognitive—via "hostility—or framing the world as a dangerous place" (p. 132). They note that just as trauma affects health adversely, so poor health can reactivate the symptoms of trauma, such as flashbacks and dissociative symptoms. Haven (2009) concludes: "It is not enough, and is actually misguided, to focus exclusively on the cognitive and emotional meaning of the experience. . . . Past traumatic experiences . . . imprinted in the deeper regions of the brain that are only marginally affected by thinking and emotion . . . are embodied in current physiological states and sensations" (p. 216). The way forward in treatment must incorporate a holistic approach.

A major concern in this book has been to explore the nature and role of empathy in the therapeutic encounter. M. L. Miller (2008) offers a significant review of the psychoanalytic literature concerning this and concludes that the emotional participation of the therapist has become the major focus in recent years. He stresses the relevance of a dynamic systems theory approach to understanding emotion, noting that emotions are self-organizing products of psychological and physiological processes that arise out of interpersonal experience. In so doing he rejects a solely cognitive appraisal approach, which stresses arousal and cognitive response to arousal and understands emotions as "an ever-present, constantly changing set of processes that influence and are influenced by the social context within which they occur" (p. 15). He understands all social interaction, including therapy, as a process "coordinating emotional-adaptive responses between participants to a social interaction [which] occurs automatically, nonconsciously, and continuously" (p. 17). Three systems, the subcortical arousal system, the cortical interpretive system, and the motor system, mutually regulate each other in response to the social environment. Miller emphasizes that "emotional processes, like all dynamic systems, have a tendency to settle into a finite number of stable patterns" (p. 16). It is these established patterns in both patient and analyst that affect the dynamics of the emotional experience within the dyad and produce change. The ventromedial prefrontal cortex, located at the interface of the cortex and subcortex, enables the necessary mind–body connections and permits emotional regulation.

Miller concludes that "dynamic systems theory casts emotion in a truly interactive context, enabling analysts to appreciate the co-constructed nature not only of the meanings attributed to the analytic interaction but also of their own and the patient's emotional states as well" (p. 20).

Although stressing his own view as one in which the emotional engagement of the therapist is paramount in therapy, M. L. Miller (2008) nevertheless voices the concerns of some who have suggested that an analyst's emotional engagement in therapy with a patient may be "an expression of the analyst's unconscious emotional conflicts" or may lead to "a traumatic reification of the patient's unconscious fantasies and fears" (p. 4). What also needs to be acknowledged is that the converse may be equally likely to be true: The disengaged, distant, abstinent therapist may be adopting that style of working because of his or her own unconscious conflicts, and it may just as likely lead to a reification of the patient's unconscious fantasies and fears. Indeed, it could be argued that the use of silence, in particular, can be extremely persecutory for the patient, as it allows so much space for persecutory fantasy and fear to flood into the room and into the relationship. Such difficulties can be guarded against only by adequate self-understanding on the part of the therapist, most fruitfully achieved through the therapist's own personal therapy, reflection, and supervision.

The field of epigenetics, which studies the effects of environmental experience on genetic expression, is yielding much information that may encourage a more proactive approach to those who have experienced early relational trauma. Inheritance and experience both play vital roles, and "parental care is revealed as a critical agent of natural selection that influences the stabilization or elimination of corticolimbic connections" in early childhood (Bradshaw & Schore, 2007, p. 429). Boes et al. (2008) suggest decreased volume in the right ventromedial prefrontal cortex as a cause of heightened impulsivity in boys and pose a host of questions that arise from the possibility of identifying neural "endophenotypes" for impulse control.

> How does one's environment interact with susceptibility genes to impact brain development in this circuit? Can therapeutic intervention be optimized if tailored to one's unique genetic vulnerability? Will biological markers of vulnerability someday be utilized to initiate preventative efforts for high-risk individuals? (p. 7)

Panksepp (1998) makes clear that maternal behavior during early childhood (e.g., rat mothers licking their pups or sea otter mothers providing for their pups) has a profound effect on the epigenetic marks on specific genes and on behavior in ways that are sustained throughout life.

In humans the earliest environments, both prenatal and postnatal, have been shown to have a profound effect on gene expression. This, in turn, has implications for our understanding of patients who have experienced early childhood trauma. A study by McGowan et al. (2009) compared a particular aspect of hippocampal gene expression (NR3C1) in brain tissue samples from suicide victims with a history of childhood abuse with samples from two control groups—victims of sudden, accidental death, and those who had committed suicide but who had no history of abuse. They found no differences in glucocorticoid receptor expression between suicide victims without a history of childhood abuse and controls, but found that this particular aspect of hippocampal gene expression was decreased in samples from those who had experienced childhood abuse. Their research indicates that "changes in glucocorticoid receptor expression are closely associated with a developmental history of familial adversity, in this case a history of childhood abuse, rather than with suicide completion" (p. 4). The researchers stress that these results, which are in keeping with earlier studies in which childhood abuse in humans and disruptions in mother–infant interactions in rodents and nonhuman primates were linked to an increase in pituitary adrenocorticotropic hormone (ACTH) responses to stress. (See Chapter 2 and the work of Shin et al., 2006, and Teicher et al., 2006, for a fuller discussion of this point.) McGowan et al. conclude that "pituitary ACTH directly reflects central activation of the HPA stress response and hippocampal glucocorticoid receptor activation dampens HPA activity" (p. 4). Stress inevitably results in symptoms that may bring the patient in search of help. Regulation of arousal levels brought about by stress becomes a central feature of work with this group. Body therapy, sensorimotor therapy, and bodily relaxation techniques have a significant part to play in the achievement of stress regulation. Psychotherapy work that focuses on affect regulation within the context of a secure relationship with the therapist will provide a different learning experience and, if underpinned by real affective engagement, will enable patients to manage their stress levels more efficiently as well as work toward some modification of their stress responses.

Panksepp (2003) encourages us to make "the evolutionary working-assumption that internally experienced affects are universal capacities of brains in all mammals" (p. 5). From a similar neuroethological stance Bradshaw and Schore (2007) emphasize the importance of early attachment and social learning and the far-reaching effects of poor early experience. They explore the abnormal behavior of the wild African elephants; these elephants have been affected by changes that led to infants "largely being reared by inexperienced, highly stressed single mothers" instead of the more traditional extended matriarchal elephant society. They note that such an upbringing impairs normative and socially mediated neuroendocrinological development and causes psychobiological dysregulation, which, if experienced "during critical periods of infant female brain growth[,] alters the developmental trajectory of successive generations." They note that new data from brain imaging, along with an understanding that "cortical and limbic structures responsible for processing and controlling emotional and social information . . . are all highly conserved evolutionarily across species," lead inevitably toward "species-inclusive models" and the emergence of "trans-species models of brain and behavior" (pp. 427–428). Such trans-species models of brain and behavior will inevitably encompass the transgenerational transmission of trauma. Changing minds in therapy will inevitably seek to break the chain by enabling patients first to experience and then to explore different ways of relating that enable affect regulation, rather than dysregulation, for them and, in turn, for their offspring. It also behooves professionals to identify as early as possible those babies and young children most at risk, and governments to have training, funding, and provision of parent–infant psychotherapy as priorities.

Turning specifically to the field of imaging, one can claim, without doubt, that it has transformed research in the field of mind–brain–body relationships. Used in conjunction with knowledge drawn from work concerning neural activity in monkeys and other species, fMRI offers the best possibility of exploring information processing in the human brain. Newer techniques are also being used to complement the findings of fMRI research. Diffusion tensor imaging, a new form of MRI, is being used to explore the axon tracts that connect regions in the human brain. Transcranial magnetic stimulation (TMS) is being used to explore whether links between a brain region and a particular behavior identified by fMRI hold true. When neural activity in a particular region is disrupted by the use of TMS, then the behavior, thought to be associated with that region on the basis of fMRI, will also be affected (G. Miller, 2008).

Of course there are limitations. Logothetis (2008) has given a masterly summary of both the strengths and weaknesses of research using fMRI. He stresses the huge amount of research that is being conducted and notes that somewhere in the region of eight papers per day have been produced in recent years. As to its value as a research tool, he asserts:

> fMRI is not and will never be a mind reader, as some of the proponents of decoding-based methods suggest, nor is it a worthless and non-informative "neophrenology" that is condemned to fail, as has been occasionally argued. Perhaps the extreme positions on both sides result from a poor understanding of the actual capacities and limitations of this technology, as well as, frequently, a confusion between fMRI shortcomings and potential flaws in modelling the organizational principles of the faculties under investigation. (p. 869)

Watt (2005) also makes several points concerning the limitations of the use of fMRI for research purposes:

- It tends to "minimally accent ventral brain areas" (p. 191).
- It produces "correlative pictures with uncertain causal connections" (p. 192).
- Emphasis on very small hot spots may be misleading and ignore the reality of "widespread and highly distributed networks in which many structures may be variably activated or inhibited, some more so than others" (p. 193).
- Studies "typically gloss over individual variations, often quite large."

Logothetis argues that, nevertheless, fMRI is the most important discovery since the X-ray and a powerful tool at our disposal, if used appropriately, for "gaining insights into brain function and formulating interesting and eventually testable hypotheses, even though the plausibility of these hypotheses critically depends on used magnetic resonance technology, experimental protocol, statistical analysis and insightful modeling" (p. 876).

From our profession's particular point of view we must also realize that time frames involved in fMRI studies are vastly different from the time frames of therapy. Modell (2005) notes the difficulty that occurs in attempts to incorporate and directly transfer information regarding emotions and feelings derived from an experimental context, such as fMRI scanning or PET imaging, into the knowledge base generated from psychoanalysis. He observes that "it is essentially a problem of the very different contexts in which feelings are experienced, and feelings are very sensitive to the context of the environmental surround" (p. 37). He further notes that "we must be mindful of the fact that named feelings and their neural correlates evoked in the context of the controlled conditions of a laboratory experiment may or may not be identical to comparable feelings evoked during a psychoanalytic session" (pp. 37–38). Others highlight the dangers of false positives and the complexities of accurate interpretation of information gained from scanning. Miller (G. Miller, 2008) notes Aron's suggestion that information accessed from fMRI should be used as "one tool in a toolbox, as a way of testing hypotheses where you have converging techniques and evidence" (p. 1414).

With all these caveats in mind, research based on imaging techniques nevertheless provides rich material for the therapist to explore in relation to clinical work, especially when used in conjunction with the complementary insights emerging from research in the fields of attachment and trauma. How links are made between these fields regarding the making of mind and how insights are used is an area that careful research, rather than speculation, will reward. In the process of changing minds, of course, our minds as therapists are also changed. While much attention is now being directed to the scanning of particular patient groups, there is also fruitful territory for research in the exploration of the effects of the therapeutic process on the mind of the therapist, particularly when there is a high risk of secondary traumatization.

I suggest that an interdisciplinary approach that values the insights from the fathers of psychoanalysis alongside insights from attachment research, parent–infant psychotherapy research, and the neurobiology of emotion should no longer be considered an optional "extra" in the world of psychotherapy for a few to pursue as a special interest. Our training venues must now embrace an interdisciplinary approach rather than shy away from one, or use it merely to bolster up outdated scientific concepts in an artificial way. Strachey (1950) notes that in 1895 Freud was at the frontier of brain science with his discovery of what he termed "contact barriers" and which Sherrington (1906) later named "synapses." Jung (1946a) pointed out that "natural science combines two worlds, the physical and the psychic, [and that] psychology does this *only in so far as it is psychophysiology*" (par. 162, emphasis in original). In the discussion that followed Jung's Second Tavistock Lecture, Bion asked Jung whether he thought there was a connection between mind and brain. Jung replied: "The psychic fact and the physiological fact come together in a peculiar way . . . We see them as two on account of the utter incapacity of our mind to think them together" (Jung, 1935, par. 135–136).

Although it can be argued cogently on the basis of empirical evidence that neuroimaging and lesion studies now make crystal clear the neural basis for theory of mind (Hirao, Miyata, et al., 2008), sadly, to a certain extent, Fonagy's (2003) argument that failure of analytic theory as a scientific theory has resulted in a failure to link theory to practice in a creative way still holds. It behooves us as a profession to seek to use the new knowledge available to us so that our discipline may truly come of age and prove even more beneficial to our patients.

Freud himself recognized this need in his own day. He observed that "a scheme of training for analysis has still to be created. It must include elements from the mental sciences, from psychology, the history of civilization and sociology, as well as from anatomy, biology, and the study of evolution" (Freud, 1959, p. 252). Many of our trainings still fall far short of Freud's breadth of vision. In arguing the importance of neurobiological teaching to underpin training, both in dynamic psychotherapy and psychiatry, to address this shortcoming, Lacy and Hughes (2006) suggest of such an approach that "rather than an attempt to justify a belief or theory, it is the establishment of core concepts that inform psychological reasoning and understanding" (p. 47). Whitehead (2006) argues that "our problem is now the true integration of two *complementary* scientific disciplines" (pp. 609–610, emphasis in the original).

The clinical process of changing minds in therapy is the central concern of this book. Emde (1999) observes that we need to "give more theoretical and empirical attention to questions regarding what kinds of emotional availability are appropriate within the professionally guarded psychoanalytic situation." He points out that "this may or may not lead to changes in technique with consequences for outcomes that can be studied" (p. 330). The positive affective aspects of intersubjective relations, rather than interpretation, appear to impact most effectively on the patient's store of implicit memories (Andrade, 2005). Research indicates that healthy interaction with others results in "increased metabolic activity, mRNA synthesis, and neural growth" and that "relationships can create an internal biological environment, supportive of neural plasticity" (Cozolino, 2006, p. 299). We have noted the effects of trauma as hypervigilance and heightened activity in the HPA axis, heightened sensitivity of the amygdala, damage to the hippocampus, and failure to develop adequate inhibitory cortical controls. However, brain plasticity and affective engagement with the therapist hold out hope for change. Such a perspective is endorsed by the body of research that points to the quality of the relationship rather than the theoretical orientation of the therapist as the effective agent for change.

In closing I would like to return to the meaning-making process at work in the clinical setting. I have been fortunate to have some patients who have chosen to express some of their trauma narrative so vividly in artwork, and I wish to thank them for their generosity in sharing these images with us. These patients have seemed unconsciously compelled to explore as yet unrecognized early trauma through the making of these visual images. Only on later reflection does the symbolic meaning become apparent. The making of such pictures indicates the dawning of the ability to move from the concrete acting-out of old trauma through the transference to a more symbolic way of experiencing. When the pictures are brought to therapy and the patient begins to talk about them, the shift from the visual to the linguistic heralds a new capacity for symbolization. It is this capacity to integrate early right-hemisphere traumatic experience, which often emerges in visual fragments, with the later developing left-hemisphere capacities that marks recovery. The shift from the visual to the linguistic that occurs not only explains why the "talking cure" has been so highly valued but also acknowledges the need for trauma to emerge from the implicit into a realm where it can be initially experienced, in this case by looking at it, and subsequently be thought about so that it can move from the "here and now" to the "there and then." Toward the close of her therapy Holly made a collage, which she then used to describe how she had come to feel about the therapeutic process (Figure 10.1). This last picture of Holly's is an extended metaphor of her experience of herself and her experience in analysis. It is rich in symbolism associated with the self. The picture, painted in glowing colors, is of a glacial, alpine lake surrounded by dark peaks under a vivid azure-blue sky. Deep in the water are hidden treasures made out of sparkling, jewel-colored sequins, stars, and glitter. Holly talked freely and easily about the picture; this was in such marked contrast to her earlier difficulties in voicing her inner world. She felt that she and I were like the two swimmers in the picture who were diving into an alpine lake to find the treasures that were in it. Tall dark mountain peaks surrounded the lake, reminiscent of the rocks that she so feared on her first visit; they spoke to her of teeth and the biting, death-dealing anger that she associated with her mother and had feared to explore in herself and in me. The glacial alpine water reminded me of the appalling chill accompanying her attachment losses, which she so feared she would experience again with me. She continued:

> I like the sheep standing near the water and in the distance. Sheep are such timid animals, and these are me; they suggest something of my feeling of fear in letting what I want to be seen. The figures struggling up the sides of the mountains are me too, on a difficult journey and not yet able to reach the water with all it can hold. There are two fishes swimming in front of the two people. They seem involved—perhaps they are like guides for us in the watery environment, perhaps they just want to be with us.

I was reminded of Jung's view of the fish as a symbol for the self. Holly continued:

> There are streams of bubbles coming from the swimmers. They are breath, oxygen, giving life and strength and endurance so that the swimmers can spend time exploring together. You said, "The picture perhaps is telling us about the journey of therapy." It's right, I have found many treasures in therapy, and the feeling of attachment is the most beautiful.

Holly's words reminded me of van der Hart, Nijenhuis, and Steele's (2006) remark that "overcoming the phobia of intimacy is perhaps the pinnacle of successful treatment" (p. 18). What was noticeable for me in the picture was that the two of us were separate, yet companionably engaged in a worthwhile and enjoyable activity, albeit with the element of challenge and uncertainty that is inherent in life. It seemed that the picture reflected Holly's approaching arrival at what Orbach (2007) has termed a "separated attachment," an attachment style characterized by connected autonomy. The making, bringing, and discussion of this picture, representative of the symbolic work that is the stuff of analysis, made crystal clear that it was the relational experience in therapy that enabled change to take place in Holly. It is this that assists the integration of activity throughout the right hemisphere and between the hemispheres of the patient's mind–brain and which then permits the development of the individual mind and of healthy attachment.

Gambini (2007) says of Jung: "He followed the silk thread that united the physical and the psychic, he fought to envisage the unity that underlies perceptible diversities and dualities" (p. 364). It is that same silk thread that we must follow as we seek to bring the best of 21st-century thinking and research to bear upon the process of changing minds in therapy.

References

Addis, D. R., Wong, A. T., & Schacter, D. L. (2007). Remembering the past and imagining the future, Common and distinct neural substrates during event construction and elaboration. *Neuropsychologia, 45*, 1363–1377.

Allen, J. G., & Coyne, L. (1995). Dissociation and vulnerability to psychotic experience: The Dissociative Experiences Scale and the MMPI–2. *Journal of Nervous and Mental Disease, 183*, 615–622.

Alvarez, A. (2006). Some questions concerning states of fragmentation, unintegration, under-integration, disintegration, and the nature of early integrations. *Journal of Child Psychotherapy, 32*, 158–180.

American Psychiatric Association (1994). *Diagnostic and statistical manual of mental disorders* (4th ed.). Washington, DC: Author.

American Psychological Association Presidential Task Force on Evidenced-Based Practice. (2006). Evidence-based practice in psychology. *American Psychologist, 61*(4), 271–285.

Andersen, S. L., & Teicher, M. H. (2004). Delayed effects of early stress on hippocampal development. *Neuropsychopharmacology, 29*(11), 1988–1993.

Andrade, V. M. (2005). Affect and the therapeutic action of psychoanalysis. *International Journal of Psychoanalysis, 86*, 677–697.

Astor, J. (2003). Empathy in use of countertransference. In Wiener, J., R. Mizen, and J. Duckham. *Supervising and being supervised: A practice in search of a theory* (pp. 49, 64). New York: Palgrave Macmillan.

Atchley, R. A., Stringer, R., Mathias, E., Ilardi, S. S., & Minatrea, A. D. (2007). The right hemisphere's contribution to emotional word-processing in currently depressed, remitted depressed, and never depressed individuals. *Journal of Neurolinguistics, 20*, 145–160.

Badenoch, B. (2008). *Being a brain-wise therapist. A practical guide to interpersonal neurobiology.* New York: Norton.

Balint, M. (1968). *The basic fault: Therapeutic aspects of regression.* London: Tavistock.

Ball, S. (2001). Performativities and fabrications in the education economy: Towards the performative society. In D. Gleeson & C. Husbands, *The performing school: Managing teaching and learning in a performance culture* (pp. 160–182). London & New York: Routledge.

Baron-Cohen, S., Wheelwright, S., Hill, J., Raste, Y., & Plumb, I. (2001). The "Reading the Mind in the Eyes" test revised version: A study with normal adults, and adults with Asperger syndrome or high-functioning autism. *Journal of Child Psychology and Psychiatry, 42,* 241–251.

Baron-Cohen. S., Wheelwright, S., & Joliffe, T. (1997). Is there a "language of the eyes"? Evidence from normal adults and adults with autism or Asperger's syndrome. *Visual Cognition, 4,* 311–331.

Bar-Yam, Y. (1993). *Sleep as temporary brain dissociation.* NECSI Research Report YB-0005. Available at necsi.org.

Bateman, A. W. & Fonagy, P. (2006). *Mentalization-based treatment for borderline personality disorder: A practical guide.* Oxford, UK: Oxford University Press.

Beaucousin, V., Lacheret, A., Turbelin, M., Morel, M., Mazoyer, B., & Tzourio-Mazoyer, N. (2006). FMRI Study of Emotional Speech Comprehension. *Cerebral Cortex, 17,* 339–352.

Beebe, B., & Lachmann, F. (2002). *Infant research and adult treatment: Co-constructing interactions.* London & Hillsdale, NJ: Analytic Press.

Beeman, M. J., Bowden, E. M., & Gernsbacher, M. A. (2000). Right and left hemisphere cooperation for drawing predictive and coherent inferences during normal story comprehension. *Brain and Language, 71,* 301–336.

Bertenthal, B. I., Proffitt, D. R., & Kramer, S. J. (1987). Perception of biomechanical motions by infants: implementation of various processing constraints. *Journal of Experimental Psychology: Human Perceptual Performance, 13,* 577–585.

Bhurruth, M. (2007). Review of Coming into Mind. *Group analysis, 40*(3), 420–421.

Bion, W. R. (1967). Notes on memory and desire. *Psychoanalytic Forum, 2,* 271–286.

Boes, A. D., Bechara, A., Tranel, D., Anderson, S. W., Richman, L., & Nopoulos, P. (2009). Right ventromedial prefrontal cortex: A neuroanatomical correlate of impulse control in boys. *Social, Cognitive and Affective Neuroscience, 4*, 1–9.

Bohleber, W. (2007). Remembrance, trauma and collective memory: The battle for memory in psychoanalysis. *International Journal of Psychoanalysis, 88*, 329–352.

Bollas, C. (1987). *The shadow of the object: Psychoanalysis of the unthought known*. London: Free Association Books.

Bowden, E. M., Jung-Beeman, M. Fleck, J. and Kounios, J. (2005). New approaches to demystifying insight. *Trends in Cognitive Sciences, 9*, 322–28.

Bowlby, J. (1958). The nature of a child's attachment to his mother. *International Journal of Psycho-Analysis, 39*, 350.

Bradshaw, G. A., & Schore, A. N. (2007). How elephants are opening doors: Developmental neuroethology, attachment, and social context. *Ethology, 113*, 426–436.

Bragin, M. (2003). The effect of terror on the capacity for symbol formation: Case studies from Afghanistan and New York. In J. A. Cancelmo, I. Tylim, J. Hoffenberg, & H. Myers (Eds.), *Terrorism and the psychoanalytic space, international perspectives from ground zero*. New York: Pace University Press.

Bragin, M. (2007). Knowing terrible things: Engaging survivors of extreme violence in treatment. *Clinical Social Work Journal, 35*, 229–236.

Braun, A. (1999). Commentary on the new neuropsychology of sleep. *Neuro-Psychoanalysis, 1*(2), 196–201.

Breuer, J., & Freud, S. (1895). *Studies on hysteria*. S. E. 2.

Bromberg, P. M. (2003). One need not be a house to be haunted: On enactment, dissociation, and the dread of "not-me"—a case study. *Psychoanalytic Dialogues, 13*(5), 689–709.

Bromberg, P. M. (2006). *Awakening the dreamer: Clinical journeys*. New York: Analytic Press.

Bromberg, P. M. (2008). MENTALIZE THIS! Dissociation, enactment, and clinical process. In E. L. Jurist, A. Slade & S. Burger (Eds.), *Mind to mind: Infant research, neuroscience, and psychoanalysis* (pp. 414–434). New York: Other Press.

Brown, A. (2001). Volcanic irruptions. In *Landmarks. Papers by jungian analysts from australia and new zealand*, compiled by Formaini, H. Australia: Australian and New Zealand Society of Jungian Analysts.

Bruner, J. (1991). The narrative construction of reality. *Critical Inquiry, 18*(1), 1–21.

Bucci, W. (1997). *Psychoanalysis and cognitive science: A multiple code theory.* New York: Guilford Press.

Bucci, W. (2001). Pathways of emotional communication. *Psychoanalytic Inquiry, 21,* 40–70.

Bugental, J. F. (1987). *The art of the psychotherapist.* New York: Norton.

Cambray, J., & Carter, L. (2004). *Analytical psychology. Contemporary perspectives in Jungian analysis.* Hove, UK, & New York: Brunner-Routledge.

Carr, L., Iacoboni, M., Dubeau, M.-C., Mazziotta, J. C., & Lenzi, G. L. (2003). Neural mechanisms of empathy in humans: A relay from neural systems for imitation to limbic areas. *Proceedings of the National Academy of Sciences USA, 100,* 5497–5502.

Charney, D., Deutsch, A., Krystal, J., Southwick, S. & Davis, M. (1993). Psychobiologic mechanisms of posttraumatic stress disorder. *Archives of General Psychiatry 50,* 294–305.

Cheavens, J., & Dreer, L. (2008, August). Hope and depression: hope as a protective factor and therapeutic agent. Paper presented at the annual meeting of the American Psychological Association, Boston.

Chodorow, J. (2006). Active imagination. In R. K. Papadopoulos (Ed.), *The handbook of jungian psychology* (pp. 215–243). London & New York: Routledge.

Chu, J. A. (1998). *Rebuilding shattered lives: The responsible treatment of complex posttraumatic and dissociative disorders.* New York: Wiley.

Chua, E. F., Schacter, D. L., Rand-Giovannetti, E., & Sperling, R. A. (2007). Evidence for a specific role of the anterior hippocampal region in successful associative encoding. *Hippocampus, 17*(11), 1071–1080.

Chugani, H., Behen, M., Muzik, O., Juhasz, C., Nagi, F., & Chugani, D. (2001). Local brain functional activity following early deprivation: A study of Romanian orphans. *NeuroImage, 14,* 1290–1301.

Chused, J. F. (2007). Nonverbal communication in psychoanalysis: Commentary on Harrison and Tronick. *Journal of the American Psychoanalytic Association, 55*(3), 875–882.

Covington, C. (1995). No story, no analysis? The role of narrative in interpretation. *Journal of Analytical Psychology, 40,* 3.

Cowan, W. M., & Kandel, E. R. (2001). A brief history of synapses and synaptic transmission. In W. M. Cowan, T. C. Sudhof, & C. F. Stevens (Eds.), *Synapses* (pp. 1–88b). Baltimore: John Hopkins University Press.

Cozolino, L. (2002). *The neuroscience of psychotherapy: Building and rebuilding the human brain*. London & New York: Norton.

Cozolino, L. (2006). *The neuroscience of human relationships: Attachment and the developing brain*. London & New York: Norton.

Crossman, A.R. & Neary, D. (2000). *Neuroanatomy. An illustrated colour text*. Edinburgh, London, New York, Oxford, Philadelphia, St Louis, Sydney & Toronto: Churchill Livingstone.

Dales, J., & Jerry, P. (2008). Attachment, affect regulation, and mutual synchrony in adult psychotherapy. *American Journal of Psychotherapy*, *62*(3), 283–312.

Damasio, A. R. (1994). *Descartes' error: Emotion, reason, and the human brain*. New York: Putnam.

Damasio, A. R. (2003) *Looking for Spinoza: Joy, sorrow, and the feeling brain*. London: Heinemann.

Decety, J., & Chaminade, T. (2003). When the self represents the other: A new cognitive neuroscience view on psychological identification. *Consciousness and Cognition*, *12*, 577–596.

de Gelder, B. (2006). Toward the neurobiology of emotional body language. *Nature*, *7*, 242–249.

de Haan, M., & Nelson, C. A. (1999). Brain activity differentiates face and object processing in 6-month-old infants. *Developmental Psychology*, *35*(4), 1113–1121.

De Laurentis, T. (1986). Feminist studies/critical studies: Issues, terms, and contexts. In T. De Laurentis (Ed.), *Feminist studies/critical studies*. Bloomington: University of Indiana Press.

Demos, K. E., Kelley, W. M., Ryan, F. C., & Whalen, P. J. (2008). Human amygdala sensitivity to the pupil size of others. *Cerebral Cortex*, *18*, 2729–2734.

Dickinson, E. (1862). There is a pain—so utter. In T. H. Johnson (Ed.), *The Complete Poems of Emily Dickinson*. Cambridge, Mass.: The Belknap Press of Harvard University.

Domhoff, G. W. (2005). Refocusing the neurocognitive approach to dreams: A critique of the Hobson versus Solms debate. *Dreaming*, *15*, 3–20.

Driver, C. (2002). The geography and topography of supervision in a group setting. In C. Driver & E. Martin (Eds.), *Supervising psychotherapy: Psychoanalytic and psychodynamic perspectives* (pp. 84–96). London & Thousand Oaks, CA: Sage.

Driver, C. (2006, October) *Response to Margaret Wilkinson's 2006 Annual Lecture of the Society of Analytical Psychology "Windows to the mind: Contemporary neuroscience—A Jungian clinical perspective."* Paper presented at the Royal Society of Medicine, London.

Eagle, M. (2000). The developmental perspectives of attachment and psychoanalytic theory. In P. Goldberg, R. Muir, J. Kerr (Eds.), *Attachment theory: Social, developmental, and clinical perspectives.* Hillsdale, NJ: Analytic Press.

Eigen, M. (2001). *Damaged bonds.* London & New York: Other Press.

Eisenberger, N. I., Lieberman, M. D., Wiliams, K. D. (2003). Does Rejection Hurt? An fMRI study of social exclusion. *Science, 302,* 290–292.

Ekstrom, S. R. (2004). Freudian, Jungian, and cognitive models of the unconscious. *Journal of Analytical Psychology, 49*(5), 657–682.

Emde, R. N. (1999). Moving ahead. *International Journal of Psycho-Analysis, 80,* 317–339.

Faust, M., & Mashal, N. (2007). The role of the right cerebral hemisphere in processing novel metaphoric expressions taken from poetry: A divided visual field study. *Neuropsychologia, 45*(4), 860–870.

Felitti, V., Anda, R., Nordenberg, D., Williamson, D., Spitz, A., Edwards, V., et al. (1998). Relationship of childhood abuse and household dysfunction to many of the leading causes of death in adults: The Adverse Childhood Experiences (ACE) Study. *American Journal of Preventative Medicine 14,* 245–258.

Ferenczi, S. (1988). *Clinical diary.* In J. Dupont (Ed.), Cambridge, Mass.: Harvard University Press.

Ferro, A. (2005). *Seeds of illness and seeds of recovery: The genesis of suffering and the role of psychoanalysis.* Hove, UK, & New York: Routledge.

Fiscalini, J. (1997). On supervisory parataxis and dialogue. In M. H. Rock (Ed.), *Psychodynamic supervision.* London & Northvale, NJ: Jason Aronson.

Fonagy, P. (1991). Thinking about thinking: Some clinical and theoretical considerations in the treatment of a borderline patient. *International Journal of Psychoanalysis, 76,* 639–656.

Fonagy, P., & Target, M. (1998). Mentalization and the changing aims of child psychoanalysis. *Psychoanalytic Dialogues, 8*(1), 87–114.

Fonagy, P., & Target, M. (2008). Attachment, trauma, and psychoanalysis. Where psychoanalysis meets neuroscience. In E. L. Jurist, A. Slade, & S. Burger (Eds.), *Mind to mind: Infant research, neuroscience, and psychoanalysis.* New York: Other Press.

Fonagy, P., Gergely, G., Jurist, E. L., & Target, M. (2004). *Affect regulation, mentalization, and the development of the self*. London: Karnac.

Fosha, D. (2003). Dyadic regulation and experiential work with emotion and relatedness. In M. F. Solomon & D. J. Siegel (Eds.), *Healing trauma, attachment, mind, body, and brain*. New York: Norton.

Fosshage, J. (2008). *Fundamental implicit and explicit pathways to psychoanalytic change*. Paper presented at the 28th spring meeting of the American Psychological Association New York.

Fowler, C., Hilsenroth, M. J., & Handler, L. (1996). A multimethod approach to assessing early dependency: The early memory dependency probe. *Journal of Personality Assessment, 67*(2), 399–413.

Fowler, C, Hilsenroth, M. J., Handler, L. (2000). Martin Mayman's early memories technique: Bridging the gap between personality assessment and psychotherapy. *Journal of Personality Assessment, 75*(1), 18–32.

Fraiberg, S., & Fraibers, L. (Eds.) (1980). *Clinical studies in infant mental health. The first year of life*. New York: Basic Books.

Freud, S. (1923). The ego and the id. *The standard edition of the complete psychological works of Sigmund Freud* (vol. 19, pp. 19–27). London: Hogarth Press.

Freud, S. (1959). Postscript to the question of lay analysis. *The standard edition of the complete psychological works of Sigmund Freud* (vol. 20, pp. 251–258). London: Hogarth Press.

Gabbard, G., Miller, L. & Martinez, M. (2008). A neurobiological perspective on mentalizing and internal object relations in traumatized borderline patients. In E. L. Jurist, A. Slade & S. Burger (Eds.), *Mind to mind: Infant research, neuroscience, and psychoanalysis* (pp. 202–224). New York: Other Press.

Gabel, S. (1990). Dreams and dissociation theory: Speculations on beneficial aspects of their linkage. *Dissociation, 3*(1), 38–47.

Gallese, V. (2007). Before and below theory of mind: Embodied simulation and the neural correlates of social cognition. *Philosophical Transactions of the Royal Society, Biological Sciences, 362*, 659–669.

Galton, G. (Ed.). (2006). *Touch papers: Dialogues on touch in the psychoanalytic space*. London: Karnac.

Gambini, R. (2007). Epilogue. Who owns the air? In A. Casement (Ed.), *Who owns Jung?* (pp. 363–367). London: Karnac.

Gergely, G., & Unoka, Z. (2008). Attachment and mentalization in humans. In E. L. Jurist, A. Slade, & S. Burger (Eds.), *Mind to mind: Infant research, neuroscience, and psychoanalysis* (pp. xx–xx). New York: Other Press.

Gerhardt, S. (2004). *Why love matters: How affection shapes a baby's brain*. Hove, UK, & New York: Brunner-Routledge.

Ginot, E. (2007). Intersubjectivity and neuroscience: Understanding enactments and their therapeutic significance within emerging paradigms. *Psychoanalytic Psychology, 24*(2), 317–332.

Gliga, T., & Dehaene-Lambertz, G. (2005). Structural encoding of body and face in human infants and adults. *Journal of Cognitive Neuroscience. 17*, 1328–1340.

Goddard, G., McIntyre, D., & Leetch, C. (1969). A permanent change in brain functioning resulting from daily electrical stimulation. *Experimental Neurology, 25*, 295–330.

Goleman, D. (1996). *Emotional intelligence*. London: Bloomsbury Press.

Grabner, R. H., Fink, A., & Neubauer, A. (2007). Brain correlates of self-related originality of ideas: evidence from event-related power and phase-locking changes in the EEG. *Behavioral Neuroscience, 121*(1), 224–230.

Greenspan, S. I. (2000). Children with autistic spectrum disorders. *Psychoanalytic Inquiry, 20*, 675–703.

Greicius, M. D., Krasnow, B., Reiss, A. L., & Menon, V. (2003). Functional connectivity in the resting brain: A network analysis of the default mode hypothesis. *PNAS, 100*(1), 253–258.

Grossman, W. (1991). Pain, aggression, fantasy and concepts of sadomasochism. *Psychoanalytic Quarterly, 60*, 22–52.

Gusnard, D. A., Akbudak, E., Shulman, G. L., & Raichle, M. E. (2001). Medial prefrontal cortex and self-referential mental activity, Relation to a default mode of brain function. *PNAS 98*(7), 4259–64.

Haft, W. L., & Slade, A. (1989). Affect attunement and maternal attachment: A pilot study. *Infant Mental Health Journal, 10*, 157–171.

Harrison, N. A., Singer, T., Rotshtein, P. Dolan, R. J., & Critchley, H. D. (2006). Pupillary contagion: Central mechanisms engaged in sadness processing. *Social, cognitive and affective neuroscience, 1*, 5–17.

Harrison, N. A., Wilson, C. E., & Critchley, H. D. (2007). Processing of observed pupil size modulates perception of sadness and predicts empathy. *Emotion, 7*(4), 724–729.

Hart, C. (2008). Affective association: An effective intervention in countering fragmentation and dissociation. *Journal of Child Psychotherapy, 34*(2), 259–277.

Hartmann, E. (2000). The psychology and physiology of dreaming: A new synthesis. In L. Gamwell (Ed.), *Dreams 1900– 2000: Science, art, and the unconscious mind*. Ithaca, NY: Cornell University Press.

Haven, T. J. (2009). 'That part of the body is just gone": Understanding and responding to dissociation and physical health. *Journal of Trauma and Dissociation, 10*(2), 204–218.

Heim, C., Mletzko, T., Purselle, D. L., & Nemeroff, C. B. (2008). The dexamethasone/corticotropin-releasing factor test in men with major depression. *Biological Psychiatry, 63*(4), 398–405.

Hershberg, S. G. (2008, April). *How do we know and how do we change what we know? Implicit and explicit learning in contemporary psychoanalysis.* Summary of panel held at the 28th spring meeting of the American Psychological Association New York.

Hirao, K., Miyata, J., Fujiwara, H., Yamada, M., Namiki, et al. (2008b). Theory of Mind and frontal lobe pathology in schizophrenia: A voxel-based morphometry study. *Schizophrenia Research, 105*, 165–174.

Hirao, K., Naka, H., Narita, H., Futamura, M., Miyata, J., Tanaka, S., et al. (2008a). *Self in conflict: Recovery from nonfluent aphasia through sand play therapy: Collaboration between subjective and objective image.* Paper presented at the 9th International Neuropsychoanalysis Congress, Montreal.

Hobson, J. A. (1999). The new neuropsychology of sleep: Implications for psychoanalysis. *Neuropsychoanalysis, 1*(2), 157–183.

Holmes, J. (1996) *Attachment, intimacy, autonomy: Using attachment theory in adult psychotherapy.* Northvale, NJ & London: Aronson.

Houdé, O., Zago, L., Crivello, F., Moutier, S., Pineau, A., Mazoyer, B., et al. (2001). Access to deductive logic depends on a right ventrome-dial prefrontal area devoted to emotion and feeling: Evidence from a training paradigm. *NeuroImage, 14*, 1486–1492.

Howard, M. F., & Reggia, J. A. (2007). A theory of the visual system biology underlying development of spatial frequency lataeralization. *Brain and Cognition, 64*, 111–123.

Hutterer, J., & Liss, M. (2006). Cognitive development, memory, trauma, and treatment: An integration of psychoanalytic and behavioral concepts in the light of current neuroscience research. *Journal of the American Academy of Psychoanalysis and Dynamic Psychiatry, 34*, 287–302.

Inderbitzin, L. B., & Levy, S. T. (1998). Repetition compulsion revisited: Implications for technique. *Psychoanalytic Quarterly, 67*, 32–53.

Jacobs, T. J. (2005). Discussion. In B. Beebe, S. Knoblauch, J. Rustin, & D. Sorter (Eds.), *Forms of intersubjectivity in infant research and adult treatment*. New York: Other Press.

Janet, P. (1889). *L'automatisme psychologique*. Paris: Alcan.

Javanbakht, A., & Ragan, C. L. (2008). A neural network model for transference and repetition compulsion based on pattern completion. *Journal of The American Academy of Psychoanalysis and Dynamic Psychiatry, 36*(2), 255–278.

Jones, B. E. (2000). The interpretation of physiology. *Behavioral and Brain Sciences, 23*(6), 955–956.

Jones, E. (1910). Remarks on Dr. Morton Prince's article "The mechanism and interpretation of dreams." *Journal of Abnormal Psychology, 5,* 328–336.

Jung, C. J. (1912). *The theory of psychoanalysis. The collected works of C. G. Jung*. Vol. 4. Freud and Psychoanalysis. Trans. R. F. C. Hull. Bollinger Series XX. Princeton, NJ: Princeton University Press.

Jung, C. J. (1928). *The therapeutic value of abreaction. The collected works of C. G. Jung*. Vol. 16. The practice of psychotherapy. Trans. R. F. C. Hull. Bollinger Series XX. Princeton, NJ: Princeton University Press.

Jung, C. J. (1934a). *A review of the complex theory. The collected works of C. G. Jung*. Vol. 8. The structure and dynamics of the psyche. Trans. R. F. C. Hull. Bollinger Series XX. Princeton, NJ: Princeton University Press.

Jung, C. J. (1934b). The meaning of psychology for modern man. *The collected works of C. G. Jung*. Vol. 10. Civilization in transition. Trans. R. F. C. Hull. Bollinger Series XX. Princeton, NJ: Princeton University Press.

Jung, C. J. (1934c). The Practical Use of Dream-Analysis. *The collected works of C. G. Jung*. Vol. 16. The practice of psychotherapy. Trans. R. F. C. Hull. Bollinger Series XX. Princeton, NJ: Princeton University Press.

Jung, C. J. (1935). The Tavistock lectures. *The collected works of C. G. Jung*. Vol. 18. The symbolic life. Trans. R. F. C. Hull. Bollinger Series XX. Princeton, NJ: Princeton University Press.

Jung, C. J. (1946a). Analytical Psychology and Education. *The collected works of C. G. Jung*. Vol. 17. The development of the personality. Trans. R. F. C. Hull. Bollinger Series XX. Princeton, NJ: Princeton University Press.

Jung, C. J. (1946b). The psychology of the transference. *The collected works of C. G. Jung*. Vol. 16. The practice of psychotherapy. Trans. R. F. C. Hull. Bollinger Series XX. Princeton, NJ: Princeton University Press.

Jung, C. J. (1951). Fundamental questions of psychotherapy. *The collected works of C. G. Jung*. Vol. 16. The practice of psychotherapy. Trans. R. F. C. Hull. Bollinger Series XX. Princeton, NJ: Princeton University Press.

Jung-Beeman, M. L., Bowden, E. M., & Gernsbacher, M. A. (2000). Right and left hemisphere cooperation for drawing predictive and coherence inferences during normal story comprehension. *Brain and Language, 71*, 310–336.

Jung-Beeman, M., Bowden, E. M., Haberman, J., Frymiare, J. L., Arambel-Liu, S., Greenblatt, R., et al. (2004). Neural activity when people solve verbal problems with insight. *PLoS Biology, 2*(4), 500–10.

Kalsched, D. (1996). *The inner world of trauma: Archetypal defenses of the human spirit*. London & New York: Routledge.

Kandel, E. R. (1999). Biology and the future of psychoanalysis: A new intellectual framework for psychiatry revisited. *American Journal of Psychiatry, 156*, 505–524.

Kendall-Tackett, K., & Klest, B. (2009). Causal mechanisms and multidirectional pathways between trauma, dissociation, and health. *Journal of Trauma and Dissociation, 10*(2), 129–134.

Kensinger, E. A., Garoff-Easton, R. J., & Schacter, D. L. (2007). Effects on emotion specificity: Memory tradeoffs elicited by negative visually arousing stimuli. *Journal of Memory and Language, 56*, 575–591.

Kimura, Y., Yoshimo, A., Takahasi, Y., & Normura, S. (2004). Interhemispheric difference in emotional response without awareness. *Physiology and Behavior, 82*, 727–731.

Kindt, M., Soeter, M. & Vervliet, B. (2009). Beyond extinction: Erasing human fear responses and preventing the return of fear. *Nature Neuroscience 12*, 256–258.

Klein, M. (1975). *Narrative of a child analysis*. London: Hogarth Press and the Institute of Psychoanalysis. (Original work published 1961).

Knickmeyer, R. C., Gouttard, S., Kang, C., Evans, D., Wilber, K., Smith, J. K., et al. (2008). A structural MRI study of human brain development from birth to 2 years. *Journal of Neuroscience, 28*(47), 12176–12182.

Knight, J. (2003). Reflections on the therapist–supervisor relationship. In J. Wiener, R. Mizen, and J. Duckham (Eds.), *Supervising and being supervised: A practice in search of a theory*. Basingstoke, UK, & New York: Palgrave Macmillan.

Knox, J. M. (2001). Memories, fantasies, archetypes: An exploration of some connections between cognitive science and analytical psychology. *Journal of Analytical Psychology, 46*(4), 613–635.

Knox, J. M. (2003). *Archetype, attachment, analysis.* London & New York: Routledge.

Knox, J. M. (2008). Response to "Report from borderland." *Journal of Analytical Psychology, 53*, 31–36.

Kradin, R. L. (2007). Minding the gaps: The role of informational encapsulation and mindful attention in the analysis of the transference. *Journal of Jungian Theory and Practice, 9*(2), 1–13.

Krowski, S. (1997). Working with adult incest survivors. In M. Lawrence & M. Maguire (Eds.), *Psychotherapy with women: Feminist perspectives* (pp. xx–xx). London: Macmillan.

Lacy, T. J., & Hughes, J. D. (2006). A systems approach to behavioral neurobiology: Integrating psychodynamics and neuroscience in a psychiatric curriculum. *Journal of the American Academy of Psychoanalysis, 34*, 43–74.

Lane, R. D. (2008). Neural substrates of implicit and explicit emotional processes: A unifying framework for psychosomatic medicine. *Psychosomatic Medicine, 70*, 214–231.

Lanius, R. (2008, October). Emotional awareness and self-reflection: Building blocks for an embodied sense of self. Paper presented at the professional seminar of the Department of Psychiatry at the Schulich School of Medicine and Dentistry, University of Western Ontario, London.

Lebovici, S. (1995). Commentaire. *Rev Fr Psychoanal, 39*, 1797–1798

LeDoux, J. E. (2002). *Synaptic self: How our brains become who we are.* London: Pan Macmillan.

Lenzi, D., Trentini, C., Pantano, P., Macaluso, E., Iacoboni, M., Lenzi, G. L., et al. (2009). Neural basis of maternal communication and emotional expression processing during infant preverbal stage. *Cerebral Cortex, 19*, 1124–1133.

Levin, F. M. (1980). Metaphor, affect and arousal: How interpretations might work. *Annual of Psychoanalysis, 8*, 231–245.

Levin, F. M. (2009). *Emotion and the psychodynamics of the cerebellum: A neuro-psychoanalytic analysis and synthesis.* London: Karnac.

Levine, P. (1997). *Waking the tiger: Healing trauma.* Berkeley: North Atlantic Books.

Lewis, T., Amini, F., & Lannon, R. (2000). *A general theory of love.* New York: Vintage Books.

Lichtenburg, J. (2004). Experience and inference: how far will science carry us? *Journal of Analytical Psychology, 49*(2), 133–142.

Logothetis, N. K. (2008). What we can do and what we cannot do with fMRI. *Nature, 453,* 869–878.

Loker, A. (2007). New facts about dreams and psychotherapy deduced from Jung's compensation theory. *Journal of Jungian Theory and Practice, 9*(2), 41–61.

Lyons-Ruth, K., & members of the Boston Process of Change Study Group. (1998). Implicit relational knowing: Its role in development and psychoanalytic treatment. *Infant Mental Health Journal, 19,* 282–289.

Lyotard, J. (1993). *Toward the postmodern.* Eds. R. Harvey & M. S. Roberts. Highlands, NJ & London: Humanities Press.

Mancia, M. (2005). Implicit memory and the early repressed unconscious. *International Journal of Psychoanalysis, 87,* 83–101.

Mander, G. (2002). Supervision, between control and collusion. In C. Driver and E. Martin (Eds.), *Supervising psychotherapy. Psychoanalytic and psychodynamic perspectives* (pp. 38–50). London & Thousand Oaks, CA: Sage.

Mar, R. A. (2004). The neuropsychology of narrative, story comprehension, story production, and their interrelation. *Neuropsychologia, 42,* 1414–1434.

Martin, E. (2002). Giving, taking, stealing: The ethics of supervision. In C. Driver and E. Martin (Eds.), *Supervising psychotherapy. Psychoanalytic and psychodynamic perspectives* (pp. 121–131). London & Thousand Oaks, CA: Sage.

Martin, E. (2003). Problems and ethical issues in supervision. In J.Wiener, R. Mizen, & J. Duckham (Eds.), *Supervising and being supervised: A practice in search of a theory* (pp. 135–150). Basingstoke, UK, & New York: Palgrave Macmillan.

Mashal, N., Faust, M., Hendler, T., & Jung-Beeman, M. (2007). An fMRI investigation of the neural correlates underlying the processing of novel metaphoric expressions. *Brain and Language, 100,* 115–126.

Mashal, N., & Faust, M. (2008). Right hemisphere sensitivity to novel metaphoric relations: Application of the signal detection theory. *Brain and Language, 104*(2), 103–112.

Mathew, M. (1998). The body as the instrument. *Journal of the British Association of Psychotherapists, 35,* 17–36.

Mayman, M. (1968). Early memories and character structure. *Journal of Projective Techniques and Personality Assessment, 32,* 303–316.

McCluskey, U., Roger, D., & Nash, P. (1997). A preliminary study of the role of attunement in adult psychotherapy. *Human Relations, 50*, 1261–1273.

McEwan, I. (2006). *Saturday*. London: Vintage.

McGowan, P. O., Sasaki, A., D'Alessio, A. C. D., Dymov, S., Labonté, B., Szy, M., et al. (2009). Epigenetic regulation of the glucocorticoid receptor in human brain associates with childhood abuse. *Nature Neuroscience 12*, 342–348.

McIntosh, D. N., Reichmann-Decker, A., Winkielman, P., & Wilbarger, J. L. (2006). When the social mirror breaks: Deficits in automatic, but not voluntary, mimicry of emotional facial expressions in autism. *Developmental Science, 9*(3), 295–302.

McQueen, D., Kennedy, R., Sinason, V., & Maxted, F. (2008). *Psychoanalytic psychotherapy after child abuse. The treatment of adults and children who have experienced sexual abuse, violence and neglect in childhood.* London: Karnac.

Meares, R. (2005). *The metaphor of play: Origin and breakdown of personal being* (3rd ed.). London: Routledge.

Mendelsohn, G. A. (1976). Associative and attentional processes in creative performance. *Journal of Personality, 44*, 341–369.

Miller, G. (2008). Growing pains for fMRI. *Science, 320*, 1412–1414.

Miller, L. (1997). Neurosensitization: A pathophysiological model for traumatic disability syndromes. *The Journal of Cognitive Rehabilitation*, 12–23.

Miller, M. L. (2008). The emotionally engaged analyst I. Theories of affect and their influence on therapeutic action. *Psychoanalytic Psychology 25*(1), 3–25.

Minagawa-Kawai, Y., Matsuoka, S., Dan, I., Naoi, N., Nakamura, K., & Kojima, S. (2009). Prefrontal activation associated with social attachment, facial-emotion recognition in mothers and infants. *Cerebral Cortex, 19*, 284–292.

Mitchell, R. L. C., & Crowe, T. J. (2005). Right hemisphere language functions and schizophrenia: The forgotten hemisphere. *Brain, 128*, 963–978.

Mizen, R., Wiener, J., & Duckham, J. (2003). From practice to theory: Evolving a theory of supervision. In J. Wiener, R. Mizen, & J. Duckham (Eds.), *Supervising and being supervised: A practice in search of a theory* (pp. 224–240). Basingstoke, UK, & New York: Palgrave Macmillan.

Modell, A. H. (2005). Commentary on "Becoming aware of feelings." *Neuro-Psychoanalysis, 7*, 36–39.

Morcom, A. M., & Fletcher, P. C. (2007). Does the brain have a baseline? Why we should be resisting a rest. *NeuroImage, 37*, 1073–1082.

Morton, J., & Johnson, M. H. (1991). CONSPEC and CONLEARN: A two-process theory of infant face recognition. *Psychological Review, 98*, 164–181.

Mundo, E. (2006). Neurobiology of dynamic psychotherapy: An integration possible? *Journal of the American Academy of Psychoanalysis and Dynamic Psychiatry, 34*(4), 679–691.

Narvaez, D. (2008). Triune ethics: the neurobiological roots of our multiple moralities. *New ideas in psychology, 26*, 95–119.

Neborsky, R. J. (2003). A clinical model for the comprehensive treatment of trauma using an affect experiencing-attachment theory approach. In M. F. Solomon & D. F. Siegel (Eds.) *Healing trauma. Attachment, mind, body and brain*. New York: Norton.

Nijenhuis, E. R. S., van der Hart, O. (1999) Forgetting and reexperiencing trauma. In J. Goodwin, J. & R. Attias (Eds.), *Splintered reflections: Images of the body in trauma* (pp. 39–66). New York: Basic Books.

Noriuchi, M., Kikuchi, Y., & Senoo, A. (2008). The functional neuroanatomy of maternal love: Mother's response to infant's attachment behaviors. *Biological Psychiatry, 63*, 415–423.

Ogden, P., Minton, K., & Pain, C. (2006). *Trauma and the body: A sensorimotor approach to psychotherapy*. New York: Norton.

Orbach, S. (1998). False memory syndrome. In V. Sinason (Ed.), *Memory in dispute* (pp. 61–71). London: Karnac.

Orbach, S. (2006). Too hot to touch. In G. Galton (Ed)., *Touch papers: Dialogues on touch in the psychoanalytic space* (pp. xiii–xviii). London: Karnac.

Orbach, S. (2009). *Bodies*. London: Profile Books Ltd.

Ortigue, S., Michel, C. M., Murray, M. M., Mohr, C., Carbonnel, S., & Landis, T. (2004). Electrical neuroimaging reveals early generator modulation to emotional words. *NeuroImage, 21*, 1242–1251.

Pace, P. (2003). *Lifespan integration: Connecting ego states through time*. Roslyn: WA Spiral Bound.

Pally, R. (2000). *The mind–brain relationship*. London & New York: Karnac.

Pally, R. (2007). The predicting brain, unconscious repetition, conscious reflection and therapeutic change. *International Journal of Psychoanalysis, 8*, 861–881.

Panksepp, J. (1998). *Affective neuroscience: The foundations of human and animal emotions*. New York & Oxford: Oxford University Press.

Panksepp, J. (2003). At the interface of the affective, behavioral, and cognitive neurosciences: Decoding the emotional feelings of the brain. *Brain and Cognition, 52,* 4–14.

Panksepp, J. (2008). The power of the word may reside in the power of affect. *Integrative Psychological Behavioral Science, 42,* 47–55.

Panksepp, J., & Bernatzky, G. (2002). Emotional sounds and the brain: The neuro-affective foundations of musical appreciation. *Behavioral Processes, 60,* 133–155.

Paus, T. (2005). Mapping brain maturation and cognitive development during adolescence. *Trends in Cognitive Sciences, 9*(2), 60–68.

Pearson, J. L., Cohn, D. A., Cowan P. A., & Cowan, C. P. (1994). Earned and continuous security in adult attachment. Relation to depressive symptomatology and poverty style. *Development and Psychopathology, 6,* 259–373.

Perry, C. (1997). Transference and countertransference. In P. Young-Eisendrath & T. Dawson (Eds.), *The Cambridge companion to Jung.* Cambridge, UK: Cambridge University Press.

Persinger, M. A., & Makarec, K. (1992). The feeling of presence and verbal meaningfulness in the context of temporal lobe function, factor analytic verification of the muses? *Brain and Cognition, 20,* 217–226.

Phan, K. L., Wager, T., Taylor, S. F., & Liberzon, I. (2002). Functional neuroanatomy of emotion: A meta-analysis of emotion activation studies in PET and fMRI. *NeuroImage, 16,* 331–348.

Porges, S. W. (1997). Emotion: An evolutionary by-product of the neural regulation of the autonomic nervous system. In C. S. Carter, B. Kirkpatrick, & I. I. Lederhendler (Eds.), *The integrative neurobiology of affiliation.* New York: Annals of the New York Academy of Sciences.

Post, R., Weiss, S. & Smith, M. (1995). Sensitization and kindling: Implications for the evolving neural substrate of post-traumatic stress disorder. In M. Friedman, D. Charney, & A. Deutsch (Eds.), *Neurobiological and clinical consequences of stress: From normal adaptation to PTSD* (pp. 203–224). Philadelphia: Lippincott-Raven Publishers.

Prince, M. (1910). The mechanism and interpretation of dreams. *Journal of Abnormal Psychology, 5,* 139–195.

Raichle, M. E., & Snyder, A. Z. (2007). A default mode of brain function: A brief history of an evolving idea. *NeuroImage, 37*(4), 1083–1090.

Rauch, S. L., van der Kolk, B. A., Fisler, R. E., Alpert, N. M., Orr, S. P., Savage, C., et al. (1996). A symptom provocation study of PTSD using PET and script driven imagery. *Archives of General Psychiatry, 53*, 380–387.

Reinders, A. A. T. S., Nijenhuis, E. R. S., Paans, A. M. J., Korf, J., Willemsen, A. T. M., & den Boor, J. A. (2003). One brain, two selves. *NeuroImage, 20,* 2119–2125.

Richardson, M. P., Strange, B. A. & Dolan, R. J. (2004). Encoding of emotional memories depends on the amygdala and hippocampus and their reactions. *Nature Neuroscience, 7*(3), 278–285.

Rosenbaum, T. (2002). *The golems of gotham.* New York: Harper Collins.

Rossi, E. L. (2004). Sacred spaces and places in healing dreams, gene expression and brain growth in rehabilitation. *Psychological Perspectives, 47*(1), 48–63.

Rowling, J. K. (1997). *Harry Potter and the philosopher's stone.* London: Bloomsbury.

Royal College of Psychiatrists and British Psychological Society. (2005). *Posttraumatic stress disorder: The management of PTSD in adults and children in primary and secondary care.* London: Gaskell and the British Psychological Society.

Samuels, A. (1985). Countertransference: The Mundus Imaginalis and a research project. *Journal of Analytical Psychology, 30*(1).

Sato, W., & Aoki, S. (2006). Right hemisphere dominance in processing unconscious emotion. *Brain and Cognition, 62,* 261–266.

Scaer, R. C. (2001a). *The body bears the burden: Trauma, dissociation, and disease.* London and New York: Haworth Press.

Scaer, R. C. (2001b). The neurophysiology of dissociation and chronic disease. *Applied Psychology and Biofeedback, 26*(1), 73–91.

Schacter, D. L., & Addis, D. R. (2007a). The cognitive neuroscience of constructive memory: Remembering the past and imagining the future. *Philosophical Transactions of the Royal Society, 362,* 773–86.

Schacter, D. L., & Addis, D. R. (2007b). The ghosts of past and future. *Nature, 445*(4), 27.

Schank, R. C., & Morson, G. S. (1990). *Tell me a story: Narrative and intelligence.* Evanston, IL: Northwestern University Press.

Schaverien, J. (2003). Supervising the erotic transference and countertransference. In J. Wiener, R. Mizen, and J. Duckham (Eds.), *Supervising and being supervised: A practice in search of a theory* (pp. 167–184). Basingstoke, UK, & New York: Palgrave Macmillan.

Schiffer, F., Teicher, M. H., & Papani-Colaou, A. C. (1995). Evoked potential evidence for right-brain activity during recall of traumatic memories. *Journal of Neuropsychiatry and Clinical Neuroscience, 7*, 169–175.

Schore, A. N. (1994). *Affect regulation and the origin of the self: The neurobiology of emotional development.* Mahwah, NJ: Erlbaum.

Schore, A. N. (2001). The right brain as the neurobiological substratum of Freud's dynamic unconscious. In D. E. Scharff (Ed.), *The psychoanalytic century: Freud's legacy for the future.* New York: Other Press.

Schore, A. N. (2002). Dysregulation of the right brain: A fundamental mechanism of traumatic attachment and the psychopathogenesis of post-traumatic stress disorder. *Australian and New Zealand Journal of Psychiatry, 36*(1), 9–30.

Schore, A. N. (2003a). *Affect dysregulation and disorders of the self.* New York: Norton.

Schore, A. N. (2003b). *Affect regulation and the repair of the self.* New York: Norton.

Schore, A. N. (2007a). Psychoanalytic research, progress, and process: Developmental affective neuroscience and clinical practice. *Psychologist–Psychoanalyst, 27*(3), 6–15.

Schore, A. N. (2007b). Review of Awakening the dreamer: Clinical journeys by Philip Bromberg. *Psychoanalytic Dialogues, 17*(5), 753–767.

Schore, A. N. (2008a, March). Paper presented at The Life Span Learning Institute Integrating attachment, affect regulation and neurobiology: Implications for research and treatment. University of California at Los Angeles.

Schore, A. N. (2008b, April). *Paradigm shift: The right brain and the relational unconscious.* Paper presented at the 28th spring meeting of the American Psychological Association, New York.

Schore, J. R., & Schore, A. N. (2008). Modern attachment theory: The central role of affect-regulation in development and treatment. *Clinical Social Work Journal, 36*, 9–20.

Schutz, L. E. (2005). Broad-perspective perceptual disorder of the right hemisphere. *Neuropsychology Review, 15*(1), 11–27.

Sherrington, C. S. (1906). *The integrative action of the nervous system.* New Haven, CT: Yale University Press.

Sherwood, D. N. (2006). Response to M. Wilkinson's paper "The dreaming mind–brain." *Journal of Analytical Psychology, 51*(1), 61–65.

Shin, L. M., Rauch, S. L., & Pitman, R. K. (2006). Amygdala, medial prefrontal cortex, and hippocampal function in PTSD. *Annals of the New York Academy of Science, 1071*, 67–79.

Sidoli, M. (2000). *When the body speaks: The archetypes in the body* (Blakemore, Ed.), London & Philadelphia: Routledge.

Sinason, V. (2006). No touch please: We're British psychodynamic practitioners. In G. Galton (Ed.), *Touch papers: Dialogues on touch in the psychoanalytic space* (pp. 49–60). London: Karnac.

Solms, M. (1999). Commentary on the new neuropsychology of sleep. *Neuropsychoanalysis, 1*(2), 183–195.

Solms, M., & Turnbull, O. (2002). *The brain and the inner world: An introduction to the neuroscience of subjective relationship.* New York: Other Press.

Solomon, H. M. (2007). *The self in transformation.* London: Karnac.

Spiegel, D. & Cardena, E. (1991). Disintegrated experience: The dissociative disorders revisited. *Journal of Abnormal Psychology, 100,* 366–378.

Spiegel, J., Severino, S. K., & Morrison, K. (2000). The role of attachment functions in psychotherapy. *Journal of Psychotherapy Practice and Research, 9,* 25–32.

Stein, M. (2006). Individuation. In R. K. Papodopoulos (Ed.), *The handbook of Jungian psychology* (pp. 196–214). Hove, UK, & New York: Routledge.

Stern, D. N. (1985). *The interpersonal world of the infant.* New York: Basic Books.

Stern, D. N., Sander, L. W., Nahum, J. P., Harrison, A. M., Lyons-Ruth, K., Morgan, A. C., Bruschweilerstern, N & Tronick, E. Z. (1998). Non-interpretive mechanisms in psychoanalytic therapy: the "something more" than interpretation. *International Journal of Psychoanalysis, 79,* 903–921.

Stern, D. B. (2008). On having to find what you don't know how to look for: Two perspectives on reflection. In E. L. Jurist, A. Slade, & S. Burger (Eds.), *Mind to mind: Infant research, neuroscience, and psychoanalysis* (pp. xx–xx). New York: Other Press.

Stewart, H. (1992). *Psychic experience and problems of technique.* London & New York: Routledge.

Stimmel, B. (1995). Resistance to awareness of the supervisor's transference with special reference to the parallel process. *International Journal of Psychoanalysis, 76,* 609.

Stokes, P. D. (1999). Novelty. In M. Runco & S. R. Pritzker (Eds.), *Encyclopedia of creativity* (pp. 297–304). San Diego, CA: Academic Press.

Strachey, J. (1950). Project for a scientific psychology (1950 [1895]). *The standard edition of the complete psychological works of Sigmund Freud, vol. 1* (1886–1899): pre-psychoanalytic publications and unpublished drafts, 231–391.

Sullivan, M. W., & Lewis, M. (2003) Emotional expressions of young infants and children. A practitioner's primer. *Infants and Young Children, 16*, 120–142.

Surtees, P., Wainwright, N., Day, N., Brayne, C., Luben, R., & Khaw, K. (2003). Adverse experience in childhood as a developmental risk factor for altered immune status in adulthood. *International Journal of Behavioral Medicine, 10*, 251–268.

Sykes, J. B. (1976). *The concise Oxford dictionary of current English.* Oxford, UK: Clarendon Press.

Teicher, M. H. (2000). Wounds time won't heal: The neurobiology of child abuse. *Cerebrum, 2*(4), 50–67.

Teicher, M. H. (2002). Scars that will not heal: The neurobiology of child abuse. *Scientific American, 286*(3), 68–75.

Teicher, M. H., Andersen, S. L., Polcari, A., Anderson, C. M., & Navalta, C. P. (2002). Developmental neurobiology of childhood stress and trauma. *Psychiatric Clinics of North America, 25*, 397–426.

Teicher, M. H., Andersen, S. L., Polcari, A., Anderson, C. M., Navalta, C. P., & Kim, D. M. (2003). The neurobiological consequences of early stress and childhood maltreatment. *Neuroscience and Biobehavioral Review, 27*(1–2), 33–44.

Teicher, M. H., Dumont, NL, Ito Y, Vaituzis, C, Giedd, JN, Andersen S. L. (2004). Childhood neglect is associated with reduced corpus callosum area. *Biological Psychiatry, 56*(2), 80–85.

Teicher, M. H., Samson, J. A., Tomoda, A., Ashy, M., & Andersen, S. L. (2006). Neurobiological and behavioral consequences of exposure to childhood traumatic stress. In B. B. Arnetz & R. Ekman, (Eds.), *Stress in health and disease* (pp. 190–205). Weinheim, Germany: Wiley-VCH.

Temperley, J. (1984). Settings in psychotherapy. *British Journal of Psychotherapy, 1*, 101–112.

Terr, L. C. (1996). True memories of childhood trauma: flaws, absences, and returns. In K. Pezdek & W. P. Banks (Eds.), *The recovered memory/false memory debate* (pp. 69–80). London & San Diego, CA: Academic Press.

Totton, N. (2006). A body psychotherapist's approach to touch. In G. Galton (Ed.), *Touch papers: Dialogues on touch in the psychoanalytic space* (pp. 145, 161). London: Karnac.

Tzourio-Mazoyer, N., DeSchonen, S., Crivello, F., Reutter, B., Aujard, S. & Mazoyer, B. (2002). Neural correlates of woman face processing by 2-month-old Infants. *NeuroImage, 15*, 451–461.

van der Hart, O., Nijenhuis, E. R. S., & Steele, K. (2006). *The haunted self: Structural dissociation and the treatment of chronic traumatization.* London & New York: Norton.

van der Kolk, B. A. (1996). The body keeps the score: Approaches to the psychobiology of posttraumatic stress disorder. In B. A. van der Kolk, A. C. McFarlane, & L. Weisaeth (Eds.), *Traumatic Stress. The Effects of Overwhelming Experience on Mind, Body and Society.* London & New York: Guilford Press.

van der Kolk, B. A., McFarlane, A. C., & van der Hart, O. (1996). A general approach to treatment of posttraumatic stress disorder. In B. A. van der Kolk, A. C. McFarlane, & L. Weisaeth (Eds.), *Traumatic stress. The effects of overwhelming experience on mind, body, and society* (pp. 417, 440). London & New York: Guilford Press.

Watt, D. F. (2003). Psychotherapy in an age of neuroscience: Bridges to affective neuroscience. In J. Corrigall & H. Wilkinson (Eds.), *Revolutionary connections: Psychotherapy and neuroscience* (pp. 79–115). London: Karnac.

Watt, D. F. (2005). Social bonds and the nature of empathy. *Journal of Consciousness Studies, 12*(8–10), 185–209.

Wharton, B. (1998). What comes out of the consulting room? The reporting of clinical material. *Journal of Analytical Psychology, 43*(2), 205–223.

Whitehead, C. C. (2006). Neo-psychoanalysis: A paradigm for the 21st century. *Journal of the American Academy of Psychoanalysis, 34*, 603–627.

Wilkinson, M. A. (2003). Undoing trauma, contemporary neuroscience: A clinical perspective. *Journal of Analytical Psychology, 48*(2), 235–253.

Wilkinson, M. A. (2004). The mind–brain relationship: The emergent self. *Journal of Analytical Psychology, 49*(1), 83–101.

Wilkinson, M. A. (2006a). *Coming into mind: The mind–brain relationship, a Jungian clinical perspective.* London & New York: Routledge.

Wilkinson, M. A. (2006b). The dreaming mind–brain: A Jungian perspective. *Journal of Analytical Psychology, 51*(1), 43–59.

Wilkinson, M. A. (2007a). Coming into mind: Contemporary neuroscience, attachment and the psychological therapies, a clinical perspective. *Attachment: New Directions in Psychotherapy and Relational Psychoanalysis, 1*(3), 323–330.

Wilkinson, M. A. (2007b). Jung and Neuroscience: The making of mind. In A. Casement (Ed.), *Who owns Jung?* (pp. 339–367). London: Karnac.

Williams, G. P. (2004, October). Response to Barry Proner's paper "Bodily states of anxiety: The movement from somatic states to thoughtfulness and relatedness." Paper presented at the scientific meeting of the Society of Analytical Psychology, London.

Winnicott, D.W. (1965). The theory of the parent-infant relationship. In D. W. Winnicott, *The maturational processes and the facilitating environment* (pp. 37–55). London: Hogarth Press. (Original work published 1960).

Winnicott, D.W. (1975a). Transitional objects and transitional phenomena. In D.W. Winnicott, *Through paediatrics to psychoanalysis: Collected papers* (pp. 229–242). London: Hogarth Press. (Original work published 1951).

Winnicott, D.W. (1954a). Metapsychological and clinical aspects of regression within the psycho-analytical set-up. In D. W. Winnicott (1975). *Through paediatrics to psychoanalysis: Collected papers* (pp. 278–294). London: Hogarth Press. (Original work published 1951).

Winnicott, D. W. (1975c). Mind and its relation to the psyche-soma. In D. W. Winnicott (1975). In D. W. Winnicott (1975). *Through paediatrics to psychoanalysis: Collected papers* (pp. 243–254). London: Hogarth Press. (Original work published 1949).

Winnicott, D. W. (1975b). Withdrawal and regression. In D. W. Winnicott (1975). *Through paediatrics to psychoanalysis: Collected papers* (pp. 255–261). London: Hogarth Press. (Original work published 1954).

Woodhead, J. (2004). "Dialectical process" and "constructive method": Micro-analysis of relational process in an example from parent–infant psychotherapy. *Journal of Analytical Psychology, 49*(2), 143–160.

Woodhead, J. (2009). *The emergence of the infant self in parent-infant psychotherapy*. The University of Essex: unpublished doctoral thesis.

World Health Organization. (1992). *The ICD–10 classification of mental and behavioral disorders*. Geneva: Author.

Young, K., & Saver, J. L. (2001). The neurology of narrative. *SubStance, 30*, 72–84.

Young, W. (1988). Psychodynamics and dissociation: All that switches is not split. *Dissociation, 1*(1), 33–38.

Zabriskie, B. (2004). Imagination as laboratory. *Journal of Analytical Psychology 49*(2), 235–242.

Zanocco, G., De Marchi, A., & Pozzi, F. (2006). Sensory empathy and enactment. *International Journal of Psychoanalysis, 87*, 145–158.

Index